Autodesk® Revit® 2018
Collaboration Tools

Learning Guide
Imperial - 1st Edition

Authorized Publisher

ASCENT - Center for Technical Knowledge®
Autodesk® Revit® 2018
Collaboration Tools
Imperial - 1st Edition

Prepared and produced by:

ASCENT Center for Technical Knowledge
630 Peter Jefferson Parkway, Suite 175
Charlottesville, VA 22911

866-527-2368
www.ASCENTed.com

Lead Contributor: Martha Hollowell

ASCENT - Center for Technical Knowledge is a division of Rand Worldwide, Inc., providing custom developed knowledge products and services for leading engineering software applications. ASCENT is focused on specializing in the creation of education programs that incorporate the best of classroom learning and technology-based training offerings.

We welcome any comments you may have regarding this learning guide, or any of our products. To contact us please email: feedback@ASCENTed.com.

Contents

© 2017, ASCENT - Center for Technical Knowledge®

Preface

Autodesk® Revit® is a Building Information Modeling (BIM) tool, which can be used by more than one person working on a new project. This is an important feature in collaboration within a project, between projects, and with other users, firms, and disciplines.

The objective of the *Autodesk® Revit® 2018: Collaboration Tools* learning guide is to enable students, who have a basic knowledge of Autodesk Revit, to increase their productivity while working with other people on a team, either in the same firm or other firms as well as with other disciplines. It also covers linking Autodesk Revit files and linking or importing other CAD files. Practices are available for each of the primary disciplines covered by Autodesk Revit: architecture, MEP, and structure.

Topics Covered

- Set up project phasing

- Create and display a variety of design options

- Use groups

- Link Autodesk Revit files

- Use multi-discipline coordination including Copy/Monitor and Coordination Review.

- Import and export vector and raster files including exporting Autodesk Revit models for energy analysis

- Understand, use, and setup worksets

Note on Software Setup

This learning guide assumes a standard installation of the software using the default preferences during installation. Lectures and practices use the standard software templates and default options for the Content Libraries.

Students and Educators can Access Free Autodesk Software and Resources

Autodesk challenges you to get started with free educational licenses for professional software and creativity apps used by millions of architects, engineers, designers, and hobbyists today. Bring Autodesk software into your classroom, studio, or workshop to learn, teach, and explore real-world design challenges the way professionals do.

Get started today - register at the Autodesk Education Community and download one of the many Autodesk software applications available.

Visit www.autodesk.com/joinedu/

Note: Free products are subject to the terms and conditions of the end-user license and services agreement that accompanies the software. The software is for personal use for education purposes and is not intended for classroom or lab use.

Lead Contributor: Martha Hollowell

Martha incorporates her passion for architecture and education into all her projects, including the learning guides she creates on Autodesk Revit for Architecture, MEP, and Structure. She started working with AutoCAD in the early 1990's, adding AutoCAD Architecture and Autodesk Revit as they came along.

After receiving a B.Sc. in Architecture from the University of Virginia, she worked in the architectural department of the Colonial Williamsburg Foundation and later in private practice, consulting with firms setting up AutoCAD in their offices.

Martha has over 20 years' experience as a trainer and instructional designer. She is skilled in leading individuals and small groups to understand and build on their potential. Martha is trained in Instructional Design and has achieved the Autodesk Certified Instructor (ACI) and Autodesk Certified Professional designations for Revit Architecture.

Martha Hollowell has been the Lead Contributor for *Autodesk Revit Collaboration Tools* since its initial release in 2008.

In this Guide

The following images highlight some of the features that can be found in this Learning Guide.

FTP link for practice files

Practice Files

The Practice Files page tells you how to download and install the practice files that are provided with this learning guide.

Learning Objectives for the chapter

Chapters

Each chapter begins with a brief introduction and a list of the chapter's Learning Objectives.

Side notes

Side notes are hints or additional information for the current topic.

Practice Objectives

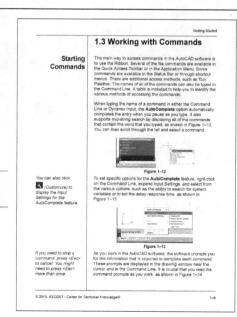

Instructional Content

Each chapter is split into a series of sections of instructional content on specific topics. These lectures include the descriptions, step-by-step procedures, figures, hints, and information you need to achieve the chapter's Learning Objectives.

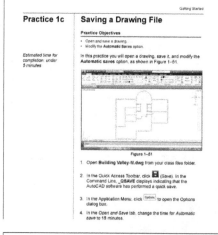

Practices

Practices enable you to use the software to perform a hands-on review of a topic.

Some practices require you to use prepared practice files, which can be downloaded from the link found on the Practice Files page.

Chapter Review Questions

Chapter review questions, located at the end of each chapter, enable you to review the key concepts and learning objectives of the chapter.

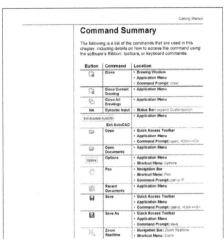

Command Summary

The Command Summary is located at the end of each chapter. It contains a list of the software commands that are used throughout the chapter, and provides information on where the command is found in the software.

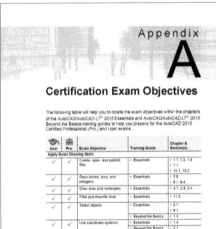

Autodesk Certification Exam Appendix

This appendix includes a list of the topics and objectives for the Autodesk Certification exams, and the chapter and section in which the relevant content can be found.

Icons in this Learning Guide

The following icons are used to help you quickly and easily find helpful information.

New in 2018	Indicates items that are new in the Autodesk Revit 2018 software.
Enhanced in 2018	Indicates items that have been enhanced in the Autodesk Revit 2018 software.

Practice Files

To download the practice files for this learning guide, use the following steps:

1. Type the URL shown below into the address bar of your Internet browser. The URL must be typed **exactly as shown**. If you are using an ASCENT ebook, you can click on the link to download the file.

Address bar

http://www.ascented.com/getfile?id=labrusca

File   Edit   View   Favorites   Tools   Help

2. Press <Enter> to download the .ZIP file that contains the Practice Files.

3. Once the download is complete, unzip the file to a local folder. The unzipped file contains an .EXE file.

4. Double-click on the .EXE file and follow the instructions to automatically install the Practice Files on the C:\ drive of your computer.

   Do not change the location in which the Practice Files folder is installed. Doing so can cause errors when completing the practices in this learning guide.

http://www.ascented.com/getfile?id=labrusca

Stay Informed!

Interested in receiving information about upcoming promotional offers, educational events, invitations to complimentary webcasts, and discounts? If so, please visit:

www.ASCENTed.com/updates/

Help us improve our product by completing the following survey:

www.ASCENTed.com/feedback

You can also contact us at: *feedback@ASCENTed.com*

Phasing, Design Options, and Groups

There are a variety of tools that can be used on complex projects:

- Phasing enables you to specify which project elements belong to a specific phase in the process of construction. You can create views that show each of these separate phases.

- Design Options enable you to create different examples for part of a building, and then display each example in separate views. Once you have decided which option to use, you can make the option part of the main model.

- Groups are sets of elements that can be inserted into a project. They can include both model and annotation elements. These groups can be saved to a separate file and then inserted or linked into multiple projects.

Learning Objectives in this Chapter

- Create and apply phases to elements.
- Create views to display different phases.
- Create Design Options.
- Add existing and new elements to Design Options.
- Create views for Design Options.
- Create groups of elements and annotations.
- Modify groups.
- Save groups as separate files.

1.1 Applying Project Phasing

Phases show distinct stages in a project's life. They are typically used with renovations and additions, as shown in Figure 1–1, or when a project involves several phases for its completion.

Phases are applied to elements. The phases you see are controlled by views.

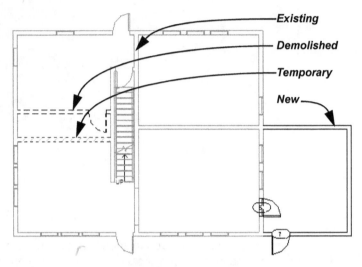

Existing

Demolished

Temporary

New

Figure 1–1

All construction elements have two phase properties, *Phase Created* and *Phase Demolished*. This creates four potential status conditions for each element regardless of how many phases you have in your project:

- **Existing:** Created in an earlier phase and exists in the current phase.

- **New:** Created in the current phase.

- **Demolished:** Created in an earlier phase and demolished in the current phase.

- **Temporary:** Created in the current phase and demolished in the current phase.

There are two default phases included in the template files: **Existing** and **New Construction**. Many projects can be completed just using these two options but you can also create additional phases for more complex projects.

When you add new elements in a view, they take on the phase set in the current view. In Properties, under the *Phasing* heading, select the *Phase* from the list, as shown in Figure 1–2.

Figure 1–2

- If you are working on a renovation project, start by modeling the building with the *Phase* set to **Existing**.

You can also move elements to a different phase. Select the element(s) and, in Properties, change the *Phase Created* as shown in Figure 1–3.

Figure 1–3

To demolish elements, select them and, in Properties, change the *Phase Demolished*. Or, in the *Modify* tab>Geometry panel,

click ![hammer icon] (Demolish) and select the elements that you want to demolish in the current phase.

- Demolishing a wall also demolishes any doors or windows associated with that wall.

- To change an element so that it is no longer demolished, set the *Phase Demolished* to **None**.

Hint: Elements that do not have phases

Annotations (tags, text, or dimensions), view elements (elevations, sections, and callout views), and datum elements (grids and levels) do not have phases.

Curtain walls and beam systems include sub-elements that do not have phases. You need to select the primary curtain wall or beam system to change the phase.

When selecting multiple elements to apply a phase, click

▽:37 (Filter) in the Status Bar and clear the check next to any annotations and curtain wall sub-elements, as shown in Figure 1–4, before modifying the phase in the properties.

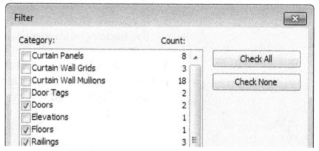

Figure 1–4

- Non-phase elements can be hidden in views where you do not want them to show. For example, in Figure 1–5, hide (by element) grids 5-8 and then modify the length of grids A-C (change the 3D icon to 2D so the change only shows in the current view.) You could also change the crop region of the view.

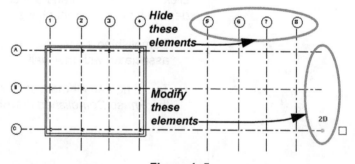

Figure 1–5

Phases and Views

The look of the elements is determined by graphic overrides assigned to each phase filter.

Duplicate a view for each phase you want to display. For example, you might want to show only the existing and demolished items in one view and the existing and new items, without the demolished items, in another view. You may also want to show the completed project without any of the previous phases, as shown in Figure 1–6.

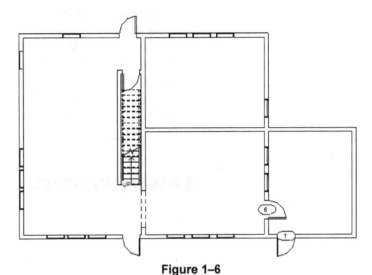

Figure 1–6

The *Phase Filter* determines which phases display in the view relative to the current phase:

- **None:** Displays all elements regardless of the current phase.

- **Show All:** Displays all phases up to the current phase, with all except the current phase, which is grayed out.

- **Show Complete:** Displays all construction up to the current phase.

- **Show Demo + New:** Displays the current phase and any demolished elements.

- **Show New:** Displays only elements created in the current view.

- **Show Previous + Demo:** Displays elements created in previous phases and any demolished elements from the current phase.

- **Show Previous + New:** Displays elements created in the previous phase and any new elements created in the current phase.

- **Show Previous Phase:** Displays elements created in any previous phases.

Creating Phases

When you create new phases, you can specify the names and time sequence, set up phase filters, and specify graphic overrides for each phase.

How To: Create New Phases

1. In the *Manage* tab>Phasing panel, click 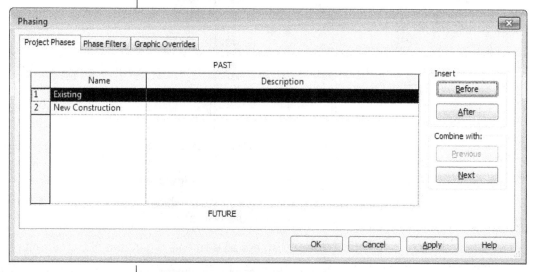 (Phases).
2. In the Phasing dialog box, *Project Phases* tab, the existing phases display. Two phases, **Existing** and **New Construction**, come with most templates, as shown in Figure 1–7.

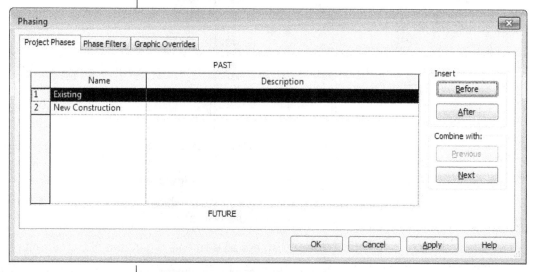

Figure 1–7

- The default phases can be renamed in this dialog box.

3. In the *Project Phases* tab, select a phase in the list. In the *Insert* area, click **Before** or **After**, as required. You cannot change the order and need to be careful as you insert phases.

- New phases are numbered (Phase 1, Phase 2, etc.). Select the name to change it. You can also add a description for each phase.

- You can combine phases, as required. Click **Previous** or **Next**. The elements on the combined phases take on the phase properties of the phase with which they were combined.

You need to add the phase in the correct time sequence. Past and Future notations are at the top and bottom of the dialog box.

4. Select the *Phase Filters* tab, as shown in Figure 1–8. Several phase filters are supplied with the program and you can add more. Once you have a new phase filter, you define which of the phases display. If listed as **Overridden**, the graphic overrides display for the phase.

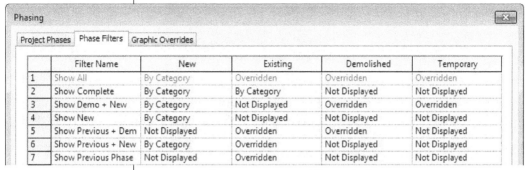

Figure 1–8

5. Select the *Graphic Overrides* tab, as shown in Figure 1–9. Set up the overrides, as required.

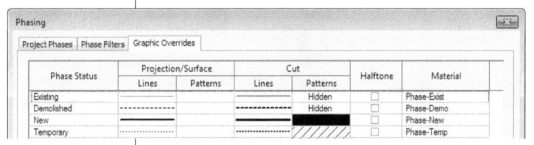

Figure 1–9

6. Click **OK** to close the dialog box.

Practice 1a

Apply Project Phasing - Architectural

Practice Objectives

- Set custom phases in a project.
- Apply phases to elements.
- Apply phases to views.

In this practice you will create several new phases and view the changes with the phase filters. You will also add some new elements in the existing building, as shown in Figure 1–10.

Estimated time for completion: 10 minutes

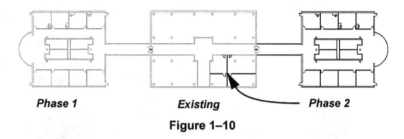

Phase 1   *Existing*   *Phase 2*

Figure 1–10

Task 1 - Set up Phases.

1. In the practice files folder, open **Office-Phases-A.rvt**.

2. In the *Manage* tab>Phasing panel, click 🗔 (Phases).

3. In the Phasing dialog box, in the *Project Phases* tab, rename the phase *New Construction* as **Phase 1** and add the description: **West Wing Addition**.

4. Insert an additional phase after the last one and accept the default name of **Phase 2**. Add the description: **East Wing Addition**, as shown in Figure 1–11.

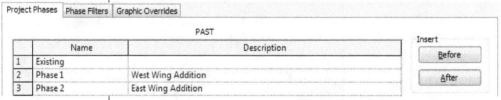

Figure 1–11

5. Click **OK** to close the dialog box.

Task 2 - Apply Phases to Views and Elements.

1. Duplicate three new views of **Level 1**. Rename them: **Level 1 - Existing**, **Level 1 - Phase 1**, and **Level 1 - Phase 2**.

2. Open the **Floor Plans: Level 1- Existing** view.

3. Select all elements in the middle building, as shown in Figure 1–12. Filter out any annotation elements, such as tags, views, and elevations.

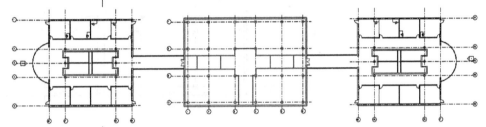

Figure 1–12

4. In Properties, change the *Phase Created* for these elements to **Existing**.

5. Click in the view to release the selection. The building elements should turn gray when you clear the selection.

6. In Properties (with no elements selected), scroll down and set *Phase Filter* to **Show Complete** and *Phase* to **Existing**, as shown in Figure 1–13.

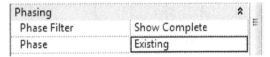

Figure 1–13

7. Click in the view. Only the central building displays but the grids on either side still display. Resize the crop region so only the main building displays as shown in Figure 1–14.

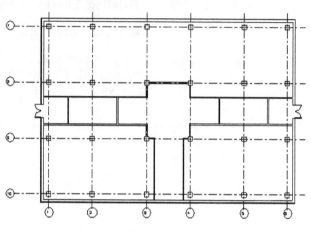

Figure 1–14

8. Open the **Floor Plans: Level 1 - Phase 1** view.

9. Select the elements in the right (east) wing, filter out any views and tags, and change the *Phase Created* of these elements to **Phase 2**. In this case, the elements are removed from the view. Resize the crop region so the east wing grids do not display, as shown in Figure 1–15.

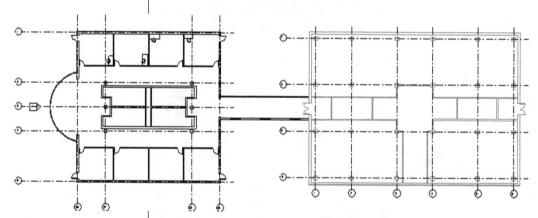

Figure 1–15

10. Without any elements selected, verify that the *Phase Filter* is set to **Show All** and the *Phase* is set to **Phase 1**.

11. In the *Modify* tab>Geometry panel, click ⚒ (Demolish). Select the four walls in the center building that cross the long horizontal hallways, as shown in Figure 1–16.

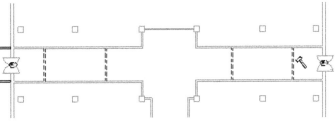

Figure 1–16

12. Click ▷ (Modify) and select one of the demolished walls. In Properties, scroll down to the *Phasing* area. Ensure that the *Phase Created* is set to **Existing** and *Phase Demolished* is set to **Phase 1**.

13. Open the **Floor Plans: Level 1 - Phase 2** view.

14. In Properties, without any elements selected, set the *Phase Filter* to **Show All** and change the *Phase* to **Phase 2**. The East Wing is added and the demolished walls are removed, while the elements in the previous two phases are grayed out, as shown in Figure 1–17.

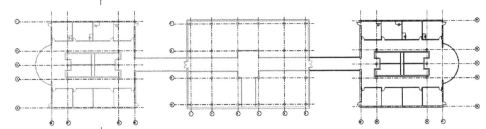

Figure 1–17

15. Modify the crop region so that it shows all of Phase 2 and part of the existing building. Hide the grids in the existing building, as shown in Figure 1–18.

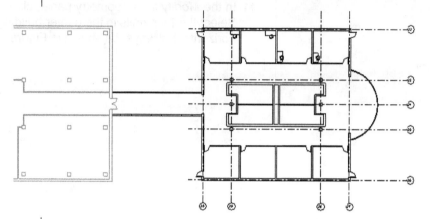

Figure 1–18

16. In the existing building add several walls and doors with some of the doors along the existing walls, as shown in Figure 1–19.

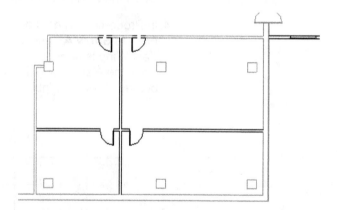

Figure 1–19

17. Open the **Floor Plans: Level 1 - Phase 1** view to see that the walls added in Phase 2 do not display.

18. Save the project.

Practice 1b

Apply Project Phasing - Structural

Practice Objectives

- Set custom phases in a project.
- Apply phases to elements.
- Apply phases to views.

In this practice you will create phases and move the elements in the project to different phases. You will then view the changes with the phase filters, as shown in Figure 1–20.

Estimated time for completion: 10 minutes

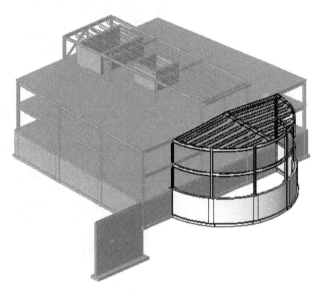

Figure 1–20

Task 1 - Set up Phases.

1. In the practice files folder, open **Office-Phases-S.rvt.**

2. In the *Manage* tab>Phasing panel, click (Phases).

3. In the Phasing dialog box there is one phase, **New Construction**. The project will now be divided into three phases. In the *Project Phases* tab, rename the phase *New Construction* as **Phase 1** and add the description **Main Building**.

4. Insert two additional phases after the last one and accept the default names of **Phase 2** and **Phase 3**. Add the description **Penthouse** to Phase 2 and **Addition** to Phase 3, as shown in Figure 1–21.

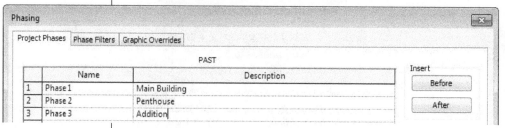

Figure 1–21

5. Click **OK** to close the dialog box.

6. Select several elements from different parts of the building. They are all in Phase 1.

7. Save the project.

Task 2 - Apply Phases to Elements.

1. Open the **Structural Plans: Penthouse** view.

2. Select all of the structural framing girders, structural columns, and structural Beam Systems (do a crossing selection and filter out everything else). In Properties, change the *Phase created* to **Phase 2**. The Phase 2 elements are removed from the view but the elevator shaft and stair shaft remain as shown in Figure 1–22.

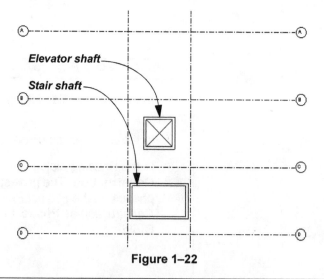

Figure 1–22

Architectural roofs do not show in some structural views. Using a structural floor ensures that the roof displays.

3. In the *Structure* tab>Structure panel, click 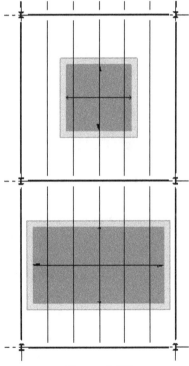 (Floor: Structural).

4. Add roof slabs to the top of the elevator and stair shafts using the **Floor: 1 1/2" Metal Roof Deck** type at a height of **8'-0"** off the Roof level. The new slabs are added to Phase 1.

5. In Properties, with no elements selected, change the *Phase* to **Phase 2**. The beams and columns now display.

6. Shade the view so you can see the roofs.

7. In the *Modify* tab>Geometry panel, click (Demolish). Zoom in and select the roof slabs, as shown in Figure 1–23. (Use <Tab> to select them.)

Figure 1–23

8. Select one of the slabs. In Properties, note that the slab is listed as **Phase Demolished** in Phase 2, as shown in Figure 1–24. The dashed edges do not display in the view because they overlap the walls.

Phasing	⌃
Phase Created	Phase 1
Phase Demolished	Phase 2

Figure 1–24

9. Open the **Structural Plans: Level 1** view.

10. Select the Structural Columns, Structural Foundations, and Walls connected to the arc area, as shown in Figure 1–25. In Properties, move these elements to Phase 3.

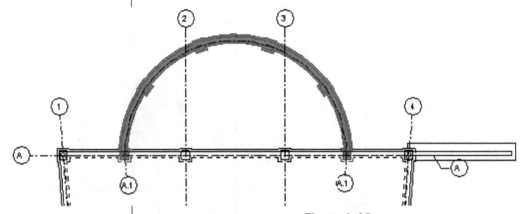

Figure 1–25

11. Hide the arc grid in the view.

12. Repeat the process in the **Structural Plans: Level 2** and **Structural Plans: Roof** views. In the Roof view, you select the beam systems first and change them to Phase 3. Then you can select the rest of the beams and columns.

13. Open the **3D Views: Front View**. It should display the existing building with the new roof slabs, as shown in Figure 1–26.

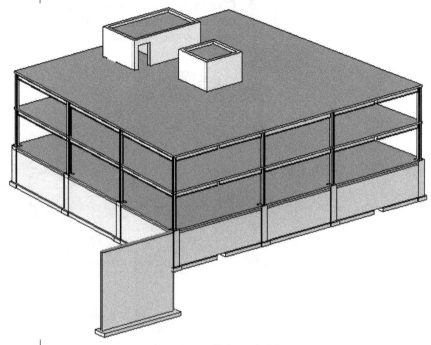

Figure 1–26

14. Save the project.

Task 3 - Apply Phases to Views.

---

1. Use **Duplicate with Detailing** and create three new views of the Front view. Rename them as **Front View - Phase 2**, **Front View - Phase 3**, and **Front View - Final**.

2. Rename Front View to **Front View - Phase 1**.

3. Open the **Front View - Phase 2** view.

4. In Properties, scroll down and change *Phase Filter* to **Show All** and *Phase* to **Phase 2** as shown in Figure 1–27.

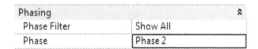

Figure 1–27

---

5. Click in the view. The existing building is grayed out and the new Penthouse phase displays with the deleted roof slabs in red, as shown in Figure 1–28.

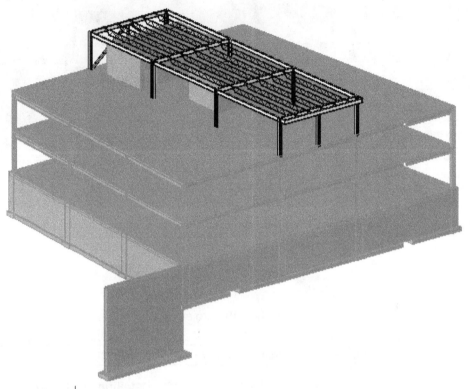

Figure 1–28

6. Open the **Front View - Phase 3** view.

7. In Properties, set *Phase Filter* to **Show All** and the *Phase* to **Phase 3**. Now the existing building and the penthouse are grayed out and the new entrance structure displays as shown in Figure 1–29.

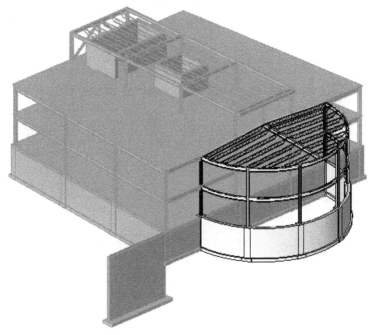

Figure 1–29

8. Open the **Front View - Final** view.

9. In Properties, set the *Phase Filter* to **Show Complete** and the *Phase* to **Phase 3**. All of the elements now display without any differences to the phases.

10. Save the project.

Practice 1c

Apply Project Phasing - MEP

Practice Objectives

- Set custom phases in a project.
- Apply phases to elements.
- Apply phases to views.

In this practice you will create phases and move the elements in the project to different phases. You will also draw new elements in different phases and view the changes with the phase filters, as shown in Figure 1–30.

Estimated time for completion: 10 minutes

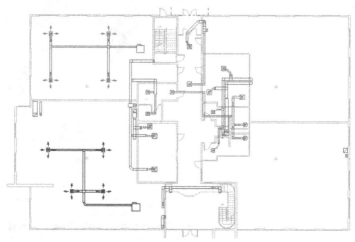

Figure 1–30

Task 1 - Set up Phases.

1. In the practice files folder, open **Office-Phases-MEP.rvt**.

2. In the *Manage* tab>Phasing panel, click (Phases).

3. In the Phasing dialog box there are two phases, **Existing** and **New Construction**. You will add two phases used for tenant build out.

4. In the *Project Phases* tab, rename *New Construction* to **Tenant 1**.

5. In the *Insert* area, click **After** once and rename that phase to **Tenant 2**, as shown in Figure 1–31.

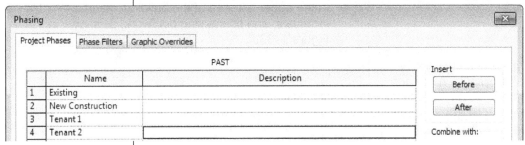

Figure 1–31

6. Click **OK** to close the dialog box.

7. Save the project.

Task 2 - Apply Phases to Elements.

1. Working in the Mechanical>HVAC>Floor Plans: **1 - Mech** view, select all of the existing ductwork and air terminals and filter out anything else.

2. In Properties, change the *Phase Created* to **Existing**. The elements turn gray, as shown in Figure 1–32.

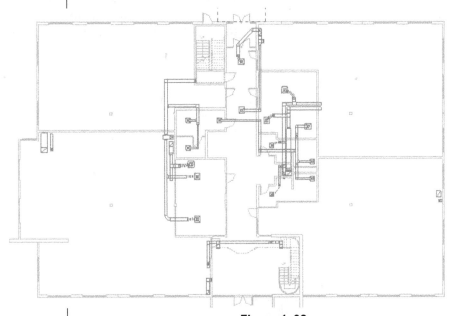

Figure 1–32

3. In Properties, with no element selected, note that the *Phase* is set to **Tenant 1**.

4. In the upper left area of the building, insert a VAV Unit, air terminals, and connecting ductwork, as shown in Figure 1–33.

In this example, the VAV Unit is set to 10'-0" and the Air Terminals to 8'-0". The exact location is not critical.

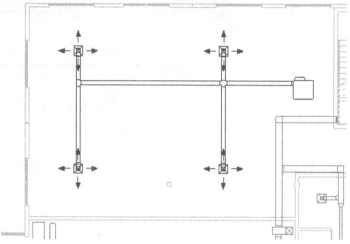

Figure 1–33

5. In Properties, with no elements selected, change the *Phase* to **Tenant 2** and draw an additional HVAC system. The Existing and Tenant 1 phases are grayed out and the current Phase displays in color, as shown in Figure 1–34.

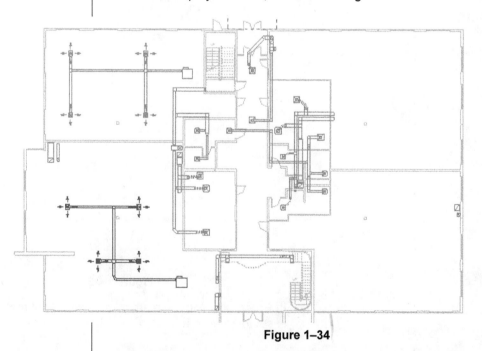

Figure 1–34

Task 3 - Apply Phases to Views.

1. Use **Duplicate with Detailing** and create three new views of **1- Mech** view. Rename them as **1 - Mech - Tenant 1**, **1 - Mech - Tenant 2**., and **1 - Mech - Final**.

2. Rename *1 - Mech* to **1 - Mech - Existing** and open it.

3. In Properties, change the *Phase* to **Existing** as shown in Figure 1–35.

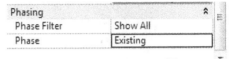

Figure 1–35

4. Open the **1 - Mech - Tenant 1** view and set the *Phase* to **Tenant 1**.

5. Open the **1 - Mech - Tenant 2** view and set the *Phase* to **Tenant 2**, if it is not already set.

6. Open the **1 - Mech - Final** view. Set the *Phase Filter* to **Show Complete** and the Phase to **Tenant 2**, as shown in Figure 1–36.

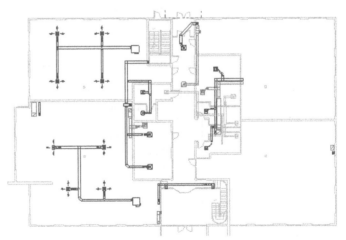

Figure 1–36

7. Save the project.

1.2 Using Design Options

Design Options provide a way to set up multiple layouts for a section of a building model. For example, you could design several roof options, window layouts, or entry areas and view each in context with the main building.

You can create a variety of *Design Option Sets* that define an area that changes and then add *Design Options* under each set. For example, you can create a Design Option Set with two options for an a-frame roof, as shown in Figure 1–37, and a curved roof, as shown in Figure 1–38.

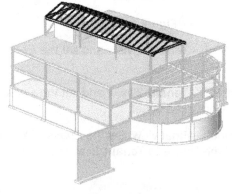

Figure 1–37   **Figure 1–38**

- The part of the building that is NOT modified by options is called the *Main Model*.

- Design Options are rarely used in MEP projects, as systems do not work in the options.

The Design Options tools are located in the *Manage* tab>Design Options panel, as shown in Figure 1–39 and with additional tools in the Status bar in Figure 1–40.

Figure 1–39

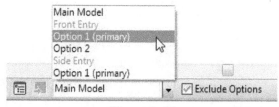

Figure 1–40

- Once you make a decision on the option to use, you can accept the primary set and delete the rest of the options.

- Design Options must be resolved before sending the model to be linked into another project. Only the primary design options display in the link.

How To: Set Up Design Options

1. In the *Manage* tab>Design Options panel, or in the Status Bar, click ▤ (Design Options). The Design Options dialog box opens, as shown in Figure 1–41.

You can have as many Option Sets and Options under a set, as required. Each set always contains one Primary option.

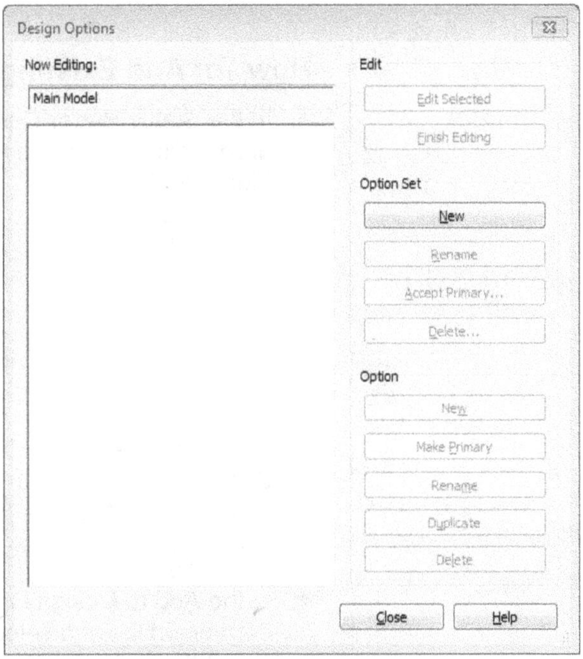

Figure 1–41

2. In the *Option Set* area, click **New**. An option set with a corresponding option is created, as shown in Figure 1–42.

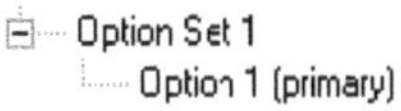

⊟ Option Set 1
    Option 1 (primary)

Figure 1–42

3. To add more options, select the Option Set title. In the *Option* area in the dialog box, click **New**.
4. Rename the option sets and options so that they convey more information. In the *Option Set* or *Option* area, click **Rename** and type a new name in the Rename dialog box.

5. Once you have defined the Option Sets and Options, you are ready to work on the various options. Close the dialog box.

• When you have added Design Options, you can set the current Design Option in the *Manage* tab or in the Status Bar, as shown in Figure 1–43.

Figure 1–43

How To: Add Existing Elements to Design Options

1. In the Status Bar or Design Option panel, verify that **Main Model** displays as the Active Design Option, as shown in Figure 1–44.

Figure 1–44

2. Select the elements that you want to include in a Design Option. The *Modify* tab displays.
3. Switch to the *Manage* tab. In the Design Options panel, click

    (Add to Set).

4. In the Add to Design Option Set dialog box, expand the drop-down list and select the **Design Option Set**. Then select the option(s) to which you want to add the selected elements, as shown in Figure 1–45. You can select more than one option.

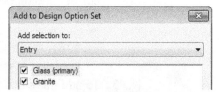

Figure 1–45

5. Click **OK** to close the dialog box. The elements are added to the option and can no longer be modified in the main model.

- Only elements in the primary Design Option display in standard views. They cannot be selected unless you clear the **Exclude Options** option in the Status bar before selecting.

- **Exclude Options** is only available in the Status Bar if Design Options have been set up in the project.

How To: Add New Elements to a Design Option

1. Set a Design Option to be current in the Active Design Option drop-down list in the Status Bar or in the Design Options panel, as shown in Figure 1–46.

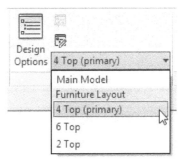

Figure 1–46

2. Only the elements that are part of the Active Design Option display in black. Elements in the main model are grayed out, as shown in Figure 1–47.

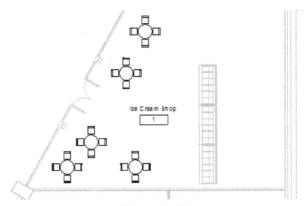

Figure 1–47

3. Use standard commands to add or modify elements in the Design Option. For example, you can move the seating and add other chairs and tables for the Ice Cream Shop shown in Figure 1–47.
4. Set the *Active Design Option* to **Main Model** when you are finished.

Viewing Design Options

You can set up views that specify Design Options. These can then be used to quickly see the various Design Options without having to edit them, as shown in Figure 1–48.

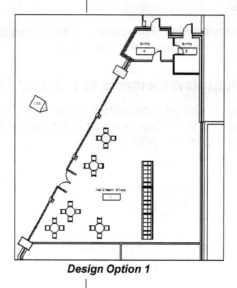
Design Option 1

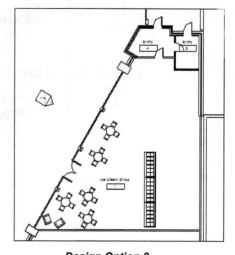
Design Option 2

Figure 1–48

How To: View Design Options

1. Create a view (a 3D view, plan, elevation, or section) that displays the information that you want to present.
2. In the view, open the Visibility/Graphic Overrides dialog box (type **VV** or **VG**).
3. In the *Design Options* tab, in the drop-down list for each Design Option Set, select a Design Option, as shown in Figure 1–49. **<Automatic>** displays the primary option or the option that is currently being edited. Setting the view to a specific choice, displays that option regardless of what is being edited.

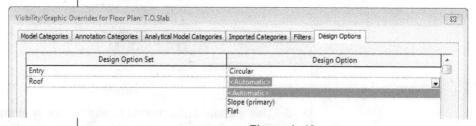

Figure 1–49

- If elements in a Design Option display in a view, you can click

  (Pick to Edit) in the Design Options panel and select one of the elements to activate that option.

How To: Delete Design Options

When you have decided on the Design Option you want to use, you can delete any other options in the project.

*If you did not set the active option to Main Model, you must select **Finish Editing** in the dialog box to continue the process.*

1. Set the *Active Design Option* to **Main Model**.
2. Open the Design Options dialog box.
3. Select the option you want to keep and click **Make Primary**.
4. Select the Option Set and click **Accept Primary...**.
5. An alert box opens as shown in Figure 1–50, warning you that all secondary options are going to be deleted. Click **Yes** if you are sure.

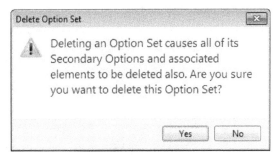

Figure 1–50

6. If views are associated with the option, you are prompted to delete the associated view, as shown in Figure 1–51. Select the view(s) and click **Delete**.

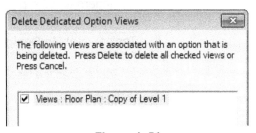

Figure 1–51

7. Close the Design Options dialog box.

Practice 1d

Use Design Options - Architectural

Practice Objectives

- Set up Design Options.
- Draw elements in each Design Option.
- Create views that show variations on the Design Options.

In this practice you will create two Design Option Sets and several Options for each set. You will modify the elements in each Design Option and create views that display the Options, such as the one shown in Figure 1–52.

Estimated time for completion: 15 minutes

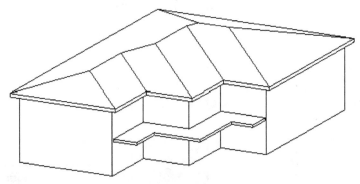

Figure 1–52

- As Design Options are rarely used with the Autodesk Revit MEP software, engineers can work through this practice to understand the process.

Task 1 - Set Up Design Options.

1. In the practice files folder, open **Office-Entry-A.rvt**.

2. In the *Manage* tab>Design Options panel or in the Status Bar, click (Design Options).

3. In the Design Options dialog box, in the *Options Set* area, click **New**. A new Option Set and a primary option is created, as shown in Figure 1–53.

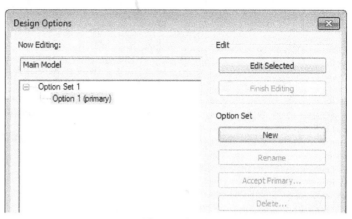

Figure 1–53

4. Select **Option Set 1** and in the *Option Set* area, click **Rename**. In the Rename dialog box set its name as **Main Roof** and click **OK**.

5. Select **Option 1 (primary)** and in the *Option* area, click **Rename**. Set its name as **Shallow Slope**.

6. In the *Option* area, click **New** twice to add two more options and name them as **Medium Slope** and **Steep Slope**.

7. Create an additional Option Set as **Entry Roof** and three options, as shown in Figure 1–54.

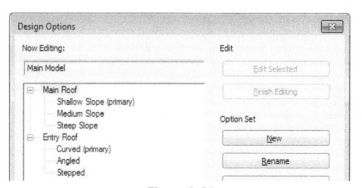

Figure 1–54

8. In the **Main Roof** option set, select **Medium Slope** and click **Make Primary**.

9. Close the Design Options dialog box.

Task 2 - Create Main Roof Design Options.

1. In the Design Options panel or in the Status Bar, in the Active Design Option drop-down list, activate the **Main Roof> Medium Slope (primary)** option. The main model is grayed out.

2. Open the **Floor Plans: Roof** view.

3. Draw a **Roof by Footprint** with a deep overhang, all edges sloped, and a medium slope angle, as shown in Figure 1–55.

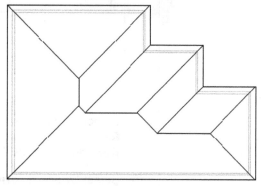

Figure 1–55

4. When prompted to attach highlighted walls to the roof, select **No**. You are prompted only for the primary option and not for other design options.

5. View the roof in elevation.

6. Set the *Active Design Option* to **Main Roof>Steep Slope**. The main model is grayed out and the medium sloped roof is toggled off.

7. Return to the **Floor Plans: Roof** view.Draw a **Roof by Footprint** using a steep slope angle.

8. Repeat the process using the **Shallow Slope** Design Option and a shallow roof slope.

9. Set the *Active Design Option* to **Main Model**.

10. Save the project.

Task 3 - Create Entry Roof Design Options.

1. Set the *Active Design Option* to **Entry Roof>Curved**. The main model and main roof are grayed out.

2. Open the **Floor Plans: Level 2** view.

3. Use **Roof by Footprint** to draw a curved flat roof over the entry area, as shown in Figure 1–56. You can use the **Spline** or **Arc** sketch options. Use a generic roof type.

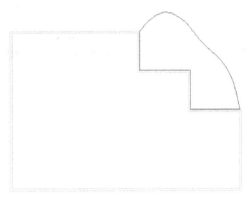

Figure 1–56

4. Create additional flat roofs similar to those shown in Figure 1–57 for the **Angled** and **Stepped** entry roof options.

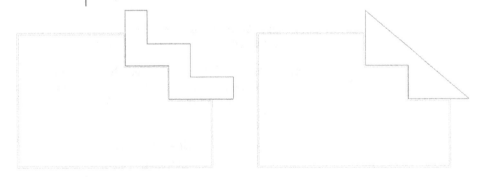

Figure 1–57

5. Return the Design Option to the **Main Model**. The curved roof displays as it is the primary design option that shows at this level.

6. Save the project.

Task 4 - Create Views of Design Options.

1. Switch to a 3D view that displays both the main and entry roofs. The primary option currently displays for each.

2. Type **VG** to open the Visibility/Graphic Overrides dialog box.

3. In the *Design Options* tab, specify the Design Options for the sets as follows and click **OK**:

   - Main Roof - Medium Slope (primary)
   - Entry Roof - Curved (primary)

4. Rename the 3D view shown in Figure 1–58, as **Medium Slope and Curved**.

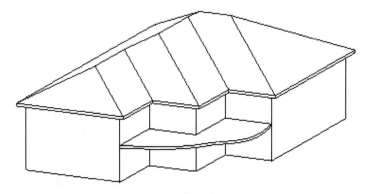

Figure 1–58

5. Duplicate the 3D view. Rename the view as **Shallow and Stepped**.

6. Open the Visibility/Graphic Overrides dialog box and in the *Design Options* tab, specify the Design Options for the sets as follows and click **OK**. The new layout displays, as shown in Figure 1–59.

   - Main Roof - Shallow Slope
   - Entry Roof - Stepped

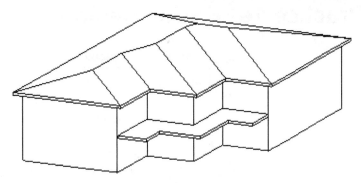

Figure 1–59

7. Repeat this with other combinations of the options if you have time.

8. Switch between the various views to see the differences.

9. Save the project.

Practice 1e

Use Design Options - Structural

Practice Objectives

- Set up Design Options.
- Draw elements in each Design Option.
- Create views that show variations on the Design Options.

In this practice you will create two Design Options. You will modify the elements in each Design Option and create views that display the Options, such as the one shown in Figure 1–60.

Estimated time for completion: 15 minutes

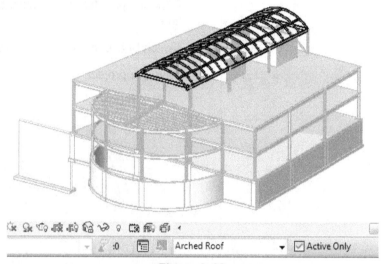

Figure 1–60

Task 1 - Set Up Design Options.

1. In the practice files folder, open **Office-Options-S.rvt**.

2. In the *Manage* tab>Design Options panel or on the Status Bar, click ▤ (Design Options).

3. In the Design Options dialog box, in the *Options Set* area, click **New**. A new Option Set and a primary option are created, as shown in Figure 1–61.

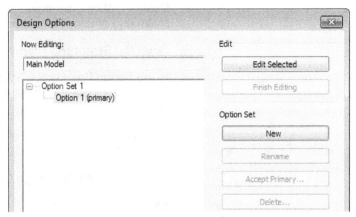

Figure 1–61

4. Select **Option Set 1** and in the *Option Set* area, click **Rename**. In the Rename dialog box, set the new name as **Penthouse Roof** and click **OK**.

5. Select **Option 1 (primary)** and in the *Option* area, click **Rename**. Set the name as **Flat Roof**.

6. In the *Option* area, click **New** twice to add two more options and rename them as **A-Frame Roof** and **Arched Roof**, as shown in Figure 1–62.

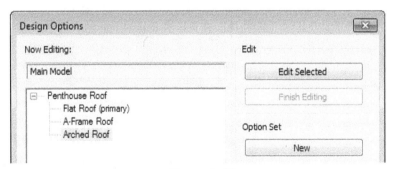

Figure 1–62

7. Close the Design Options dialog box.

8. Save the project.

Task 2 - Add structural elements to Design Options.

1. In the Design Options panel or in the Status Bar, in the Active Design Option drop-down list, activate the **Flat Roof (primary)** option. The model is grayed out.

2. Open the **Structural Plans: Penthouse** view.

3. In the Status Bar, clear the **Active Only** option. This enables you to select elements that are not in the current design option.

4. Select all of the structural elements but not the tags, openings, and walls.

5. In the *Manage* tab>Design Options panel or the Status Bar, click 🖳 (Add to Set).

6. Switch to a 3D view that displays the elements in this design option, as shown in Figure 1–63.

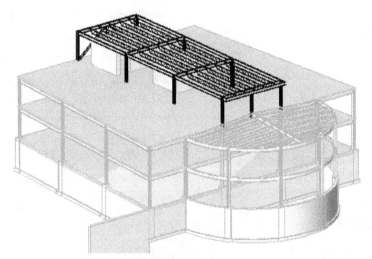

Figure 1–63

7. While still in the 3D view, switch to the **A-Frame Roof** design option. The elements in the previous design option are also available for this design option.

8. Create two additional penthouse roofs similar to those shown in Figure 1–64 for the **A-Frame Roof** and **Arched Roof** options.

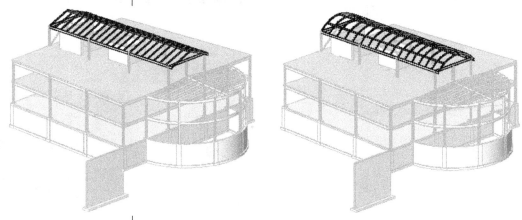

Figure 1–64

9. Return the Design Option to the **Main Model**. The flat roof displays as it is the primary design option that shows at this level.

10. Save the project.

Task 3 - Create Views of Design Options.

1. Open the 3D view **Front View**. All of the building with the Flat Roof (primary) design option should display.

2. Duplicate the view and rename it **Design Option Flat Roof**.

3. Type **VG** to open the Visibility/Graphic Overrides dialog box.

4. In the *Design Options* tab, set the Design Option for the Penthouse roof to **Flat Roof (primary)**. Click **OK** and the view remains as is.

5. Duplicate this 3D view and rename it **Design Option A-Frame Roof**.

6. In the Visibility/Graphic Overrides dialog box, change the Design Option to **A-Frame Roof**. Click **OK** and note that the building updates with the A-Frame Roof design option in place of the flat roof as shown in Figure 1–65.

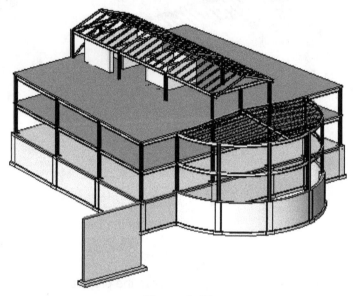

Figure 1–65

7. Repeat one more time creating a 3D View for the **Arched Roof** design option.

8. Switch between the various views to see the differences.

9. Save the project.

1.3 Working with Groups

Groups enable you to gather elements together to work as one unit. They can be used multiple times in a project. For example, if you are creating a hotel lobby, you can create a seating group, as shown in Figure 1–66, and then copy the group rather than place the individual furniture components.

Groups are rarely used in MEP projects, as systems do not work in groups.

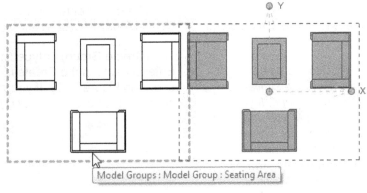

Model Groups : Model Group : Seating Area

Figure 1–66

There are three types of groups:

- **Model Groups:** Consists of model elements only.

- **Detail Groups:** Consists of detail or annotation elements only, including detail components, dimensions, tags, etc.

- **Model Groups with Attached Detail Groups:** Consists of a model group with the associated detail group attached to it.

New
in **2018**

- Model groups can be scheduled including the Count, Types, Reference Level and Origin Level Offset, as shown in Figure 1–67

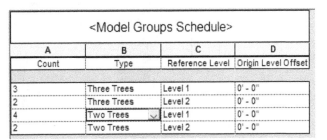

<Model Groups Schedule>			
A	B	C	D
Count	Type	Reference Level	Origin Level Offset
3	Three Trees	Level 1	0' - 0"
2	Three Trees	Level 2	0' - 0"
4	Two Trees	Level 1	0' - 0"
2	Two Trees	Level 2	0' - 0"

Figure 1–67

Creating Groups

You can create groups by selecting elements and then using the **Group** command or by starting the command first and then adding the elements to the group. If you start the command first, anything you insert or draw during the process of creating the group is added to it.

How To: Create a Group using Preselected Elements

1. Select the elements you want to include in the group.
2. In the *Modify | Multi-Select* tab>Create panel, click
   (Create Group) or type **GP**.
3. Enter a name in the Create Model Group dialog box, as shown in Figure 1–68. If you want to modify the group before creating it, select **Open in Group Editor**.

If only Detail elements are selected, a similar dialog box opens. If you select both Model and Detail elements, you are prompted to name both the Model Group and the Attached Detail Group.

Figure 1–68

4. Click **OK** to create the group.
5. By default, the group origin is at the center of the group. Click and drag the origin to a new location, as shown in Figure 1–69. The new origin is used by any new instances of the group.

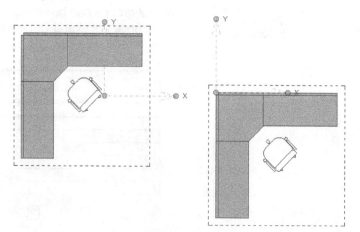

Figure 1–69

- Most elements can be grouped, including walls, components, and annotation, as long as the elements are compatible with each other.

- If you include a window, door, or other host-based element in a group, you need to place it on the type of host it is looking for.

How To: Create a Group and Add Elements

1. In the *Architecture* or *Structure* tab>Model panel, expand

   (Model Group) and click (Create Group).

2. In the Create Group dialog box, name the group and specify the type of group, either **Model** or **Detail**, as shown in Figure 1–70.

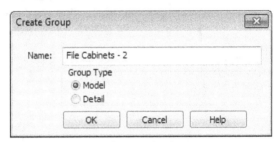

Figure 1–70

3. Click **OK**.
4. The Group Editor opens with the Edit Group panel, as shown in Figure 1–71.

Elements that are not part of the group are grayed out.

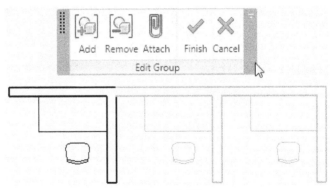

Figure 1–71

5. Add elements to the group.

- Click (Add) or type **AP** and select any existing elements you want to include in the group.

*The type of elements that you can select or insert depends on the Group Type (**Model** or **Detail**).*

- Anything you draw or insert while in the Group Editor is added to the group.

- You can copy elements which become part of the group.

- Click 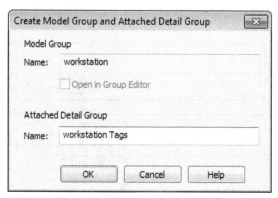 (Remove) or type **RG** to remove existing elements from the group. The elements are not removed from the project unless you delete them.

- To add or remove multiple elements from the group, hold <Ctrl> when selecting the elements.

- Click (Attach) or type **AD** to add detail elements to a model group. The Create Model Group and Attached Detail Group dialog box displays as shown in Figure 1–72. The *Model Group Name* is preset and you are required to add the *Attached Detail Group Name*.

*You cannot select detail elements with **Add** when editing a model group.*

Figure 1–72

Using Groups in a Project

You can add groups to a project by selecting them in the Project Browser, in the *Groups* node, and dragging them into the view, as shown in Figure 1–73. You can also use the Place Group commands.

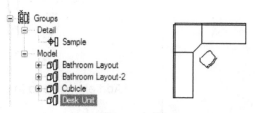

Figure 1–73

- If a model group has a detail group, you need to attach it separately.

How To: Add Groups from the Ribbon

1. **Model Groups:** In the *Architecture* or *Structure* tab>Model panel, expand

    ⬚ (Model Group) and click ⬚ (Place Model Group).
    Detail Groups: In the *Annotate* tab>Detail panel, expand

    ⬚ (Detail Group) and click ⬚ (Place Detail Group).
2. In Properties, in the Type Selector, select the group you want to add.
3. Click in the drawing screen to place the group. You can add multiple copies.

- If you selected a model group with a hosted element (such as a door or window) that does not include the host (wall), you can only place one group at a time.

- In some cases, when there are hosted and non-hosted elements in the same group, pick in the model to place the group and then move it so that the hosted element is on the correct host as shown in Figure 1–74. In the *Modify | Model Groups* tab>Edit Pasted panel, click ✓ (Finish).

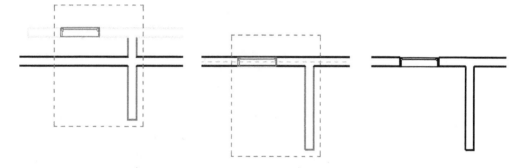

Figure 1–74

How To: Attach Detail Groups to Model Groups

1. Select a model group that has a related detail group.
2. In the *Modify | Model Groups* tab>Group panel, click

    ⬚ (Attached Detail Groups).

3. In the Attached Detail Group Placement dialog box, select the detail groups that you to want attach to the model group, as shown in Figure 1–75.

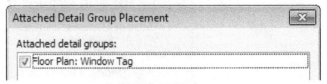

Figure 1–75

4. Click **OK**.

- Remove detail groups from the model group by following the same process, but clearing the checkmark next to the group name in the dialog box.

Modifying Groups

Groups can be copied, moved, mirrored, and rotated like most elements in the program. You can also cut, copy, and paste them to the clipboard. Individual instances of groups can be changed, but you can also change a group definition that impacts all instances of that group.

- If you no longer want an instance of a group to act as a group, as shown in Figure 1–76, select it and click

   (Ungroup) in the Group panel or type **UG**.

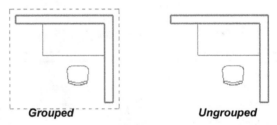

Grouped   *Ungrouped*

Figure 1–76

- To delete a group definition from the project, you must first delete all instances of the group in the project. You can then select the group name in the Project Browser, right-click, and select **Delete**.

- To modify individual instances of a group, use <Tab> to select one element in a group. Then, click on the *Group Member* icon (as shown in Figure 1–77), to remove the element from that instance of the group

Figure 1–77

- To replace one group with a different group, select a group. In Properties, select another group's name, as shown in Figure 1–78. The selected groups are replaced.

If you are replacing groups, it helps to match the groups' origin and rotation.

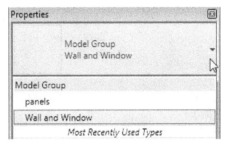

Figure 1–78

- To make duplicates of groups, in the Project Browser, *Groups* node, right-click on the group and select **Duplicate**, or in Properties, click

  (Edit Type) and **Duplicate...**. When you have copied the new group, make any changes as shown in Figure 1–79.

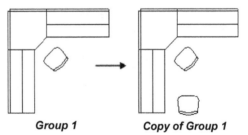

Group 1   *Copy of Group 1*

Figure 1–79

- To modify all instances of a group definition, in the *Modify |*

  Model Groups tab>Group panel, click (Edit Group) or type **EG**. In the Group Editor, make changes to the group as required. Use the floating Edit Group toolbar to add, remove, and attach elements.

- To change the name of a group, right-click on the group in the Project Browser and select **Rename**.

Groups in Other Projects

You can save groups to a project file to use in other projects. Groups can also be converted to links. This creates an additional project file but also changes the group in your project to link to the new project file.

How To: Save a Group as a File

1. In the *File* tab, expand (Save As), expand

    (Library), and click (Group).
2. In the Save Group dialog box, in the Group To Save drop-down list, select a group as shown in Figure 1–80.

*Alternatively, right-click on the group name in the Project Browser and select **Save Group**.*

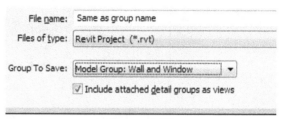

Figure 1–80

3. Navigate to the folder in which you want to store the group.
4. Click **Save**.

How To: Use a File as a Group in a Project

1. Open the file in which you want to load the group.

2. In the *Insert* tab>Load from Library panel, click (Load As Group).
3. In the Load File as Group dialog box, navigate to the folder in which the file is stored and select the file.
4. Click **Open**. The file is added as a group definition in the current project.
5. Insert the group in the project using one of the methods for placing a group.

- Any Autodesk® Revit® project or family file can be loaded as a group.

- Because a group can be saved as a standard RVT project file, the groups can be edited externally from any project.

- When you reload the group into a project, an alert box opens if you are loading a file with the same name as an existing group in your project, as shown in Figure 1–81.

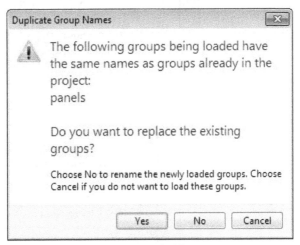

Figure 1–81

- Click **Yes** to replace all instances of the group with the new information.
- Click **No** to bring in the group with a new name incremented from the previous name.
- Click **Cancel** to stop the process.

How To: Use an Open File as a Group in Another Open File

1. Open a project file in which you want to place a group.
2. Open the file that you want to use as a group.
3. In the *Architecture* or *Structure* tab> Model panel, expand ⬚ (Model Group) and click ⬚ (Load as Group into Open Projects).
4. In the Load into Projects dialog box, select the projects into which you want the currently active project to be loaded as a group.
5. Click **OK**. The group is now available for use in the other projects.

How To: Convert a Group to a Link

1. Select the group that you want to convert to a link.
2. In the *Modify | Model Groups* tab>Group panel, click 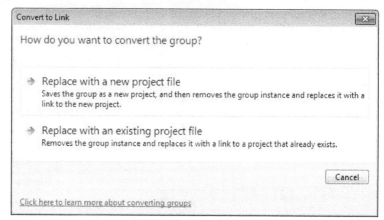 (Link).
3. In the Convert to Link dialog box shown in Figure 1–82, select the method that you want to use.

Convert to Link

How do you want to convert the group?

→ Replace with a new project file
Saves the group as a new project, and then removes the group instance and replaces it with a link to the new project.

→ Replace with an existing project file
Removes the group instance and replaces it with a link to a project that already exists.

Cancel

Click here to learn more about converting groups

Figure 1–82

4. If you create a new project file, the Save Group dialog box opens. Specify the name and location of the file and click **Save**. The group becomes a linked model in the host project.

5. If you replace it with an existing project file, the Open dialog box opens. Locate the file you want to use to replace the existing group, and click **Open**. The new project file becomes a linked model in the host project.

Practice 1f

Work with Groups - Architectural

Practice Objectives

- Create a group.
- Place instances of a group in a project.
- Edit a group definition.
- Modify an instance of a group.

In this practice you will group components, copy the group, modify the group, and modify one instance, as shown in Figure 1–83. You will also save the group to be used in another project.

Estimated time for completion: 10 minutes

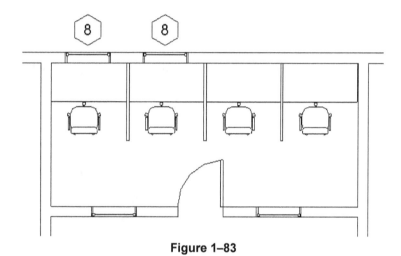

Figure 1–83

Task 1 - Create a Group.

1. In the practice files folder, open **Testing-Room-A.rvt**.

2. Add the component **Desk: 60" x 30"** against the left back wall.

3. Place a **Chair-Executive** in front of the desk and a **Cube Panel: 60" x 66"** to the right of it. These components are already loaded into the project.

Click (Thin Lines) in the Quick Access Toolbar to help you see the exact placement of the panel.

4. Place a window with a tag in the wall directly in front of the desk, as shown in Figure 1–84.

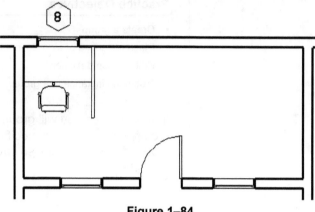

Figure 1–84

5. Select the three components, the window, and the tag.

6. In the *Modify | Multi-Select* tab>Create panel, click (Create Group).

7. Name the Model Group as **Test Station**, and the Attached Detail Group as **Tags**, as shown in Figure 1–85.

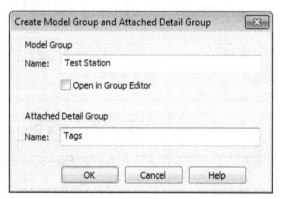

Figure 1–85

8. Click on the Modify Group Origin control and drag it to the upper left corner of the desk, as shown in Figure 1–86.

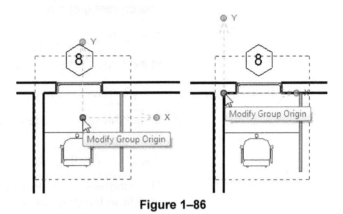

Figure 1–86

Task 2 - Place Instances of the Group.

1. In the *Architecture* tab>Model panel, expand [icon] (Model Group) and click [icon] (Place Model Group).

2. In the Type Selector, verify that the name of the current group is **Test Station**.

3. Place a copy of the group directly to the right of the original group. Everything but the tag should be inserted.

4. Click [icon] (Finish) to complete the process.

5. Select the new group.

6. In the *Modify | Model Groups* tab>Group panel, click [icon] (Attached Detail Groups).

7. In the Attached Detail Group Placement dialog box, select the **Floor Plan: Tags** detail group and click **OK**. The tag is added to the instance of the group.

Because this is a model group that includes hosted elements (the window) without the host element (the wall), you can only place one group at a time.

Task 3 - Edit the Group Definition.

1. The current group is still selected. In the *Modify | Model Groups* tab>Group panel, click 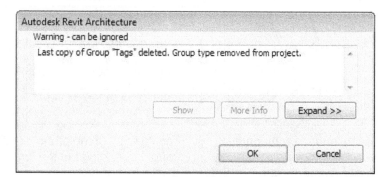 (Edit Group).

2. In the Group Editor, in the floating Edit Group panel, click (Remove).

3. Select the window to remove it from the group.

4. Click (Finish).

5. The windows are no longer involved in the groups but they are still in the drawing. A warning box opens indicating that the attached detail group is removed, as shown in Figure 1–87. Click **OK**.

Autodesk Revit Architecture

Warning - can be ignored

Last copy of Group "Tags" deleted. Group type removed from project.

Show   More Info   Expand >>

OK   Cancel

Figure 1–87

6. Place two more copies of the model group **Test Station** in the project. The new groups do not include the window.

Task 4 - Modify an Instance of a Group.

1. The last group does not need the last cubicle wall. Hover over the element that you want to exclude, press <Tab> until it highlights, and select the element, as shown in Figure 1–88.

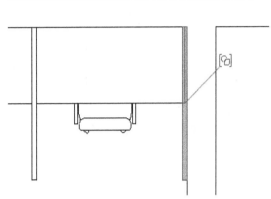

Figure 1–88

2. Click the icon to only exclude the wall from that group. Click in empty space to complete the process. The cubicle wall is only excluded from that group.

Task 5 - Save the Group as a File.

1. In the Project Browser, in the *Groups*>**Model** node> right-click on the **Test Station** group name and select **Save Group**.

2. In the Save Group dialog box, navigate to your practice files folder and save the group with the same name as the group.

3. Save and close the project.

Practice 1g | Work with Groups - Structural

Practice Objectives

- Create a group of model and annotation elements.
- Add copies of the group to a project.
- Modify the elements of one group.

In this practice you will place bracing in a framing elevation and then group the bracing and its associated tags as shown in Figure 1–89. You will also add the group to another bay and copy it to further bays. You will ungroup and modify one group and use the elements to create another group.

Estimated time for completion: 15 minutes

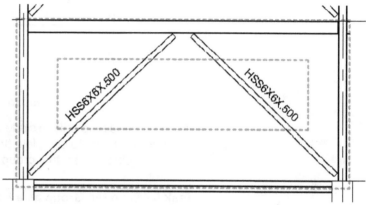

Figure 1–89

Task 1 - Add bracing.

1. In the practice files folder, open **Syracuse-Suites-Groups-S.rvt**.

2. Open the **Elevations (Framing Elevation): West Bracing** view.

3. Zoom in to display the **00 GROUND FLOOR** and **TOS-1ST FLOOR** level heads.

4. In the *Structure* tab>Structure panel, click ⊠ (Brace).

5. In the *Modify | Place Brace* tab>Tag panel, click ⌐① (Tag on Placement) to toggle it on.

6. In the Type Selector, select **HSS Hollow Structural Section: HSS6X6X.500**.

7. Draw from the midpoint of the beam located on the 1st Floor to the centerline of the column at the base, as shown in Figure 1–90. Do the same on both sides.

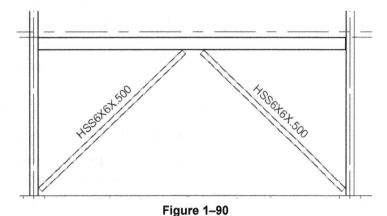

Figure 1–90

8. Press <Esc> or click 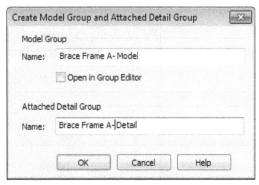 (Modify) to end the command.

Task 2 - Create and place groups.

1. Select the braces and the tags.

2. In the *Modify | Multi Select* tab>Create panel, click [Create Group icon] (Create Group).

3. Name the groups **Brace Frame A-Model** and **Brace Frame A-Detail**, as shown in Figure 1–91.

Figure 1–91

4. Click **OK**.

5. Move the blue control to the lower left corner, as shown in Figure 1–92, to change the insertion point of the group.

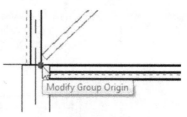

Figure 1–92

6. In the *Structure* tab>Model panel, expand ⬚ (Model Group) and click ⬚ (Place Model Group).

7. In the Type Selector, verify that the name of the current group is **Brace Frame A - Model**.

The group moves into the correct location once you complete the process.

8. In the *Modify | Model Groups* tab>Edit Pasted panel, click ✓ (Finish).

9. Select the group. In the *Modify | Model Groups* tab>Group panel, click 🗐 (Attached Detail Groups).

10. In the Attached Detail Group Placement dialog box, select **Elevation: Brace Bay A-Detail**.

11. Click **OK**. The bracing is labeled.

12. Select both the brace group and the attached detail group.

13. In the *Modify | Multi-Select* tab>Modify panel, click ⬚ (Copy).

14. In the Options Bar, select **Multiple** and **Constrain** (this forces the copy to only move horizontally or vertically).

15. Copy the groups to every level up to the 13th floor.

16. Zoom in on the 13th Floor bay, as shown in Figure 1–93. This bay requires a modification because of the difference in elevation.

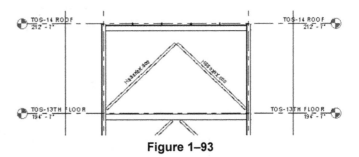

Figure 1–93

17. Select the bracing, and in the *Modify | Model Groups* tab> Group panel, click 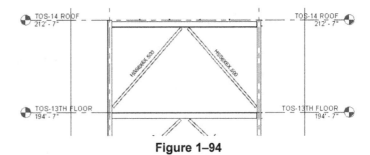 (Ungroup).

18. Modify the braces so that they extend up to the framing, as shown in Figure 1–94.

Figure 1–94

19. Select the revised braces and tags. Create two groups named **Brace Frame B-Model** and **Brace Frame B-Detail**.

20. Save the project.

Chapter Review Questions

1. When you want to demolish some elements, as shown in Figure 1–95, in what phase should the elements be?

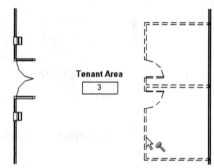

Figure 1–95

  a. New Construction

  b. Existing

  c. Demolition

2. When creating a view that displays the *Phase* **New Construction** along with the existing and demolished elements, as shown in Figure 1–96, which of the Phase Filters do you use?

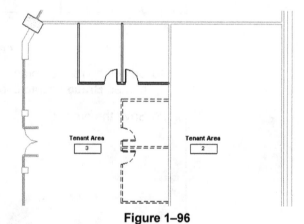

Figure 1–96

  a. Show All

  b. Show Complete

  c. Show Previous + New

  d. Show Previous Phase

3. What is the difference between *Option Set* and *Option*, as shown in Figure 1–97?

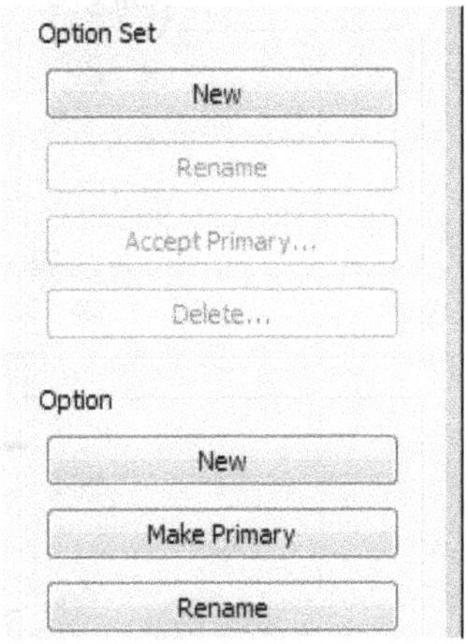

Figure 1–97

a. You can have multiple Options but only one Option Set.

b. You can have multiple Options without any Option Set.

c. You can have multiple Option Sets without any Options.

d. You can have multiple Option Sets with multiple Options in each set.

4. What method do you use to set up a view to display specific Design Options?

a. Set the Active Design Option.

b. Select the Primary Design Option in the Design Options dialog box.

c. Open the Visibility/Graphics dialog box and select the options.

d. Right-click in the view and select **Override Graphics** in view>By Element.

5. Which are the type of groups that can be created in the Autodesk Revit software? (Select all that apply.)

a. Annotative

b. Component

c. Detail

d. Model

6. While in the Group Editor, how do you add tags to an existing group, as shown in Figure 1–98, so that it creates a related detail group?

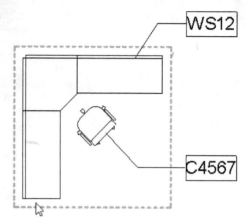

Figure 1–98

a. Drag and drop the tags group from the Project Browser on to the group.

b. In the Edit Group panel, click (Add) and select existing tags.

c. In the Edit Group panel, click (Attach) and specify the tags group.

d. Add the tags using (Tag by Category).

7. You can use the contents of an entire open project as a group in another project.

a. True

b. False

Command Summary

Button	Command	Location
Phases		
	Demolish	• **Ribbon**: *Modify* tab>Geometry panel
	Phases	• **Ribbon**: *Manage* tab>Phasing panel
Design Options		
Main Model ▼	**Active Design Option**	• **Ribbon**: *Manage* tab>Design Options panel • **Status Bar**
	Add to Set	• **Ribbon**: *Manage* tab>Design Options panel • **Status Bar**
	Design Options	• **Ribbon**: *Manage* tab>Design Options panel • **Status Bar**
	Pick to Edit	• **Ribbon**: *Manage* tab>Design Options panel
Groups		
	Add to Group	• **Floating Panel:** Edit Group • **Shortcut**: AP (when a group is in edit mode)
	Attach Detail	• **Floating Panel:** Edit Group • **Shortcut:** AD (when a group is in edit mode)
	Attached Detail Groups	• **Ribbon:** *Modify	Model Groups* tab>Group panel
	Create Group (Detail)	• **Ribbon:** *Annotate* tab>Detail panel>expand Detail Group • **Shortcut: GP**
	Create Group (elements selected)	• **Ribbon:** *Modify* contextual tab>Create panel • **Shortcut: GP**
	Create Group (Model)	• **Ribbon:** *Architecture* or *Structure* tab>Model panel>expand Model Group • **Shortcut: GP**
	Edit Group	• **Ribbon:** *Modify	Model (or Detail) Groups* tab>Group panel • **Shortcut: EG** (when a group is selected)

	Load as Group	• **Ribbon:** *Insert* tab>Load from Library panel
	Load as Group into Open Projects	• **Ribbon:** *Architecture* or *Structure* tab>Model panel> expand Model Group
	Place Detail Group	• **Ribbon:** *Annotate* tab>Detail panel> expand Detail Group
	Place Model Group	• **Ribbon:** *Architecture* or *Structure* tab>Model panel> expand Model Group
	Remove from Group	• **Floating Panel:** Edit Group • **Shortcut: RG** (when a group is in edit mode)
	Ungroup	• **Ribbon:** *Modify	Model* (or *Detail*) *Groups* tab>Group panel • **Shortcut: UG** (when a group is selected)

Linking Models

Autodesk® Revit® models can be linked into other projects. Linking models can be used to create multiple copies of one building that are placed in a site plan, or to link an architectural model into a structural or MEP project. Once models are linked, you can copy and monitor elements between the linked model and the host project. If a change is made to the linked file, the software alerts you to do a Coordination Review. You can also check for interferences between the linked and host projects.

Learning Objectives in this Chapter

- Link Autodesk Revit models into a host project.
- Modify link display settings in views.
- Copy and monitor elements from linked models
- Use a Coordination Review to identify breaks in monitoring.
- Check interferences between elements in linked projects.

2.1 Linking Models

You can link an Autodesk® Revit® project into any other project. A linked model automatically updates if the original file is changed. This method can be used in many ways. For example, use this method when you have a number of identical buildings on one site plan, as shown in Figure 2–1.

The more links that are in a project, the longer it can take to open.

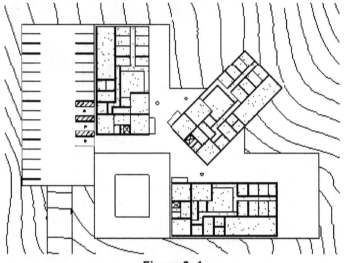

Figure 2–1

For architectural projects you can use links for multiple floors of one building that are identical to each other, or for repeated elements in a floor, such as identical room plans in a hospital, hotel, or apartment building. You can create one link and then copy the link to the host project.

Structural and MEP projects typically use the architectural model as the base for their projects. But there are times when an architect should link consultants files into the architectural file as well.

Standard practice on collaborative projects is that the architect and all consultants are on the same release.

- Architectural, structural, and MEP models created in the Autodesk® Revit® software can be linked to each other as long as they are from the same release cycle.

- When you use linked models, clashes between disciplines can be detected, and information can be passed between disciplines.

- Elements can be copied and monitored for even better coordination.

- Linked models can be constrained to elements in the host project and to each other. You can select references in linked models as a work plane and can schedule elements from the linked model in the host project.

Hint: Project Base Point

The origin of a project coordinate system is specified by the project base point, as shown in Figure 2–2. This should be set early in the project and before you start linking files together. It can be (but is not always) connected with the Survey Point, a secondary coordinate system used with shared coordinates.

Site : Project Base Point

Figure 2–2

- Project base points and survey points are visible in the Site view of the default architectural template. You can toggle them on in any view. In the Visibility/Graphic Overrides dialog box, in the *Model Category* tab, expand the **Site** category.

- Spot Coordinates and Spot Elevations are relative to the project base point.

How To: Add a Linked Model to a Host Project

1. In the *Insert* tab>Link panel, click (Link Revit).
2. In the Import/Link RVT dialog box, select the file that you want to link. Before opening the file, set the *Positioning*, as shown in Figure 2–3.

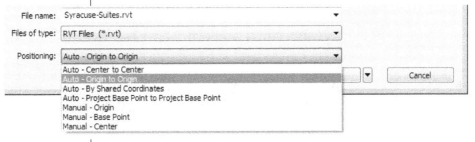

File name: Syracuse-Suites.rvt

Files of type: RVT Files (*.rvt)

Positioning: Auto - Origin to Origin

Auto - Center to Center
Auto - Origin to Origin
Auto - By Shared Coordinates
Auto - Project Base Point to Project Base Point
Manual - Origin
Manual - Base Point
Manual - Center

Cancel

Figure 2–3

3. Click **Open**.
4. Depending on how you decide to position the file, it is automatically placed in the file or you can manually place it with the cursor.

- The default positioning is **Auto - Origin to Origin**. The center of a linked model is the center of the geometry. Therefore, if you modify the extents of the original model, its exact location changes in the host project if you link **Center to Center**.

- **Auto - Project BasePoint to Project Base Point** aligns the base points of the projects rather than the default origins.

- The software remembers the most recently used positioning type as long as you are in the same session of Autodesk Revit. (The CAD Links dialog box remembers the last positioning used as well, but separately from RVT Links)

- As the links are loading, do not click on the screen or click any buttons. The more links that are present in a project, the longer it takes to load.

- Linked models can be moved once you have placed them in the project. If you want to return them to the original location, right-click on the link and select either **Reposition to Project Base Point** or **Reposition to Internal Origin**, as shown in Figure 2–4

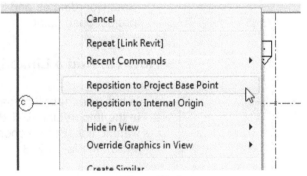

Figure 2–4

Hint: Preventing Linked Model from being moved

Once a linked model is in the correct location, you can lock it in place to ensure that it does not get moved by mistake, or prevent the linked model from being selected.

- To toggle off the ability to select links, in the Status Bar, click ⬚ (Select Links).

- To pin the linked model in place, select it and in the *Modify* tab>Modify panel, click ⬚ (Pin).

- To prevent pinned elements from being selected, in the Status Bar, click ⬚ (Select Pinned Elements).

Multiple Copies of Links

Copied instances of a linked model are typically used when creating a master project with the same building placed in multiple locations, such as a university campus with several identical student residences.

- Linked models can be copied, rotated, arrayed, and mirrored.

- You only link a model once, but you can place as many copies as are required into the host project. The copies are numbered automatically, and the name can be changed in Properties when the instance is selected. There is only one linked model, and the copies are additional instances of that link.

- When you have placed a link in a project, you can use the Project Browser, as shown in Figure 2–5, to drag and drop additional copies of the link into the project.

Figure 2–5

Annotation and Linked Models

Many annotations can be added to the host model that reference elements in the linked model. For example, in Figure 2–6, the walls columns and grids are part of the linked model but the dimensions and tags are placed in the host project.

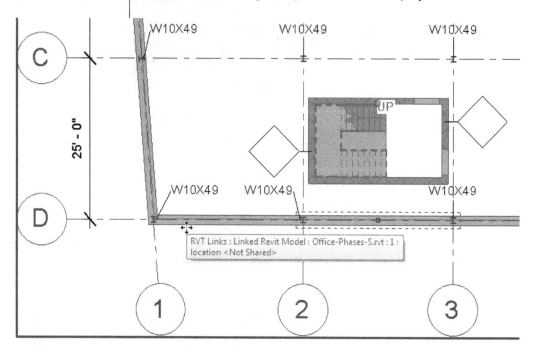

Figure 2–6

- Elements in the linked model can also be scheduled in the host project.

Managing Links

A linked model reloads each time the host project is opened. You can also reload the model by right-clicking on the Revit Link in the Project Browser, and then selecting **Reload** or **Reload From**, as shown in Figure 2–7.

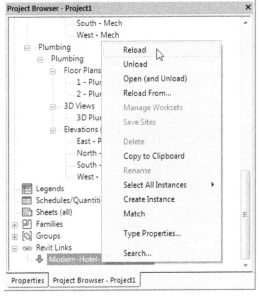

Figure 2–7

The Manage Links dialog box (shown in Figure 2–8) enables you to reload, unload, add, and remove links. Additionally, it provides access to other options. To open the Manage Links dialog box, in the *Insert* tab>Link, panel click (Manage Links). The Manage Links dialog box also displays when you select a link in the *Modify | RVT Links* tab.

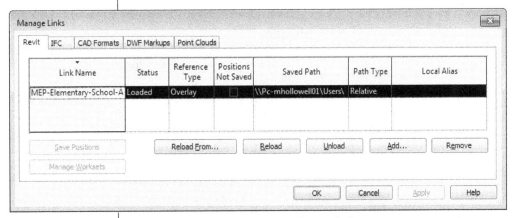

Figure 2–8

The options available in the Manage Links dialog box include the following:

- **Reload From:** Opens the Add Link dialog box, which enables you to select the file you want to reload. Use this if the linked file location or name has changed.

- **Reload:** Reloads the file without additional prompts.

- **Unload:** Unloads the file so that it the link is kept, but the file is not displayed or calculated in the project. Use **Reload** to restore it.

- **Add:** Opens the Import/Link RVT dialog box, which enables you to link additional models into the host project.

- **Remove:** Deletes the link from the file.

Links can be nested into one another. How a link responds when the host project is linked into another project depends on the option in the *Reference Type* column:

- **Overlay:** The nested linked model is not referenced in the new host project.

- **Attach:** The nested linked model displays in the new host project.

The option in the *Path Type* column controls how the location of the link is remembered:

- **Relative**

  - Searches the root folder of the current project.
  - If the file is moved, the software still searches for it.

- **Absolute**

  - Searches the entire file path where the file was originally saved.
  - If the original file is moved, the software is not able to find it.

- Other options control how the linked file interfaces with Worksets and Saved Positioning.

- In the Manage Links dialog box, when you have multiple links, you can sort rows by clicking the column header.

Linked Model Properties

Linked models have both instance properties and type properties. Instance Properties, as shown in Figure 2–9, include the *Name* for the individual copy of the link. This is automatically updated as you insert more than one. You can also change the name to help you identify it later. It also shows if it is part of a *Design Option* and if it is set to a *Shared Site*.

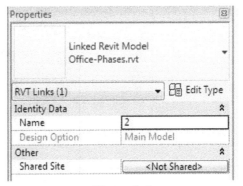

Figure 2–9

Type Properties, as shown in Figure 2–10, include *Room Bounding* which is required if you want to be able to place rooms or spaces from the information in the linked model. It also includes *Reference Type* (Overlay or Attachment) and *Phase Mapping*.

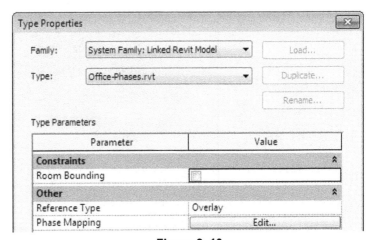

Figure 2–10

The phases in linked models can be mapped to the host project phasing so that the phasing schemes from different projects can be displayed consistently. Edit the Type Properties of the linked model and next to *Phase Mapping*, click **Edit...**. In the Phases dialog box, as shown in Figure 2–11, select the Phase from the linked model to match the corresponding phase in the host project.

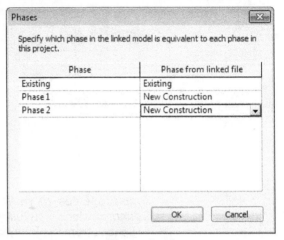

Figure 2–11

Hint: Shared Positioning

Each project has a set of internal coordinates that are used only by that project. If you are linking projects together, it helps to have one coordinate system that is referenced throughout the connected projects. For example, when you have a site plan with multiple linked buildings, as shown in Figure 2–12, you typically use the coordinates of the site and publish the coordinates from the host to the linked model.

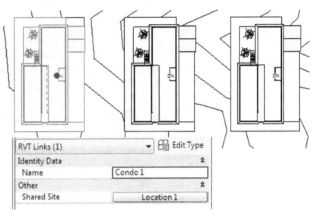

Figure 2–12

When working with an architectural model linked into your host project, obtain the coordinates from the architectural model, as shown in Figure 2–13.

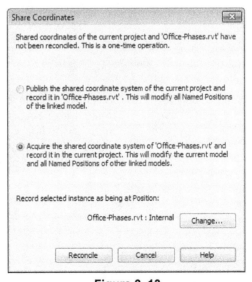

Figure 2–13

2.2 Views and Linked Models

Linked files can be very large and include a lot of information that is not required when all you want is the base building model. Depending on the standards of your office, it can help to clean up the linked file by deleting unneeded views or sheets and purging out all unused families. If required, you can request the original creator to set up coordination views that can be used specifically as a base view in the project.

Preparing Views for Other Disciplines

If you are working with consultants from other disciplines, it can be helpful to create coordination views for them that include only the element types that they require. For example, in Figure 2–14, the architect created plans for the first and second floors as a base for MEP and Structural projects. These views display only the architectural elements that other disciplines require as a background for their own elements.

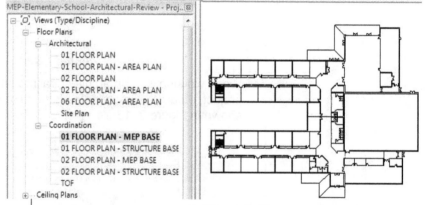

Figure 2–14

- When a model is linked to a host project, any changes you make in the Visibility/Graphic Overrides dialog box are also made in the linked model by default. For example, if you toggle off the visibility of the grids in the host project, it also toggles off the visibility of the grids in linked models.

Hint: Hiding Individual Elements in Linked Models

Individual elements in linked models can be hidden in the host project as shown in Figure 2–15. To select an element in a linked model, hover the cursor over the element and press <Tab> until only that element highlights. Then, right-click and select **Hide in View>Elements**. You can do this in plans, sections, elevations, and 3D views.

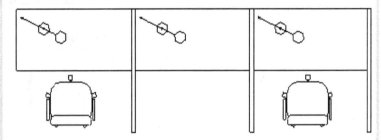

Three instances of a linked model with the chair hidden in one instance

Figure 2–15

- You can only modify the graphic overrides of elements in linked models by category, not by element.

- Hiding elements in the linked model By Category, has the same effect as hiding elements By category in the main model. All elements of that category are hidden in the main model and in all instances of all links, unless other link(s) have overrides attached to them.

Display Settings in Linked Models

To further customize views in projects with links, you can modify the Display Settings of the link. By default, the link displays using the host view parameters, but you can change it to use a view in the linked file or a custom view where you can specify every aspect of its appearance.

For example, in Figure 2–16, an MEP model has been linked into an architectural model and the Display Settings are set to **By Host View**. Only a couple of MEP elements display by default, such as the lights and some piping.

*If a graphic override has been applied to categories in a project, the linked files are also modified if their display setting is set to **By host view**.*

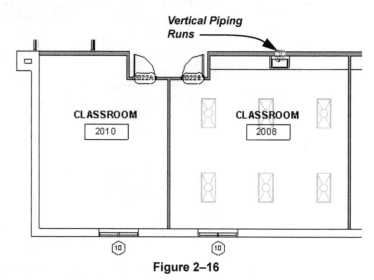

Figure 2–16

In Figure 2–17, the Display Settings have been changed to **By Linked View** with a mechanical view selected. The duct work and air terminals display, the lights remain grayed out and piping is toggled off.

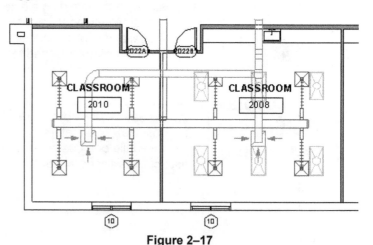

Figure 2–17

In Figure 2–18, the Display Settings have been customized. The Mechanical view is still selected but all of the duct elements are toggled off while the air terminals display.

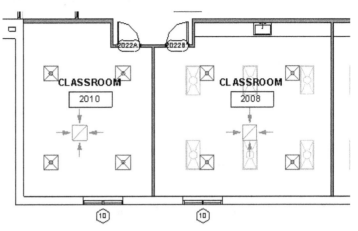

Figure 2–18

How To: Modify Display Settings in a Linked View

1. Type **VV** or **VG** to open the Visibility/Graphics Overrides dialog box.
2. Switch to the *Revit Links* tab.
3. Set the *Display Settings* for the linked model or an instance of the linked model, as shown in Figure 2–19.

Figure 2–19

4. In the RVT Link Display Settings dialog box, in the *Basics* tab, select **By linked view** or **Custom**.

If you have more than one copy of a link, you can have them all update together by clicking on the Display Settings next to the link name rather than the instance name.

- If you select **By linked view**, you can select from a list of views in the linked model, as shown in Figure 2–20.

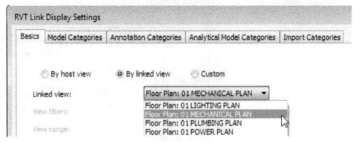

Figure 2–20

- If you select **Custom**, you can specify each setting independently, as shown in Figure 2–21.

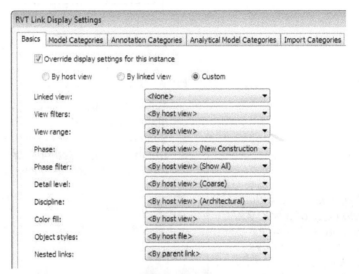

Figure 2–21

- When **Custom** is selected, you can also customize the display of specific categories using other tabs in the RVT Link Display Settings dialog box.

- If a linked model contains phases that are not in the host project, they can still be displayed by overriding the display settings for that instance of the linked model. The phases from the linked model display in the Phase drop-down list.

Practice 2a

Link Models - All Disciplines

Practice Objectives

- Link several models into a host project.
- Make copies of linked models in a project.
- Modify the visibility graphics overrides of the copied links.

Estimated time for completion: 15 minutes

In this practice you will link architectural, structural, and MEP models into a host building site project. You will make copies of the linked models and modify the Visibility/Graphics Overrides for several of the instances. You will also modify one of the linked models and then reopen the site model to see how the changes automatically update in the final project, as shown in Figure 2–22.

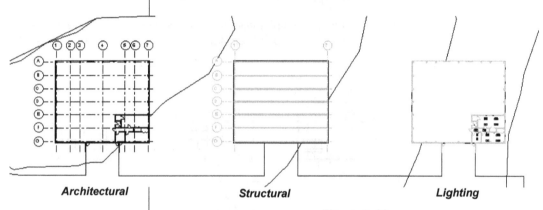

| Architectural | Structural | Lighting |

Figure 2–22

Task 1 - Link several models into a host project.

1. In the practice files folder, open **Industrial-Park.rvt**. The site has six rectangular pads for warehouse buildings.

2. In the *Insert* tab>Link panel, click (Link Revit).

The links do not come in directly on a pad. They need to be moved to the correct location.

3. In the Import/Link RVT dialog box, select the file **Industrial-Building-A.rvt**. Verify that the Positioning is set to **Auto - Origin to Origin.**

4. Click **Open**.

5. Select the new link. In Properties, verify that the *Name* of this instance is **1**. This makes tracking the rest of the instances easier.

6. Click 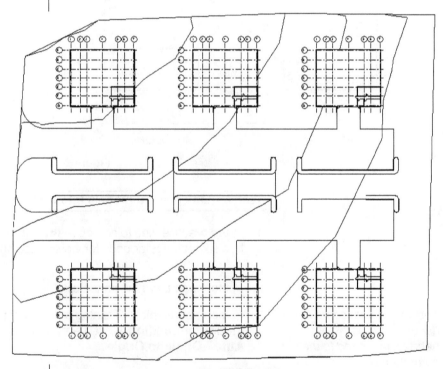 (Link Revit) again and link in **Industrial-Building-MEP.rvt** at the same position.

7. An alert box opens, warning you that the model has another model linked to it and that it is not visible in this project. This is because it was linked in that file as an overlay rather than an attachment. Close the dialog box.

8. Repeat the process one more time and link in **Industrial-Building-S.rvt** at the same position.

9. Select all of the linked models that are on top of each other and move them to one of the pads at the top of the site. You might need to zoom in to place it precisely.

10. Copy the linked models to the other pads on the same side of the parking lot.

11. Mirror the links from the north side of the parking to the south side and move them into place, as shown in Figure 2–23.

Figure 2–23

12. Save the project.

Task 2 - Modify the Visibility/Graphics of the links.

1. Zoom in to see the top group of warehouses.

2. Type **VG** to open the Visibility/Graphics Overrides dialog box. In the *Revit Links* tab, next to the main MEP and S links, select **Halftone**. Click **Apply** and move the dialog box out of the way slightly so that you can see the changes, as shown in Figure 2–24.

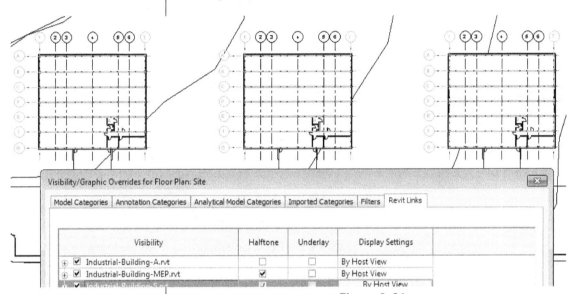

Figure 2–24

3. Remain in the Visibility/Graphic dialog box, *Revit Links* tab. Set up the first pad location so that it displays the architectural information, as shown in Figure 2–25. Expand the lists beside each of the links and clear the first instance of MEP (2) and S (3) links. Click **Apply**. Only the architectural information displays in this one instance

4. Set up the second pad location to display only the structural information, as shown in Figure 2–25. Clear the second architectural instance (4) and the second MEP instance (5). Click **Apply**. Only the structural information displays in this instance.

5. Set up the third pad location to display the MEP lighting information. Clear the third architectural (7) and structural (9) instances. Click **Apply**. Not enough information displays in this instance, as shown in Figure 2–25.

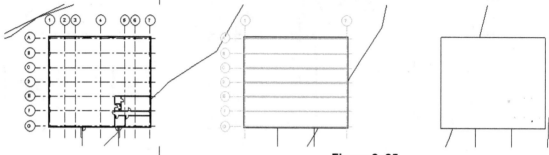

Figure 2–25

6. Select the third architectural instance (7) again and change only this one instance to **Halftone**.

7. Clear the **Halftone** option for the main MEP link.

8. Override the Display Settings of the third MEP instance (8). In the RVT Link Display Settings dialog box, in the *Basics* tab, select **Override display settings for this instance**. Set it to **By linked view** and select **Floor Plan: 1 - Lighting** for this view, as shown in Figure 2–26.

Figure 2–26

9. Click **OK** twice to close the dialog boxes.

10. Zoom in to see the lighting layout in the office area as shown in Figure 2–27.

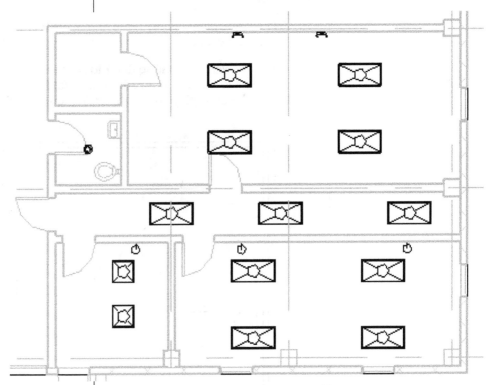

Figure 2–27

11. If you have time you can repeat the MEP steps for another instance and set up one using the view **Floor Plans: 1 - Mech**.

12. Save and close the project.

Task 3 - Modify linked models.

1. Open **Industrial-Building-A.rvt** from your practice files folder.

2. Add several other interior walls and doors to the office area of the warehouse, similar to that shown in Figure 2–28.

3. Duplicate without detailing, the **Floor Plan: Level 1** view and rename it to **Level 1 - Coordination**. Verify that the tags and grids are not displaying, as shown in Figure 2–28.

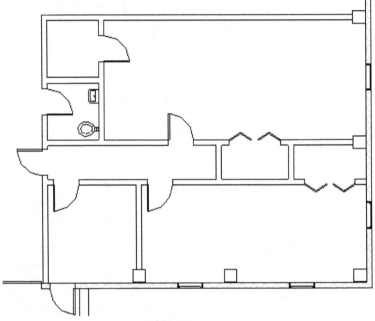

Figure 2–28

4. Save and close the project.

5. Open **Industrial-Building-MEP.rvt** from your practice files folder. The linked architectural model is automatically updated in this project.

6. Open the Electrical>Lighting>**Ceiling Plans: 1 - Ceiling Elec** view.

7. Modify the lighting locations, as required.

8. Save and close the file.

9. Reopen the project **Industrial-Park.rvt**. The new walls and the modified lighting locations display in the linked files, as shown in Figure 2–29 for the office section at the third pad location.

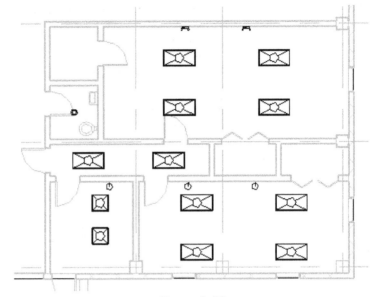

Figure 2–29

10. Type **VG** and for the third architectural instance (7) override the Display Settings by linked view. Select **Floor Plan: Level 1 - Coordination**. The grids no longer display in this instance.

11. Save and close the project.

12. If you have time, you can link the structural model into the architectural model and delete the columns and extra grids because the structural model uses a wide-span structural system.

13. In the structural model, you can also add more beams and other structural elements to finish the project. Test it in the Industrial Park project.

2.3 Copying and Monitoring Elements

When working with linked files, such as an architectural model linked into a structural or MEP project, you can coordinate information between the files using the **Copy/Monitor** tool. When you monitor an item in the linked file with an identical or similar one in the host project, the program tracks these two items, looking for changes in location, existence, height, etc. It always requires two elements to compare.

Items that are monitored display the ⟨⟩ icon when selected, as shown in Figure 2–30.

Copy/Monitor works with grids, levels, columns, walls, and floors, as well as MEP fixtures in the same file or in a linked file.

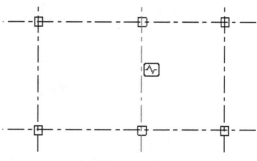

Figure 2–30

- **Monitor:** Compares two elements of the same type (in the same project or in a project and a linked model) to ensure that the correct relationship between them is maintained. For example, you can monitor two grid lines in the project that you want to keep a specific distance apart or an architectural level in a linked model and the T.O. Steel level in the structural host project.

- **Copy:** Duplicates elements from the linked model into the host project and monitors those elements against the linked model. For example, you may want to copy and monitor plumbing fixtures from the linked architectural model into the MEP host project.

What is Typically Copied/Monitored:

- **Architecture:** The **Copy/Monitor** tool is not heavily used by architects, although they might on occasion monitor elements in their project. For some projects they might use the structural engineer's linked model to control the grids and column locations or the plumbing engineer's linked model to control the location of the plumbing fixtures.

- **Structure:** Structural consultants copy/monitor levels, grids, columns, floors, and bearing walls from the architectural project.

- **MEP:** Mechanical consultants monitor levels and grids from the architectural model. They also copy/monitor some elements including plumbing and lighting fixtures.

- It is especially important to agree who controls datum elements, such as levels and grids, and not to modify them without explicit communication with others using that project as a link.

How To: Monitor Elements

1. In the *Collaborate* tab>Coordinate panel, expand

   (Copy/Monitor) and click (Use Current Project) or

   (Select Link).

2. In the *Copy/Monitor* tab>Tools panel, click (Monitor).
3. Pick the first element to monitor and then the corresponding element to monitor.
4. The icon displays on the first element of the selected pair.
5. If you want to monitor other pairs you can continue selecting the element to monitor and then the corresponding element.
6. When you have finished selecting elements, click

   (Finish).

- If you move or otherwise modify one of the monitored elements, the related elements highlight and a warning displays alerting you of the change as shown in Figure 2–31.

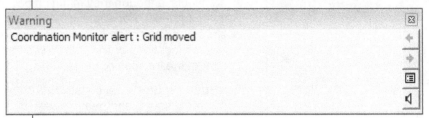

Figure 2–31

How To: Copy Elements from a Linked File into a Host File

1. Have a linked file in the host drawing.
2. In the *Collaborate* tab>Coordinate panel, expand (Copy/Monitor) and click (Select Link).
3. In the project, select the linked file.
4. In the *Copy/Monitor* tab>Tools panel, click (Copy).
5. Pick the elements that you want to copy into the host project.
   - Click on them one at a time.
   - Select **Multiple** in the Options Bar, select all of the elements you need, and click **Finish**.
6. When you have finished selecting elements to copy into the host project, in the *Copy/Monitor* tab>Copy/Monitor panel, click (Finish).
7. The elements become part of your host drawing and you can manipulate them, as required. The originals remain in the linked file with a monitoring watch set between them.

Copy/Monitor Options

Before starting the copy/monitor process, you can modify settings for the types of elements. In the *Copy/Monitor* tab>Tools panel, click 🔧 (Options). In the Copy/Monitor Options dialog box, select the tab for the type of element that you want to copy: *Levels*, *Grids*, *Columns*, *Walls*, or *Floors*, as shown in Figure 2–32.

Tabs display for the categories that exist in the linked project.

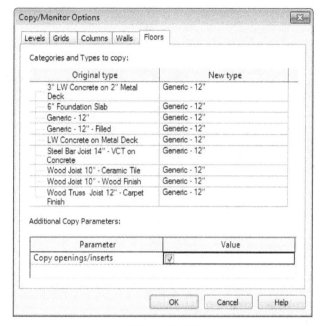

Figure 2–32

- By default, hosted elements such as shaft openings in floors and door, and window openings in walls (as shown in Figure 2–33) are automatically copied with their host elements. You can change this response in the Copy/Monitor Options dialog box, in the *Floors* tab *Additional Copy Parameters* area, as shown in Figure 2–32.

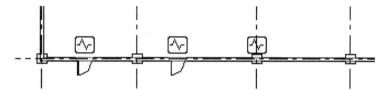

Figure 2–33

- MEP projects have additional options for Coordination Settings where you specify the copy and mapping behavior for different HVAC, Plumbing, Electrical equipment and fixtures, and other related devices, as shown in Figure 2–34. These elements can also be batch copied into the host project from the linked model.

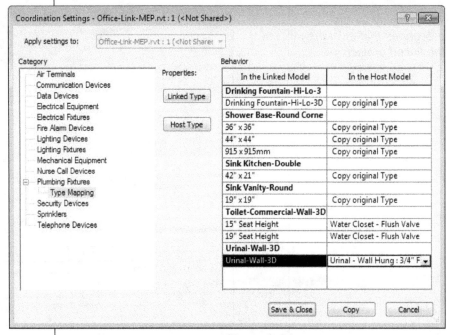

Figure 2–34

Working with Copy/Monitor Elements

- When you open a project with a linked file that includes changes to elements that are monitored, the warning dialog box opens as shown in Figure 2–35.

Figure 2–35

- When you work in a host project and move an element that is copied into the host file, you see a warning as shown in Figure 2–36. This does not prevent you from making the change, but alerts you that this is a monitored element that requires further coordination with the other disciplines involved.

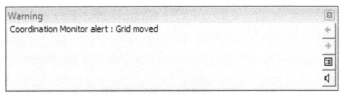

Figure 2–36

- If you make a change to a monitored host element, such as adding a door in a wall, a warning opens as shown in Figure 2–37.

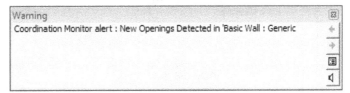

Figure 2–37

- If you no longer want an element to be monitored, select it and in the associated *Modify* tab>Monitor panel, click

 (Stop Monitoring).

2.4 Coordinating Linked Projects

Coordination Review

When you are working with projects or elements that are monitored, you can run a Coordination Review of the selected elements. In the *Collaborate* tab>Coordinate panel, expand

(Coordination Review) and click (Use Current Project) or

(Select Link). The Coordination Review dialog box lists any conflicts detected as shown in Figure 2–38.

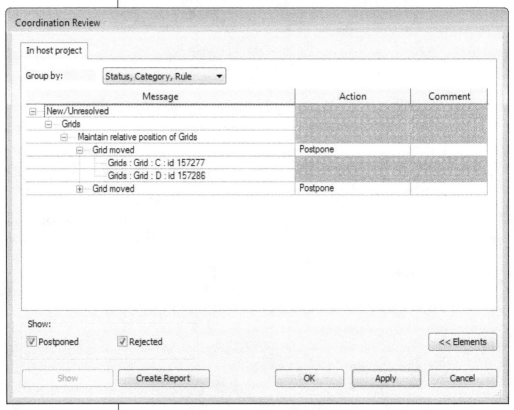

Figure 2–38

If there are no conflicts, the Message area is empty.

- You can group the information by *Status*, *Category*, and *Rule* in a variety of different ways in the **Group by:** drop-down list. This is important if you have many elements to review.

- Next to each conflict is a place for an **Action** and a **Comment**. The Action can be: *Postpone*, *Reject*, *Accept Difference*, or *Rename/Modify/Move/Delete Element* in relationship to the elements involved.

- To display items in conflict, select the element names and click **Show**. The view changes to center the elements in your screen.

- Click **Create Report** to create an HTML report that you can share with other users.

Reconcile Hosting

If the owner of a linked file deletes or moves a host, such as a wall and the current project had elements hosted to it, such as a light fixture, the connection between the two is lost, as shown in Figure 2–39.

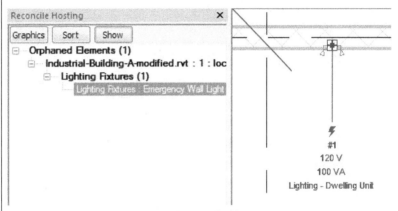

Figure 2–39

How To: Reconcile Hosting

1. When you open a project or reload a linked file, an alert box might be displayed, as shown in Figure 2–40.

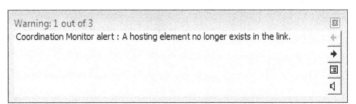

Figure 2–40

2. In the *Collaborate* tab>Coordinate panel, click 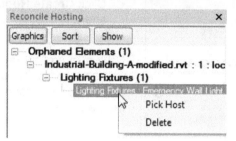 (Reconcile Hosting).
3. The Reconcile Hosting palette displays as shown in Figure 2–41.
4. Expand the list, select the element, and click **Show** to zoom in on the element that is orphaned.
5. To correct the issue, right-click on the element name, as shown in Figure 2–41, and select **Pick Host** or **Delete**.

Figure 2–41

- You can also select the element and in the *Modify* contextual tab>Work Plane panel, click (Pick New) and select a new host or delete it as required.

6. When you are finished correcting the elements, close the Reconcile Hosting palette.

- If you have control of the host elements in your project and you want to use a different wall type, do not delete and redraw the wall, just select it and in the Type Selector, select the new type. This does not create issues for others who are using the model as a link which has objects hosted on it.

- Because of this issue, many hosted elements are face-based rather than wall (or other host type) based. These elements do not notify you if a host is moved so you need to be aware to look for these orphaned elements.

Interference Checking

Interference Checking can be used when there are potential overlaps between disciplines, such as the structural column and stair shown in Figure 2–42.

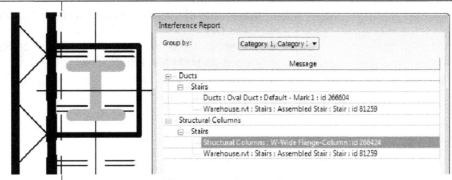

Figure 2–42

- Typical items to check include structural elements against architectural columns, walls, door or window openings, floors and roofs, specialty equipment and floors, and any elements in a linked file with the host file.

- For more complex projects and those that include files from other software, the Navisworks software provides a much more powerful solution than this basic interference checking.

How To: Run an Interference Check

1. In the *Collaborate* tab>Coordinate panel, expand (Interference Check) and click (Run Interference Check).

   - To filter out unneeded elements, select the elements first and then run the interference check.

2. In the Interference Check dialog box, as shown in Figure 2–43, in the *Categories From* drop-down list, select the projects that you want to compare. This can be the same project or any linked projects.

Select only the categories that you need to review. In a large project, selecting all categories can take a very long time to process.

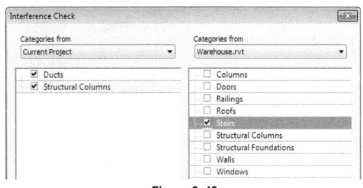

Figure 2–43

3. Select the element types that you want to compare.
4. Click **OK**.
5. If there are interferences, the Interference Report dialog box opens as shown in Figure 2–44.

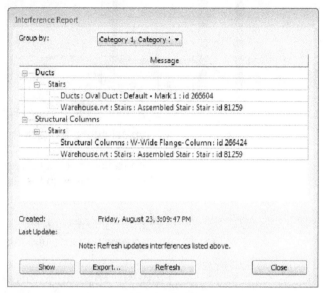

Figure 2–44

6. To see the elements that are interfering, select an element in the list and click **Show**.
7. If you need to create a report that can be viewed by other users, click **Export...**. This creates an HTML file listing the conflicts.
8. The dialog box can remain open while you make changes or you can click **Close** and then expand (Interference Check) and click (Show Last Report) to see the report again.
9. In the Interference Report dialog box, click **Refresh** to display any changes.
10. Refreshing the report only reviews the elements selected when the report was first run. If you need to select other elements, run a new report.

Practice 2b

Coordinate Linked Projects - Architectural and Structural

Practice Objectives

- Copy and monitor elements.
- Review and correct issues when coordination relationships established with Copy/Monitor are broken.

In this practice you will start a new structural project and link in an architectural model. You will then Copy/Monitor the grids, setup Column options to use structural columns, and Copy/Monitor in the columns, as shown in Figure 2–45. Finally, you will make changes to the architectural project and then use Coordination Review to match the structural project with the link.

Estimated time of completion: 20 minutes

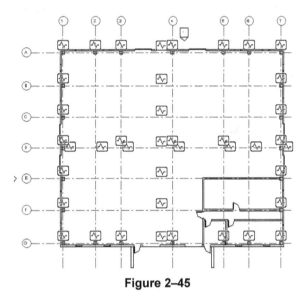

Figure 2–45

Task 1 - Link a file and copy/monitor elements

1. Start a new project based on the Structural template and save the project as **Warehouse-Structural.rvt**.

2. Open the **Structural Plans: Level 1** view.

3. In the *Insert* tab>Link panel, click (Link Revit).

4. In the Import/Link RVT dialog box, navigate to the practice files folder and select **Warehouse-A.rvt**. Verify that the *Positioning* is set to **Auto - Origin to Origin** and click **Open**.

5. The columns and grids of the linked model, and the doors and foundation elements display, while the walls do not because they are not structural.

6. In the View Control Bar, click ⬚ (Temporary View Properties) and select **Temporarily Apply Template Properties**.

7. In the Temporarily Apply Template Properties dialog box select **Architectural Plan** and click **OK**.

8. In the *Collaborate* tab>Coordinate panel, expand ⬚ (Copy/Monitor) and click ⬚ (Select Link).

9. Select the linked warehouse model.

10. In the *Copy/Monitor* tab>Tools panel, click ⬚ (Copy).

11. In the Options Bar, select **Multiple**. Select all of the grids using any selection method, such as that shown in Figure 2–46. Hold <Ctrl> and select additional grids, as required. In the Options Bar, click **Finish**.

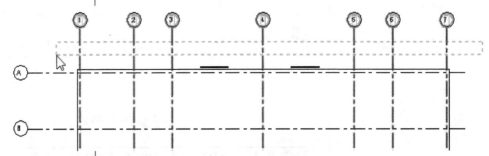

Figure 2–46

12. The grids are copied into the host project and monitored in place, as shown in Figure 2–47.

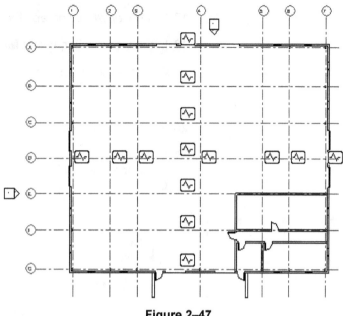

Figure 2–47

13. Click ⬡ (Modify) to release the grids.

14. Return to the *Copy/Monitor* tab. In the Tools panel, click
    🔧 (Options).

15. In the Copy/Monitor Options dialog box, select the *Columns* tab. The types of columns in the linked file are listed on the left. Verify that the architectural columns are set to a structural column type. For the *Pipe-Column*, select **Copy original Type** as shown in Figure 2–48.

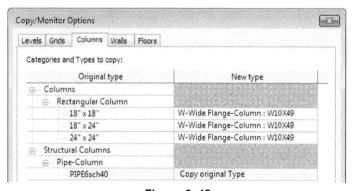

Figure 2–48

16. Click **OK**.

17. In the *Copy/Monitor* tab>Tools panel, click 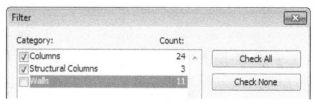 (Copy).

18. In the Options Bar, select **Multiple**.

19. Create a window around the entire building to select everything but the grids.

20. In the Status Bar or Options Bar, click (Filter).

21. In the Filter dialog box, select **Columns** and **Structural Columns**. Clear **Walls** as shown in Figure 2–49 and click **OK**.

Filter		
Category:	Count:	
☑ Columns	24	Check All
☑ Structural Columns	3	
☐ Walls	11	Check None

Figure 2–49

22. In the Options Bar, click **Finish**.

23. The columns are copied into the project as shown in Figure 2–50.

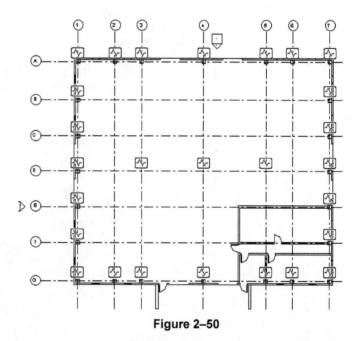

Figure 2–50

24. In the *Copy/Monitor* tab, click ✔ (Finish).

25. Zoom into the columns. There should be structural columns at the location of the square architectural columns, as shown in Figure 2–51, and pipe columns in the center of the building.

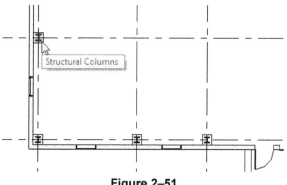

Figure 2–51

26. Save and close the project.

Task 2 - Modify the Architectural project.

1. Open **Warehouse-A.rvt** from your practice files folder.

2. Zoom in to check that there are no structural columns where the architectural columns are, as shown in Figure 2–52.

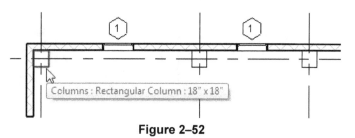

Figure 2–52

3. Zoom out.

4. Select grid line 3 and change it so it is **12'-0"** from grid line 2, as shown in Figure 2–53.

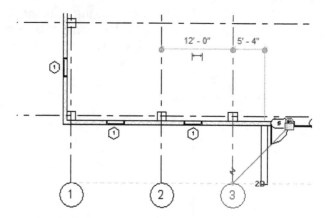

Figure 2–53

5. Repeat the process with grid line 5 and move it **12'-0"** from grid line 6. The associated architectural columns move with the grid line.

6. Save and close the project.

Task 3 - Coordinate the host file with the linked file.

---

1. Open the project **Warehouse-Structure.rvt** that you created earlier. The warning about needing a coordination review, as shown in Figure 2–54, displays.

Figure 2–54

2. Click **OK**.

3. You can see the change between the host project and linked model as shown in Figure 2–55.

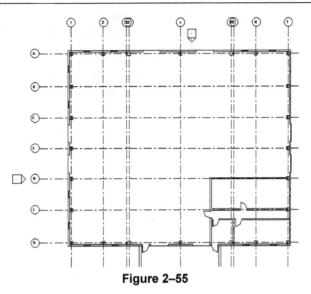

Figure 2–55

4. In the *Collaborate* tab> Coordinate panel, expand
   (Coordination Review) and click (Select Link).

5. Select the linked model.

6. In the Coordination Review dialog box, review the issues as shown in Figure 2–56.

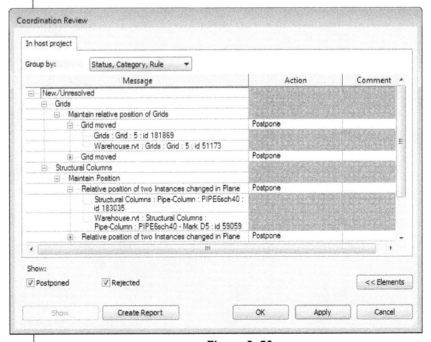

Figure 2–56

7. In the *Action* column, next to the grid issues, select **Modify Grid '5'** and **Modify Grid '3'**.

8. Click **Apply**. The grid lines move over, and because columns move with grid lines, the issues with the structural columns are resolved and are not listed in the Coordination Review dialog box.

9. Click **OK** and the host file matches up with the linked file.

10. Save and close the project.

Practice 2c

Coordinate Linked Projects - MEP and Architectural

Practice Objectives

- Copy and monitor elements.
- Review and correct issues when coordination relationships that were established with **Copy/Monitor** are broken.

In this practice you will create a new systems project and link in an architectural model. You will then Use Copy/Monitor to monitor levels and draw some ductwork that references one of the levels as shown on the top in Figure 2–57. You will then change the level in the architectural model and use Coordination Review to update the change in the systems model as shown on the bottom in Figure 2–57.

Estimated time for completion: 10 minutes

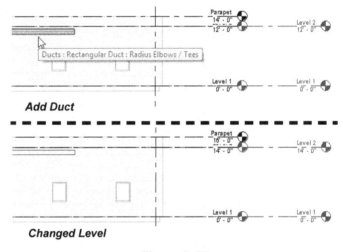

Figure 2–57

Task 1 - Link a file and copy/monitor elements

1. Start a new project based on the Mechanical or Systems template and save the project as **Warehouse-MEP.rvt**.

2. In the *Insert* tab>Link panel, click ⬚ (Link Revit).

3. In the Import/Link RVT dialog box, navigate to the practice files folder and select **Warehouse-A.rvt**. Verify that the *Positioning* is set to **Auto - Origin to Origin** and click **Open**.

4. Open the Mechanical>HVAC>**Elevations (Building Elevation): South - Mech** view. The current project has two levels and the architectural model has three, as shown in Figure 2–58.

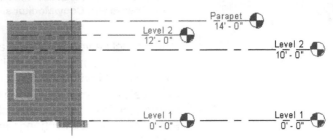

Figure 2–58

5. Align Level 2 of the current project with Level 2 of the linked project.

6. In the *Collaborate* tab>Coordinate panel, expand (Copy/Monitor) and click (Select Link).

7. Select the linked warehouse model.

8. In the *Copy/Monitor* tab>Tools panel, click (Monitor).

9. Select Level 1 in the project and then Level 1 in the linked model.

10. Repeat the process with Level 2 and click (Finish).

Task 2 - Add Ductwork (and Lighting).

1. Open the Mechanical>HVAC>Floor Plans>**1 - Mech** view.

2. In the *Systems* tab>HVAC panel, click (Duct).

3. In Properties, set the *Reference Level* to **Level 2** and the *Offset* to (negative) **-1'-0"**. Draw several ducts.

4. Return to the elevation view to see the location of the ducts, as shown in Figure 2–59.

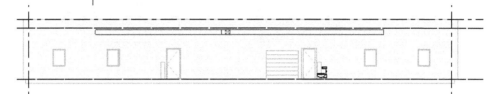

Figure 2–59

5. Save and close the project.

Task 3 - Modify the Architectural project.

1. Open **Warehouse-A.rvt** from your practice files folder.

2. Open the **Elevations: South** view.

3. Change the height of Level 2 to **14'-0"**.

   - The parapet level automatically changes height because it has been dimensioned and locked to Level 2.

4. Save and close the project.

Task 4 - Coordinate the host file with the linked file.

1. Open the project **Warehouse-MEP.rvt** that you created earlier. The warning about needing a coordination review displays, as shown in Figure 2–60.

Figure 2–60

2. Click **OK**.

3. You can see the change between the host project and linked model as shown in Figure 2–61.

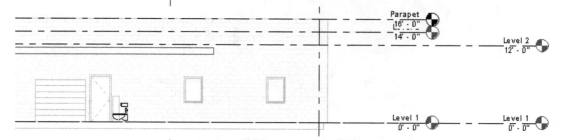

Figure 2–61

4. In the *Collaborate* tab> Coordinate panel, expand ![icon] (Coordination Review) and click ![icon] (Select Link).

5. Select the architectural link.

6. In the Coordination Review dialog box, expand the options in the *Action* column and select **Move Level 'Level 2'**, as shown in Figure 2–62.

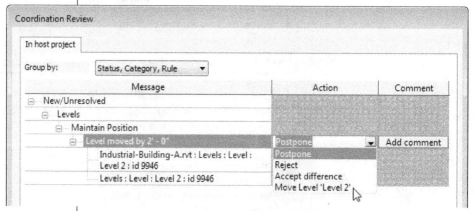

Figure 2–62

7. Click **OK** and the host file matches up with the linked file. The duct work moves as well because it was referenced to the level that was changed.

8. Save and close the project.

Chapter Review Questions

1. When linking an Autodesk Revit model into another project, which of the positioning methods keeps the model in the same place if the extents of the linked model changes in size?

    a. Auto - Center to Center

    b. Auto - Origin to Origin

    c. Manual - Basepoint

    d. Manual - Center

2. If you want to toggle off all the grids in a linked file but still display them in the host file, what do you need to do?

    a. Select one of the grids in the linked file and select **Hide in View>Category**.

    b. Select one of the grids in the host file and, in the View Control Bar, expand 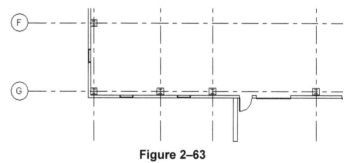 (Temporary Hide/Isolate) and select **Isolate Category**.

    c. In the Visibility Graphics Overrides dialog box change the link's *Display Settings* to **Custom** and in the *Annotation Categories* tab, clear **Grids**.

    d. In the Visibility Graphics Overrides dialog box, change the link's *Display Settings* to **By linked view** and in the *Annotation Categories* tab, clear **Grids**.

3. Which of the following elements, as shown in Figure 2–63, can be copied and monitored? (Select all that apply.)

Figure 2–63

    a. Grids

    b. Walls

    c. Columns

    d. Doors

4. When working with nested links, which of the following describes the Reference Type that is NOT included when its host project is linked into another project?

    a. Attach

    b. Bind

    c. Import

    d. Overlay

5. What type of element(s) is created when you bring links permanently into a host file?

    a. The elements come in individually

    b. A block

    c. A group

    d. An import

6. When working with a linked file, as shown in Figure 2–64, what property do you need to set to be able to add rooms or spaces?

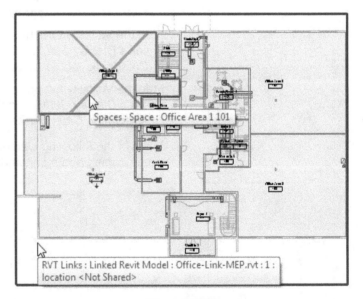

Figure 2–64

    a. Reference Type

    b. Room Bounding

    c. Phase Mapping

    d. Shared Site

7. In Figure 2–65, a wall in the link has been moved but the monitored wall in the host file has not been moved. How do you align the wall in the host file with the wall in the linked file? (Select all that apply.)

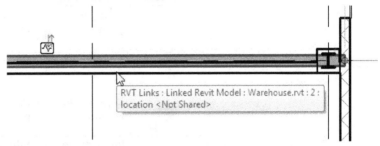

Figure 2–65

a. Move the wall in the host file so it matches the location in the linked file.

b. Run Coordination Review and select **Accept the difference**.

c. Run Coordination Review and select **Modify Wall**.

d. Run Interference Check and select **Match Centerlines**.

Command Summary

Button	Command	Location
	Bind Link (convert link to group)	• **Ribbon**: *Modify	RVT Links* tab>Link panel>Bind Link
	Copy/Monitor	• **Ribbon**: *Collaborate* tab>Coordinate panel
	Coordination Review	• **Ribbon**: *Collaborate* tab>Coordinate panel
	Interference Check	• **Ribbon**: *Collaborate* tab>Coordinate panel
	Link (convert group to link)	• **Ribbon**: *Modify	Model Groups* tab> Group panel>Link • **Shortcut**: LG (when a group is selected)
	Link Revit	• **Ribbon**: *Insert* tab>Link Panel>Link Revit
	Manage Links	• **Ribbon**: *Insert* tab>Link panel> Manage Links or *Modify RVT Links* tab>Link panel>Manage Links (if selected)
	Reconcile Hosting	• **Ribbon**: Collaborate tab>Coordinate panel> Reconcile Hosting

Importing and Exporting

Files from other CAD programs can be imported (and in some cases linked) into an Autodesk® Revit® project. These elements can be traced over or used as is to create a hybrid project. Imported CAD files can be manipulated and even exploded into individual elements which can then take on Revit properties. Raster images can also be imported into a Revit project. Similarly, information stored in Autodesk Revit files can be exported for use in other CAD programs. The detailed building information that is stored in a project can be exported to other file formats that include DWF, ADSK, and IFC. Further, information that is exported to a gbXML file can be used in energy analysis programs.

Learning Objectives in this Chapter

- Import or link files that were created in other CAD programs into an Autodesk Revit project.
- Query elements and delete layers in imported/linked CAD files.
- Explode imported CAD files.
- Import and modify raster images.
- Export Autodesk Revit projects to other file formats, including CAD formats and DWF files.
- Export information contained in a project to gbXML that can be used in other energy analysis software.

3.1 Importing and Linking Vector Files

You can print a hybrid drawing - part Autodesk Revit project and part imported/linked drawing.

Many firms have legacy drawings from vector-based CAD programs and could be working with consultants that use them. For example, you may want to link a DWG plan into your project, as shown in the Link CAD Formats dialog box in Figure 3–1, that you would then trace over using Autodesk Revit tools. Other non-CAD specific file formats including ADSK, IFC. Point clouds can also be opened or linked into Autodesk Revit projects.

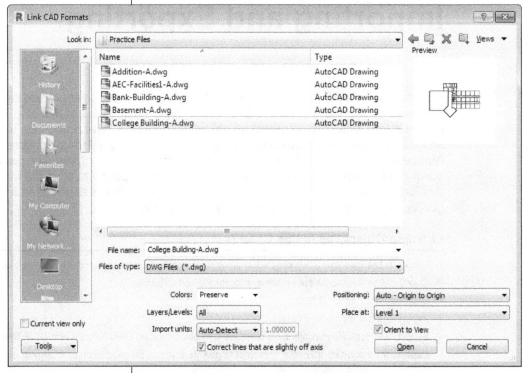

Figure 3–1

CAD Files can be either linked or imported into a project.

- **Link:** A connection is maintained with the original file and the link updates if the original file is updated.
- **Import:** No connection is maintained with the original file. It becomes a separate element in the Autodesk Revit model.

- CAD file formats that can be imported or linked include: AutoCAD® (DWG and DXF), MicroStation® (DGN), Trimble® SketchUp® (SKP and DWG), Standard ACIS Text format (SAT), and Rhinoceros® (3DM).

How To: Import or Link a CAD File

1. In the *Insert* tab>Import panel, click 🔗CAD (Import CAD), or in the *Insert* tab>Link panel, click 🔗CAD (Link CAD).
2. Fill out the Import CAD (or Link CAD) dialog box. The top part of the dialog box holds the standard select file options. The bottom outlines the various options for importing or linking, as shown in Figure 3–2.

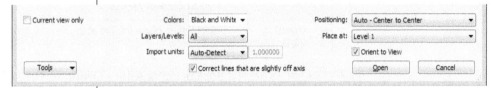

Figure 3–2

3. Click **Open**.
4. Depending on the selected Positioning method, the file is automatically placed or you can place it with the cursor.

Import/Link Options

Current view only	If selected, the file is imported/linked into the current view and not into other views. You might want to enable this option if you are just working on a floor plan and do not want the objects to display in 3D and other views.
Colors	The Autodesk Revit software works mainly with black lines of different weights on a white background to describe elements, but both AutoCAD and MicroStation use a variety of colors. To make the move into the Autodesk Revit software easier, you can select to turn all colors to Black and White, Preserve colors, or Invert colors
Layers	You can select which layers from the original drawing are imported/linked. The options are All, Visible (those that are not off or frozen), and Select. Select opens a list of layers or levels from which you can select when you import the drawing file.
Import units	Autodesk Revit software can auto-detect the units in the imported/linked file. You can also specify the units that you want to use from a list of typical Imperial and Metric units or set a Custom scale factor.

Correct lines that are slightly off axis	Corrects lines that are less than 0.1 degree of axis so that any elements based on those line are created correctly. It is on by default. Toggle it off if you are working with site plans.
Positioning	Select from the methods to place the imported/linked file in the Autodesk Revit host project. 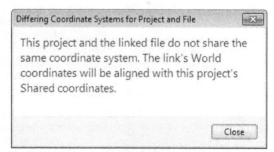
Place at:	Select a level in the drop-down list to specify the vertical positioning for the file. This is grayed out if you have selected Current view only.
Orient to View	Select this to place the file at the same orientation as the current view.

- The default positioning is **Auto - Origin to Origin**. The software remembers the most recently used positioning type as long as you are in the same session of Autodesk Revit. (The CAD Links dialog box remembers the last positioning used separately from the RVT Links dialog box.)

- If you are linking a file, an additional Positioning option, **Auto-By Shared Coordinates**, is available. It is typically used with linked Autodesk Revit files. If you use it with a CAD file, an alert box opens, as shown in Figure 3–3, containing information about the coordinate systems and what the Autodesk Revit software does.

Differing Coordinate Systems for Project and File

This project and the linked file do not share the same coordinate system. The link's World coordinates will be aligned with this project's Shared coordinates.

Close

Figure 3–3

- When you link a DWG file that includes reference files (XREFS), as shown in AutoCAD in Figure 3–4, only files whose *Type* is set to **Attach** display. Files whose *Type* is set to **Overlay** do not display.

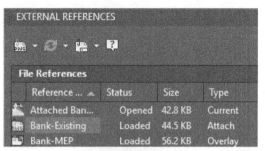

Figure 3–4

- When you import a DWG file, all XREFS display no matter how they are setup in the DWG file.

Importing Line Weights

One significant setting for imported drawings is the line weight. Both AutoCAD and MicroStation can use line weights as well as colors. Typically, AutoCAD line weights are associated with a color. Therefore, the Autodesk Revit software imports them by color.

How To: Import Line Weights

1. Before you import a CAD file, in the *Insert* tab>Import panel,

   click (Import Line Weights), as shown in Figure 3–5.

Clicking in the title bar of a panel typically opens a settings dialog box related to the commands in the panel.

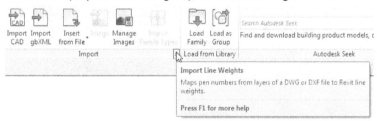

Figure 3–5

2. In the Import Line Weights dialog box shown in Figure 3–6, load a text file that holds the relationships or type them in the dialog box. You can then save them for later use.

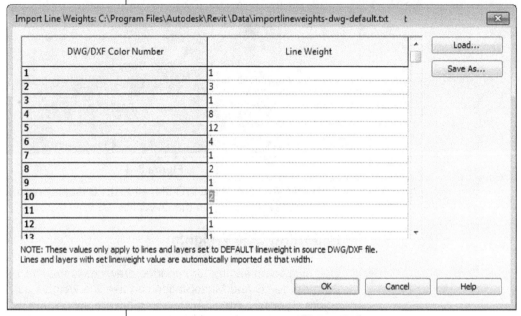

Figure 3–6

3. Click **OK** and then import the CAD file.

- To load information from an existing text file, click **Load...** and select the file that you want to use. Several files are included in the *Data* folder, as shown in Figure 3–7.

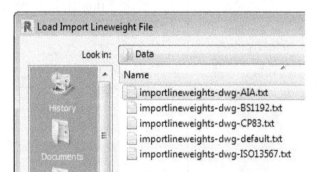

Figure 3–7

- To create a custom text file for specific projects, set up a sequence and click **Save As...**.

- Save your custom import line weight text files to a folder that is accessible to everyone that might need to use it. Do not save any custom files to the Autodesk Revit folders because they might be deleted if the program is upgraded or reinstalled.

Hint: Linking AutoCAD Civil 3D DWG Files

AutoCAD Civil 3D creates DWG files but the process of using them accurately in Autodesk Revit requires some extra steps. The Project Base Point in Revit is basically the same as the 0,0,0 origin point in an AutoCAD DWG. However, Civil 3D files typically use real world site locations established by surveyors. You can request a reference point (Northing, Easting, Elevation) from the civil engineer and add that information to the Survey Point in the Revit project before linking the site into the model.

Working with Other File Formats

There are additional file formats that can be opened or linked into Autodesk Revit projects, including IFC (Industry Foundation Class) elements, ADSK (Autodesk Exchange) files and point clouds.

IFC (Industry Foundation Classes)

The IFC specification is an international data neutral format. Models created in any building design program can be saved or exported to this file format. You can open IFC files directly (*File* tab>Open> (IFC)) or link them into the current project (in the *Insert* tab>Link panel, click (Link IFC)).

- If you are opening an IFC file, first setup the default template and manage the mapping of IFC classes to Revit Categories (*File* tab>Open> (IFC Options).

- Autodesk Revit models can be exported to IFC.

Autodesk Exchange Files

Building Component files, such as the blower created in Inventor shown in Figure 3–8, can be imported as a family into an Autodesk Revit project. They display the real size of the equipment and can also include connectors to related MEP elements. They must first be saved in the original program as an Autodesk® Exchange (ADSK) file.

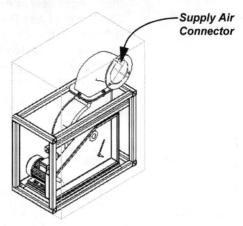

Supply Air Connector

Figure 3–8

- To use an ADSK file, first load it into the project (*Insert* tab> Load from Library panel, click ⬇️ (Load Family)) and then use the **Component** command to place it.

- ADSK files can be saved as an RFA family file. In the *File* tab, expand 📂 (Open), expand 🏗️ (Building Component) and select the ADSK file to open. Then, in the *File* tab, expand 💾 (Save As) and click 🗐 (Family).

Point Clouds

Point clouds are created using 3D laser scanners and are frequently used to establish accurate existing information. Once you link a point cloud (in the *Insert* tab>Link panel click

(Point Cloud)) into a project, as shown in Figure 3–9, you can snap to alignment planes and individual points.

Figure 3–9

There are three file formats that you can link:

- **RCS** - Individual indexed scanned models.
- **RCP** - Groups of indexed scanned models.
- **Raw** - Non-indexed scans from multiple types of scanners.

- If you are using one of the raw formats, Revit will automatically index it. You will then need to return to the original command to load the new RCS or RCP.

- In the Visibility/Graphic Overrides dialog box, in the *Point Clouds* tab, you can change the visibility and set a color mode. Each individual scan can be controlled individually.

Coordination Models

New
in 2018

Many construction projects include designs from a variety of software programs. Navisworks (R) enables you to link together files from these different programs to create a coordination model. You can then link the models saved in Navisworks as a NWD or NWC file into your Autodesk Revit model, to help you coordinate the larger project, as shown in Figure 3–10.

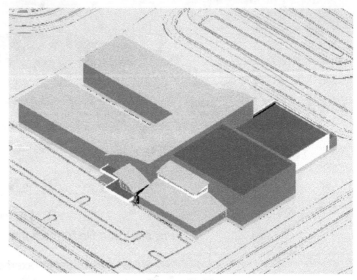

Figure 3–10

How To: Link a Coordination Model

1. In the *Insert* tab>Link panel, click ![icon] (Coordination Model).
2. In the Coordination Model dialog box, specify the *Positioning* (**Origin to Origin** or **By Shared Coordinates**), as shown in Figure 3–11, and click **Add...**.

Figure 3–11

3. Navigate to the correct file folder, select the Navisworks document (NWD or NWC), and click **Open**.

4. In the Coordination Model dialog box (shown in Figure 3–12), modify the *Path Type* if required and click **Apply** if you want to remain in the dialog box. Otherwise, click **OK**.

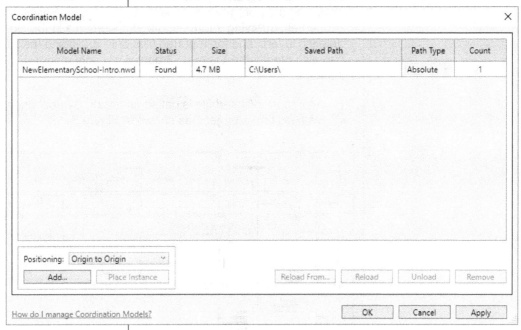

Coordination Model

Model Name	Status	Size	Saved Path	Path Type	Count
NewElementarySchool-Intro.nwd	Found	4.7 MB	C:\Users\	Absolute	1

Positioning: Origin to Origin

Add...   Place Instance   Reload From...   Reload   Unload   Remove

How do I manage Coordination Models?   OK   Cancel   Apply

Figure 3–12

- You can add copies of the coordination model if required. Select the *Model Name*, specify the *Positioning* and click **Place Instance**.

- You can also use the buttons to **Reload From...**, **Reload**, **Unload**, and **Remove** coordination models.

3.2 Modifying Imported Files

When you select an imported/linked file, you can modify it by arranging the Foreground/Background status, modifying its Type Properties, querying information about elements in the file, deleting layers, and for imported files only, exploding the file. You can also modify the Visibility/Graphics of each imported/linked instance.

- An imported/linked file is called an Import Symbol once it is inserted into a project, as shown in Figure 3–13.

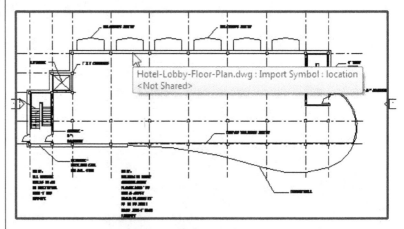

Figure 3–13

Arranging Imported Files

*These options display if the imported/linked instance was imported by **Current View Only** or into a Drafting View.*

When you import/link a CAD file into the current view, it is view-specific and you can arrange it with respect to the model elements in the project. To do this, in the Options Bar or in Properties, change the *Draw Layer* to either **Background** or **Foreground**, as shown in Figure 3–14.

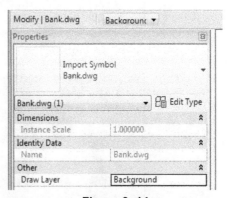

Figure 3–14

- You can also move imported/linked files incrementally using **Bring to Front** and **Send to Back** in the Arrange panel, as shown in Figure 3–15.

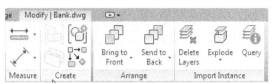

Figure 3–15

Modifying Type Properties

The *Instance Scale* and the *Name* of the file are Type Properties.

Select the import instance you want to modify and click 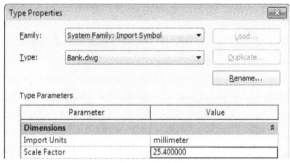 (Edit Type) to open the Type Properties dialog box, as shown in Figure 3–16.

Figure 3–16

- If you change the *Import Units*, the *Scale Factor* is automatically updated. If the *Import Units* are the same type as the host units, you can change the *Scale Factor* independently. You might need to do this if the original file was scanned and not necessarily accurately to scale.

- You can also change the scale using ⬚ (Scale). This command is not typically used on other Autodesk Revit elements.

- Imported/linked instances can be part of a group. If they are placed in the current view, they are the only ones to be considered detail elements, otherwise they will be considered model elements.

Querying Imported Files

When working with imported/linked files, it often helps to know what type of objects you are dealing with, without having to modify the file in any way. The **Query** command gives you this information and also enables you to delete or hide the layer of the selected object.

How To: Query Imported/Linked Files

1. Select the imported/linked file that you want to query.
2. In the *Modify* contextual tab>Import Instance panel, click
   ![Query icon] (Query).
3. Select the element in the imported/linked file about which you want to inquire. The Import Instance Query dialog box displays information about the objects, as shown in Figure 3–17.

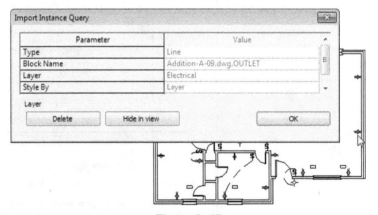

Figure 3–17

- Click **OK** if you just want to look at the object's information.
- Click **Delete** to remove all objects on the layer referenced by the selected object.
- Click **Hide in View** to hide (but not delete) all objects on the layer referenced by the selected object.
4. You are still in the **Query** command and can select other items in the file.
5. Press <Esc> to end the command.

Deleting Layers

If you are creating a hybrid file and there are layers or levels in the imported/linked file that you do not need in the project, you can delete them without exploding the imported file.

- Only items on the selected layers are removed. What is actually on those layers depends on how well the original drafters followed the layering guidelines.

- If deleting layers from a linked file, the layers and items on them are deleted inside the Autodesk Revit project only. The original file is not changed.

How To: Delete Layers in Imported/Linked Files

1. Select the imported/linked file.
2. In the *Modify* contextual tab>Import Instance panel, click

   (Delete Layers).
3. The Select Layers/Levels to Delete dialog box displays a list of all layers or levels in the drawing, as shown in Figure 3–18.

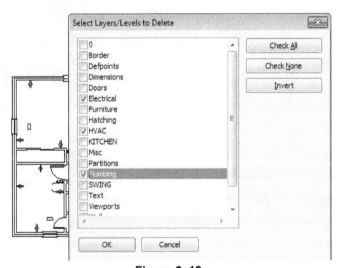

Figure 3–18

4. Select the layers or levels that you want to delete from the imported/linked file and click **OK**.

Exploding Imported Files

If hiding or deleting layers in the imported file does not give the required results, you can explode the file to convert it to Autodesk Revit lines, text, curves, and filled regions. There are two steps to exploding an imported vector file in the Autodesk Revit software: select the imported file and then select the method that you want to use in the Import Instance panel.

 Partial Explode: Converts all top-level objects but does not explode reference files or blocks in the imported drawing as shown in Figure 3–19.

 Full Explode: Converts everything to Autodesk Revit objects.

Exploding importing files increases the file size of the project.

Linked files cannot be exploded.

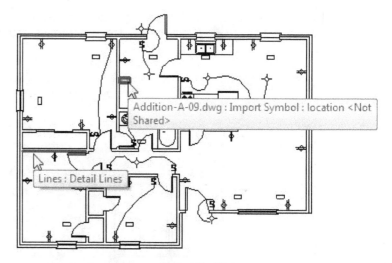

Addition-A-09.dwg : Import Symbol : location <Not Shared>

Lines : Detail Lines

Figure 3–19

- Text becomes Autodesk Revit text objects when the file is exploded.

- Each object that is broken into lines retains its layer/level name as well as its line type.

Modifying the Visibility of Imported Files

If you have used the imported/linked file as a guideline for tracing, you can toggle off the visibility of the entire image without removing it from the project in case you need it later. You can also toggle off individual layers or levels.

How To: Hide individual Layers

1. Open the Visibility/Graphic Overrides dialog box.
2. Switch to the *Imported Categories* tab. It displays a list for each imported instance, as well as its layers/levels, as shown in Figure 3–20.

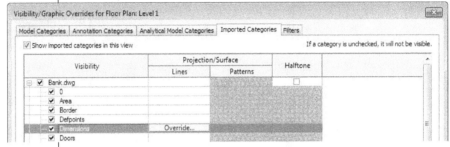

Figure 3–20

3. Click the plus sign beside the name to open a list of the layers or levels in that file.
4. Clear the checkmark from the individual layers that you do not want to display.

   - Typically, these layers contain similar information, such as all windows or all notes in a drawing. However, it is not as definite as using Autodesk Revit elements. An item might have been misplaced on a different layer and if so, it does not toggle off.

5. Close the dialog box.

- To toggle off the entire file, clear the checkmark next to the filename.

- You can also use (Hide in View) and (Override Graphics in View) in the View Graphics panel or in the shortcut menu to modify the view graphics of an imported/linked file.

3.3 Importing Raster Image Files

Raster images are made up of pixels or dots in a file that create a picture. For example, a raster file is created when you scan a blueprint. A logo used in a title block is often a raster image made in a graphics program, as shown in Figure 3–21. You can add raster images to any 2D view, including sheet files. They can be used as a background view or as part of the final drawing. Imported images are placed behind model objects and annotation.

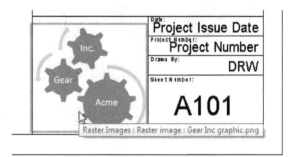

Figure 3–21

How To: Import a Raster Image

1. On the *Insert* tab>Import panel, click 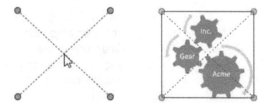 (Image).
2. In the Open dialog box, select the image you want to insert. You can insert bmp, jpg, jpeg, png, and tif files.
3. Click **Open**. Four blue dots and an "x" illustrate the default size of the image file, as shown on the left in Figure 3–22. Click on the screen to place the image. It displays with the shape handles still visible, as shown on the right in Figure 3–22.

Figure 3–22

4. Drag the shape handles to resize the graphic, as required.

Editing Raster Files

Select an image to make changes. Once it is selected, you can resize the image as you did when you first inserted it or in Properties, specify *Width* and *Height* values.

- Select **Lock Proportions** in the Options Bar to ensure that the length and width resize proportionally to each other when you adjust the size of an image.

- Use the standard modification tools to **Move**, **Copy**, **Rotate**, **Mirror**, **Array**, and **Scale** images. Images can also be grouped together into Detail Groups

- Use the *Arrange* tools, as shown in Figure 3–23, to move images to the front or back of other images or objects.

You can also set the Foreground/Background status in the Options Bar and in Properties.

- You can snap to edges of images, as shown in Figure 3–24.

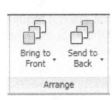

Figure 3–23

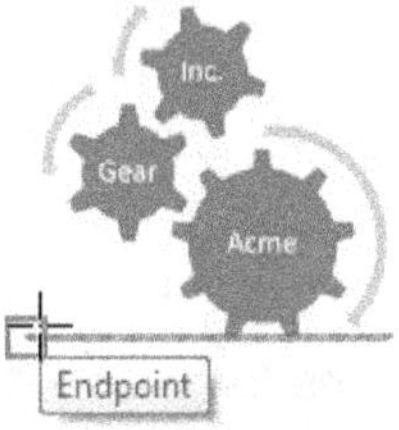

Figure 3–24

- In the *Insert* tab>Import panel, click (Manage Images) to open the Manage Images dialog box, as shown in Figure 3–25. In this dialog box, you can delete images from your file. If you have several instances, it deletes all of them.

You can also select an image and delete it. This removes that instance of the image, but does not remove it from the images associated with the project.

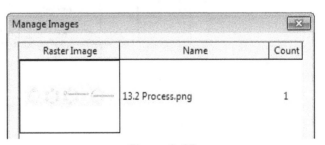

Figure 3–25

Practice 3a

Work with Vector Files - Architectural

Practice Objectives

- Import an AutoCAD file into an Autodesk Revit project and use it as a basis to add elements for a hybrid drawing.
- Query elements in the imported file and delete extraneous layers as well as explode and delete elements.
- Create a sheet and add a rendered raster image to the sheet.

In this practice you will create a hybrid CAD/Autodesk Revit project for an addition to an existing building. You will import an AutoCAD file into a project and add some Autodesk Revit elements, as shown in Figure 3–26. You will then query elements in an imported file, toggle off layers, and delete layers from the file. You will explode the imported file so that you can remove items that are not required. Finally, you will set up a sheet with a copy of the floor plan and add a rendered image of the new entrance.

Estimated time for completion: 15 minutes

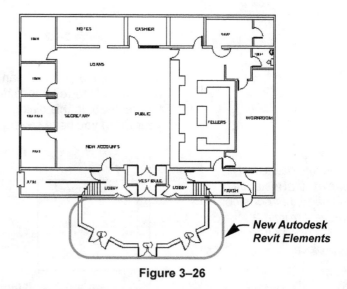

Figure 3–26

Task 1 - Import a CAD file.

1. Start a new project based on the Architectural template.

2. Save the project as **Bank Addition Architectural.rvt**.

3. Verify that you are in the **Floor Plans: Level 1** view.

The CAD file is not going to change. So you can Import rather than link this file.

4. In the *Insert* tab>Import panel, click 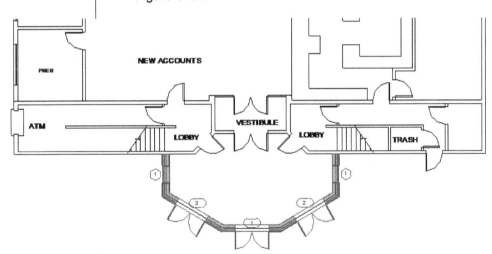 (Import CAD).

5. In the Import CAD dialog box, in the practice files folder, select the AutoCAD drawing file **Bank-Existing.dwg** and set the following options:

    • Select **Current View Only**.
    • *Colors:* **Black and White**
    • *Layers:* **All**
    • *Import Units:* **Auto-Detect**
    • Select **Correct lines that are slightly off axis**.
    • *Positioning:* **Auto-Center to Center**

6. Click **Open**.

7. Switch to an elevation view. No elements are in that view—the imported information is 2D only.

8. Switch back to the **Floor Plans: Level 1** view.

9. Use the outline to draw walls (with a Height to Level 2). Add doors and windows in front of the existing entrance of the building as a new entrance, similar to that shown in Figure 3–27.

Figure 3–27

10. Switch to the **Elevations (Building Elevations): South** view. You should see the Autodesk Revit objects in the view.

11. Save the project.

Task 2 - Query Elements in an Imported File.

1. Return to the **Floor Plans: Level 1** view.

2. Select the imported file. In the *Modify | Bank-Exisiting.dwg* tab>Import Instance panel, click 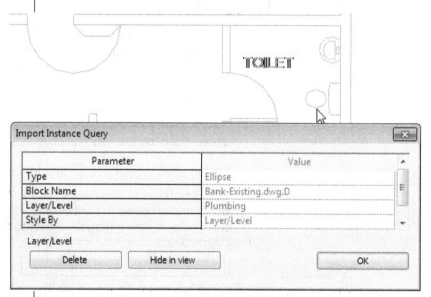 (Query).

3. Select one of the objects in the toilet room. It is a block from AutoCAD on the layer **Plumbing**, as shown in Figure 3–28.

Figure 3–28

4. Click **Hide in View**. This and the other block are removed from the view.

5. Press <Esc> to end the query.

Task 3 - Modify the Visibility of Graphics in an Imported File.

1. Type **VG** to open the Visibility/Graphic Overrides dialog box. Switch to the *Imported Categories* tab.

2. Click the "+" next to **Bank-Existing.dwg** to expand the layers. Toggle off the layers **Text** and **Furniture**. Click **OK**.

3. The cabinetwork of the tellers' booths is toggled off but the text still remains, as shown in Figure 3–29.

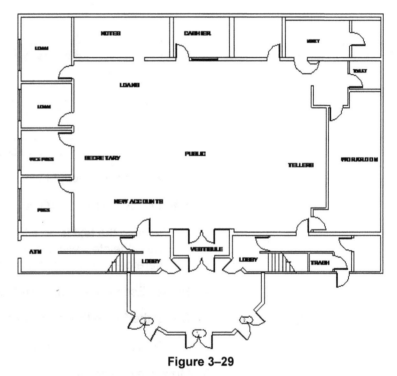

Figure 3–29

- The text in the AutoCAD drawing was not placed on the layer **Text**.

Task 4 - Delete Objects in an Imported File.

1. Elements on several layers are not required for this project. Select the imported file in the drawing. In the Import Instance panel, click ⬛ (Delete Layers).

2. Select the layers **Header**, **Furniture**, and **Plumbing** in the dialog box, as shown in Figure 3–30, and click **OK**.

Select Layers/Levels to Delete

☐ 0	Check All
☐ Area	
☐ Border	Check None
☐ Defpoints	
☐ Dimensions	Invert
☐ Doors	
☐ Electrical	
☑ Furniture	
☐ Hatching	
☑ Header	
☐ HVAC	
☐ Misc	
☐ Partitions	
☑ Plumbing	
☐ Stairs	
☐ Text	

OK   Cancel

Figure 3–30

3. The text that you thought would be on one layer is on a different layer. Use 🔲 (Query) to find out which layer it is on.

   • Because the text is on a layer with other elements, you cannot delete it without impacting the rest of the drawing. Therefore, you need to explode the imported instance.

4. Press <Esc> twice to end the Query and exit the command.

5. Select the file. In the Import Instance panel, click 🔲 (Partial Explode). The file is exploded.

6. Move the cursor over elements in the project, as shown in Figure 3–31.

Most elements in the imported file become detail lines, but the text becomes Autodesk Revit text objects and can be modified. The doors are imported symbols because they were blocks.

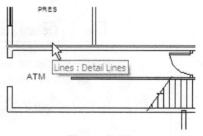

Figure 3–31

7. Delete the text. (Select everything and use (Filter) to select only the Text Notes.)

8. Save the project.

Task 5 - Importing Raster Files.

1. In the Floor Plans: **Level 1** view, toggle off the elevation markers so that they do not display when the view is placed on a sheet.

2. Create a new sheet using the default title block.

3. Drag and drop the **Level 1** view onto the sheet, leaving room for other information.

4. In the *Insert* tab>Import panel, click (Image). Select the image file **Entrance.jpg** (from your practice files folder) and place it on the sheet.

5. Move and resize it so that it fits on the sheet, as shown in Figure 3–32.

The design of the rendered image might not match the design of the walls you created earlier.

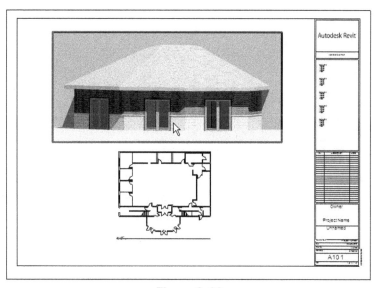

Figure 3–32

6. Save the project.

Practice 3b

Work with Vector Files - Structural

Practice Objectives

- Import an AutoCAD file into an Autodesk Revit project and use it as a basis to add elements for a hybrid drawing.
- Query elements in the imported file and delete extraneous layers as well as explode and delete elements.

Estimated time for completion: 10 minutes

In this practice you will create a hybrid CAD/Autodesk Revit project for an addition to an existing building. You will import an AutoCAD file into a project and add some Autodesk Revit elements, as shown in Figure 3–33. You will then query elements in an imported file, toggle off layers, and delete layers from the file. You will explode the imported file so that you can remove items that are not required.

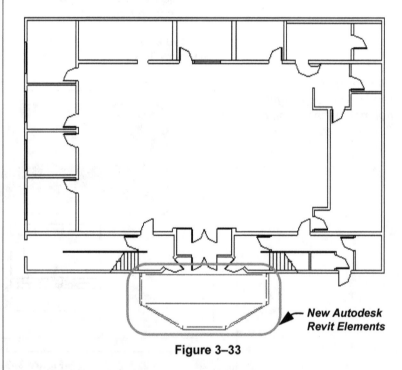

New Autodesk Revit Elements

Figure 3–33

Task 1 - Import a CAD file.

1. Start a new project based on the Structural template.

2. Save the project as **Bank Addition Structural.rvt**.

3. Verify that you are in the **Structural Plans: Level 2** view.

4. In the *Insert* tab>Import panel, click 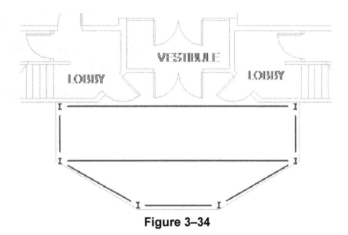 (Import CAD).

5. In the Import CAD dialog box, in the practice files folder, select the AutoCAD drawing file **Bank-Existing.dwg** and set the following options:

   - Select **Current View Only**.
   - *Colors*: **Black and White**
   - *Layers:* **All**
   - *Import Units:* **Auto-Detect**
   - Select **Correct lines that are slightly off axis**.
   - *Positioning*: **Auto-Center to Center**

6. Click **Open**.

7. Switch to an elevation view. No elements are in that view—the imported information is 2D only.

8. Switch back to the **Structural Plans: Level 2** view.

9. Select the imported CAD file and change it to half-tone.

10. Add columns (with a *Depth* set to **Level 1**) and beams to the top of them using the outline in front of the existing entrance of the building for a new entrance, similar to that shown in Figure 3–34.

Figure 3–34

11. Switch to the **Elevations (Building Elevations): South** view. You should see the Autodesk Revit objects in the view.

12. Save the project.

Task 2 - Query Elements in an Imported File.

1. Return to the **Structural Plans: Level 2** view.

2. Select the imported file. In the *Modify | Bank-Existing.dwg* tab>Import Instance panel, click 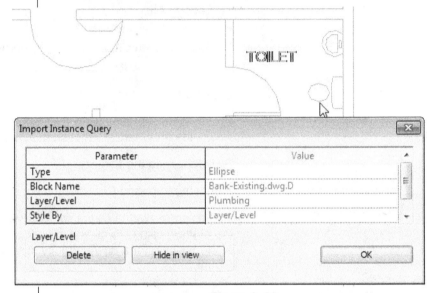 (Query).

3. Select one of the objects in the toilet room. It is a block from AutoCAD on the layer **Plumbing**, as shown in Figure 3–35.

Figure 3–35

4. Click **Hide in view**. This and the other block are removed from the view.

5. Press <Esc> to end the query.

Task 3 - Modify the Visibility of Graphics in an Imported File.

1. Open the Visibility/Graphic Overrides dialog box. Switch to the *Imported Categories* tab.

2. Click the "+" next to **Bank-Existing.dwg** to expand the layers. Toggle off the layers **Text** and **Furniture**. Click **OK**.

3. The cabinetwork of the tellers' booths is toggled off but the text still remains, as shown in Figure 3–36.

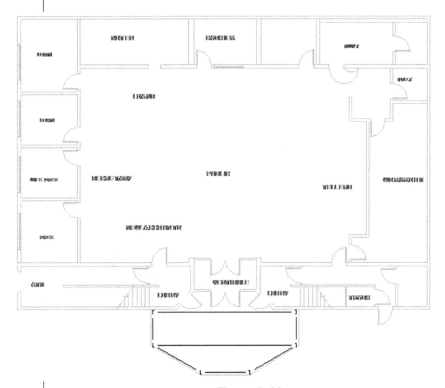

Figure 3–36

- The text in the AutoCAD drawing was not placed on the layer **Text**.

Task 4 - Delete Objects in an Imported File.

1. Elements on several layers are not required for this project. Select the imported file in the drawing. In the Import Instance panel, click (Delete Layers).

2. Select the layers **Header**, **Furniture**, and **Plumbing** in the dialog box, as shown in Figure 3–37, and click **OK**.

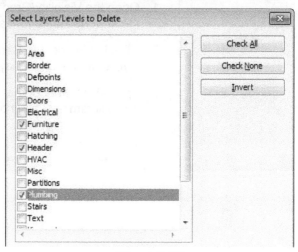

Figure 3–37

3. The text that you thought would be on one layer is on a different layer. Use (Query) to find out which layer it is on.

   - Because the text is on a layer with other elements, you cannot delete it without impacting the rest of the drawing. Therefore, you need to explode the imported instance.

4. Press <Esc> twice to end the Query and exit the command.

5. Select the file. In the Import Instance panel, click (Partial Explode). The file is exploded.

6. Move the cursor over elements in the project, as shown in Figure 3–38.

Most elements in the imported file become detail lines, but the text becomes Autodesk Revit text objects and can be modified. The doors are imported symbols because they were blocks.

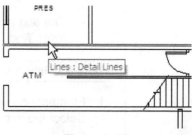

Figure 3–38

7. Delete the text. (Select everything and use 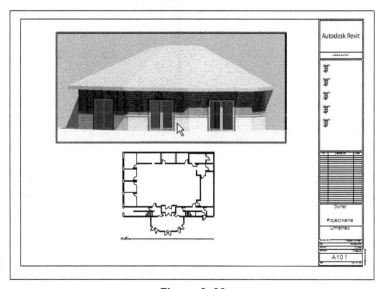 (Filter) to select only the Text Notes.)

8. Save the project.

Task 5 - Importing Raster Files.

1. In the **Structural Plans: Level 2** view, toggle off the elevation markers so that they do not display when the view is placed on a sheet.

2. Create a new sheet using the default title block.

3. Drag and drop the **Level 2** view onto the sheet, leaving room for other information.

4. In the *Insert* tab>Import panel, click (Image). Select the image file **Entrance.jpg** (from your practice files folder) and place it on the sheet.

5. Move and resize it so that it fits on the sheet, as shown in Figure 3–39.

The design of the rendered image might not match the design of the walls you created earlier.

Figure 3–39

6. Save the project.

Practice 3c

Work with Vector Files - MEP

Practice Objectives

- Import an AutoCAD file into an Autodesk Revit project and use it as a basis to add elements for a hybrid drawing.
- Query elements in the imported file and delete extraneous layers as well as explode and delete elements.

In this practice you will create a hybrid CAD/Autodesk Revit project for an addition to an existing building. You will import an AutoCAD file and link an Autodesk Revit model into a project and add some Autodesk Revit elements, as shown in Figure 3–40. You will then query elements in an imported file, toggle off layers, and delete layers from the file. You will explode the imported file so that you can remove items that are not required.

Estimated time for completion: 10 minutes

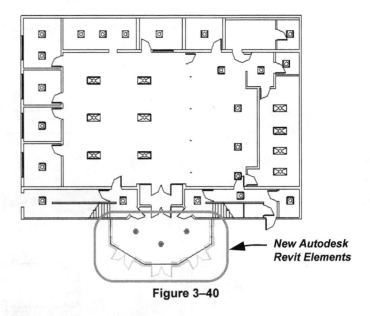

New Autodesk Revit Elements

Figure 3–40

Task 1 - Import a CAD file.

1. Start a new project based on the Electrical or Systems template. (To access these templates, in the New Project dialog box, click **Browse...** and select the required template from the Autodesk Revit templates library.)

2. Save the project as **Bank Addition-MEP.rvt**.

3. Open the Electrical>Lighting> **Floor Plans: 1- Lighting** view.

 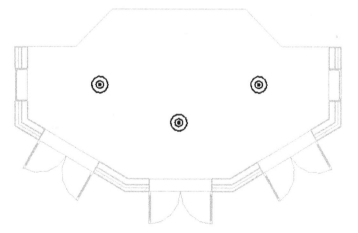

4. In the *Insert* tab>Import panel, click (Import CAD).

5. In the Import CAD dialog box, in the practice files folder, select the AutoCAD drawing file **Bank-MEP.dwg** and set the following options:

   - Select **Current View Only**.
   - *Colors*: **Black and White**
   - *Layers:* **All**
   - *Import Units:* **Auto-Detect**
   - Select **Correct lines that are slightly off axis**.
   - *Positioning*: **Auto-Origin-to-Origin**

6. Click **Open**.

7. Switch to an elevation view. No elements are in that view—the imported information is 2D only.

8. Switch back to the **Floor Plans: 1 - Lighting** view.

9. Link in the Autodesk Revit model, **Bank-Addition-A**.rvt from your practice files folder using Origin - to - Origin positioning.

10. Open the Electrical>Lighting>Ceiling Plans>**1 - Ceiling Elec** view. The linked Autodesk Revit elements display in this view but the imported CAD elements do not.

11. Add several new lights in the new entry area similar to that shown in Figure 3–41. (This example uses pendant lights placed on the ceiling face.)

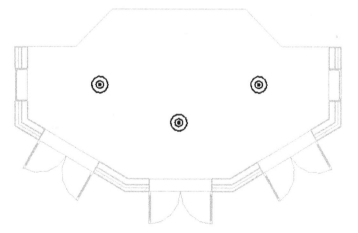

Figure 3–41

12. Switch to the **Elevations (Building Elevations): North- Elec** view. You should see the Autodesk Revit objects in the view.

13. Save the project.

Task 2 - Query Elements in an Imported File.

1. Return to the **Floor Plans: 1 - Lighting** view.

2. Select the imported file. In the *Modify | Bank-Existing.dwg* tab>Import Instance panel, click (Query).

3. Select one of the lighting fixtures. It is a block from AutoCAD on the layer **E-LITE-EQPM**, as shown in Figure 3–42. Click **OK**.

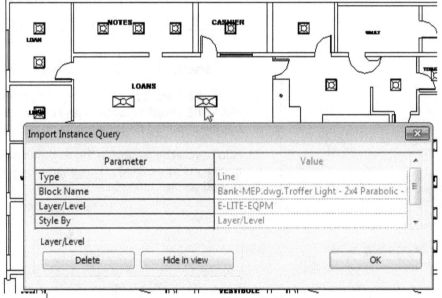

Figure 3–42

4. Select one of the elements in the toilet room. It is also a block on layer **Plumbing**. Click **Hide in view**. This and the other block are removed from the view.

5. Press <Esc> to end the query.

Task 3 - Modify the Imported File.

1. Open the Visibility/Graphic Overrides dialog box. Switch to the *Imported Categories* tab.

2. Click the "+" next to **Bank-MEP.dwg** to expand the layers. Toggle off the layers **Text** and **Furniture**. Click **OK**.

3. The cabinetwork of the tellers' booths is toggled off but the text still remains, as shown in Figure 3–43.

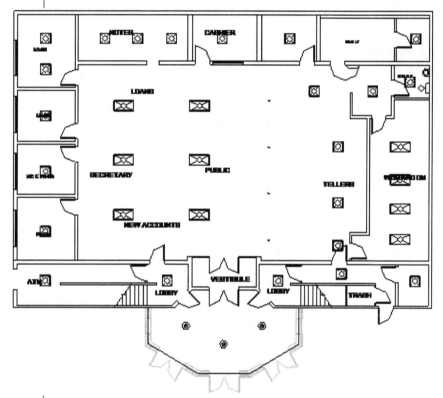

Figure 3–43

4. The text that you thought would be on one layer is on a

   different layer. Use (Query) to find out which layer it is on.
   - Because the text is on a layer with other elements, you cannot delete it without impacting the rest of the drawing. Therefore, you need to explode the imported instance.

5. Press <Esc> twice to end the Query and exit the command.

6. Select the file. In the Import Instance panel, click 📦 (Partial Explode). The file is exploded.

7. Move the cursor over elements in the project, as shown in Figure 3–44.

Most elements in the imported file become detail lines, but the text becomes Autodesk Revit text objects and can be modified. The doors are imported symbols because they were blocks.

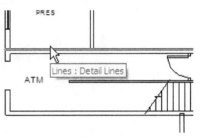

Figure 3–44

8. Delete the text. (Select everything and use 🔽 (Filter) to select only the Text Notes.)

9. Save the project.

3.4 Exporting Files

If your company uses multiple CAD programs or works with consultants who use other CAD programs, prepare your Autodesk Revit files so that the other programs can use them as well. The Autodesk Revit software provides ways to export Autodesk Revit vector data to CAD formats, DWF, Building Site, Images and Animations, Reports, FBX, gbXML, IFC (Industry Foundation Classes), and ODBC databases, as shown in Figure 3–45.

Scroll down the Export list to see additional options.

Figure 3–45

*   Find out if the users for which you are exporting need a 2D or 3D view. You can export any view, but only 3D views export the entire building model; other views create 2D files.

*   Text character size, location, and other text related properties is rendered faithfully when exported to other CAD file formats.

Export Types

- **CAD Formats:** Exports projects to AutoCAD DWG or DXF, MicroStation DGN, or ASIC SAT files for 3D modeling.

- **DWF/DWFx:** Exports views and sheets to DWF or DWFx files to be used in Autodesk® Design Review for review and redlining.

- **Building Site:** Exports ADSK exchange files that can be used with Civil Engineering programs.

- **FBX:** Exports 3D files for Autodesk® MotionBuilder®, as well as Autodesk® Maya®, Autodesk® 3ds Max®, and Viz plug-ins. You must be in a 3D view for this to display.

- **Family Types:** Exports family type information to a text (.txt) file that can be imported into a spreadsheet program to verify that all of the parameters for each type are correct. You must be in a family file for this to display.

- **gbXML:** Exports model information that can be used in other programs for energy or load analysis.

- **IFC:** Exports the Autodesk Revit model to Industry Foundation Class objects. These can be used by CAD programs that do not use RVT file formats. It uses established standards for typical objects in the building industry. For example, an Autodesk Revit wall element translates to an IfcWall object. Additional mapping for specialty items can be set up.

- **ODBC Database:** Exports Autodesk Revit information to an Open Database Connectivity database file. It creates tables of the model element types and instances, levels, rooms, key schedules, and assembly codes.

- **Images and Animations:** Exports walkthroughs, solar studies, and images.

- **Reports:** Exports information from Schedules and Room/Area. Schedules are exported as delimited text files that can be imported into a spreadsheet. You must be in a schedule view to export. Room/Area reports are saved as HTML files.

- **Options:** Sets up the options for Export Setups for DWG/DXF, DGN, and IFC options.

Exporting CAD Format Files

Exporting Autodesk Revit Projects to various CAD file formats is a common need in collaboration with consultants and engineers. Using this process, you can export individual views or sheets, or sets of views or sheets to DWG, DXF, DGN, and SAT files. You can also create and save sets of views/sheets.

How To: Export a CAD Format File

1. If you are exporting only one view, open the view you want to export. If you are exporting the model, open a 3D view.

2. In the *File* tab, expand ⬚ (Export), click

   ⬚ (CAD Formats), and select the type of format you want to export as shown in Figure 3–46.

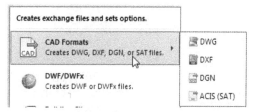

Figure 3–46

- The examples in this section show the process for DWG files. It is the same for other types of files.

3. The Export CAD Formats dialog box displays, as shown in Figure 3–47.

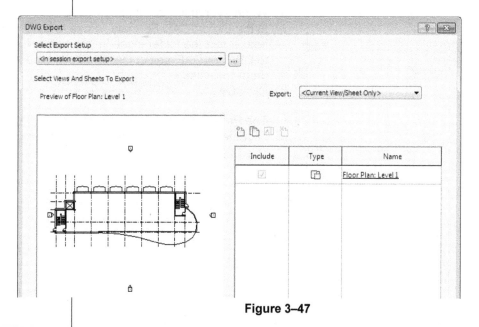

Figure 3–47

4. If you have an existing export setup, you can select it from the drop-down list as shown in Figure 3–48, or click 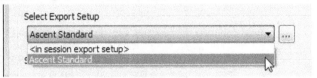 (Modify Export Setup) to create a new one.

Figure 3–48

5. Select the view(s) you want to export from the Export drop-down list as shown in Figure 3–49.

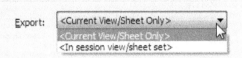

Figure 3–49

- To export only the active view, select **<Current View/ Sheet Only>**.
- To export any views or sheets that are open in the session of the Autodesk Revit software, select **<In session view/sheet set>**.
- To export a predefined set of views or sheets, select the name from the list if it is available. You can create new sets of views and sheets to export.

6. When everything is set up correctly, click **Next...**.
7. In the Export CAD Formats - Save to Target Folder dialog box, select the folder location and name. If you are exporting to DWG or DXF, select the version in the Files of type drop-down list.
8. Click **OK.**

- The Project Base Point of the Autodesk Revit project becomes the 0,0 coordinate point in other CAD formats.

How To: Create an Export Setup

1. In the DWG, DXF, or DGN Export dialog box, next to the Select Export Setup list, click ⬚ (Modify Export Setup) or in the *File* tab, expand ⬚ (Export), scroll down to ⬚ (Options), expand it, and select ⬚ (Export Setups DWG/DXF) or ⬚ (Export Setups DGN).

2. The Modify DWG/DXF or Modify DGN Export Setup dialog box contains all of the elements and types you can export. You can select an existing Layer standard provided with the program (as shown in Figure 3–50), or create a new one.

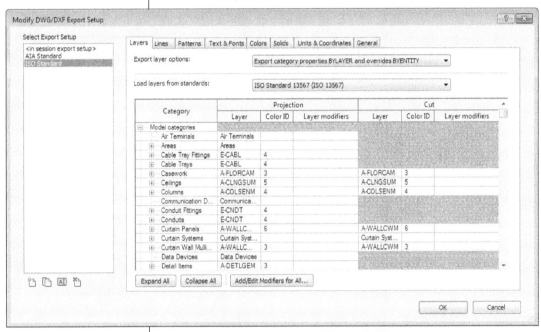

Figure 3–50

3. Select each of the tabs and apply the appropriate information.

    *   In the *Layers* tab, map the Categories in the Autodesk Revit software to the Layers (or Levels).

    *   In the *Lines*, *Patterns*, and *Text & Fonts* tabs map the styles required.

    *   In the *Colors* tab, select to export either Index colors (255 colors) or True color (RGB values).

    *   In the *Solids* tab (3D views only), select to export to either Polymesh or ACIS solids.

- In the *Units & Coordinates* tab, specify what unit type one DWG unit is and the basis for the coordinate system.
- In the *General* tab, you can set up how the rooms and room boundaries are exported, what to do with any non-plottable layers, how scope boxes, reference planes, coincident lines, and unreferenced view tags are handled, how views on sheets and links are treated, and which version of the DWG file format to use.

- Export setups can be created in a template file or shared between open projects using Transfer Project Standards.

How To: Create a New Set of Views/Sheets to Export

1. Start the appropriate Export CAD Formats command.
2. In the Export CAD Formats dialog box, click ⬚ (New Set).
3. In the New Set dialog box, type a name and click **OK**.
4. The tab displays with the new set active and additional information, as shown in Figure 3–51.

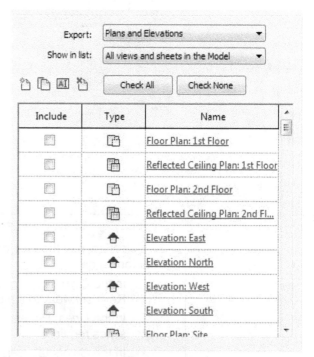

Figure 3–51

5. Use *Show in List* to limit the number of items that display in the table.
6. Select the views and/or sheets that you want to export from the project.
   - Use **Check all** or **Check none** to aid in selection.
7. When you finish with the set, continue the export process.

Exporting to DWF

Exporting DWF/DWFx (Design Web Format) files gives you a safe and easy way to share Autodesk Revit project information without sending the actual file. For example, a client does not have to have the Autodesk Revit software on their machine to view the file and they cannot make any changes directly to it. DWF/DWFx files are also much smaller than project files and are therefore easier to email or post on a website. DWF/DWFx files can include element data that can be viewed in Autodesk Design Review.

The process of exporting a DWF file is similar to CAD Format exports. You can export individual views or sheets, as shown in Figure 3–52, or you can create sets of multiple views/sheets.

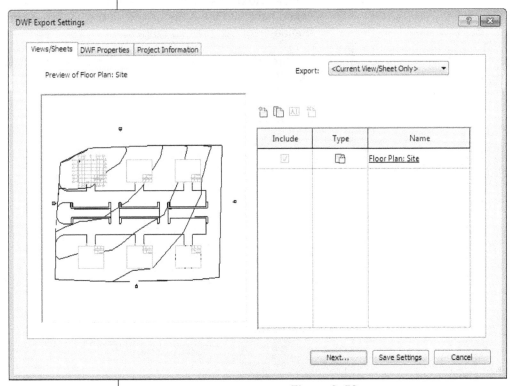

Figure 3–52

- In the *DWF Properties* tab, set up the export object data, the graphics settings, and print setup.

- The *Project Information* tab, shown in Figure 3–53, can be updated and included in a DWF export.

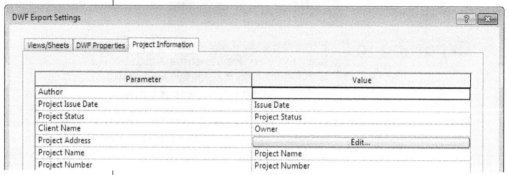

Figure 3–53

- Files can be exported to the DWF or DWFx format.

- You can mark up (redline) DWF/DWFx files using a program such as Autodesk Design Review. The markups can then be linked back into the Autodesk Revit project, where the original user can make changes.

- Textures, line patterns, line weights, and text are included in 3D DWF exports.

Practice 3d

Export Files - All Disciplines

Practice Objective

- Export views to AutoCAD drawing files and DWF viewing files.

Estimated time for completion: 5 minutes

In this practice you will export several views to AutoCAD drawing files and to DWF files, as shown in Autodesk Design Review in Figure 3–54.

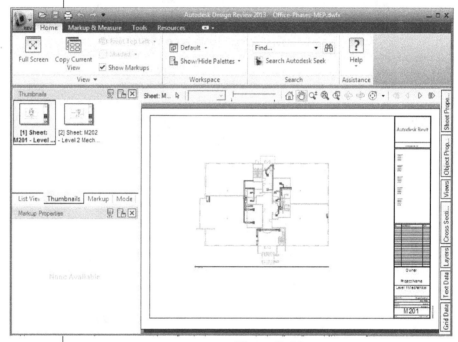

Figure 3–54

Task 1 - Set up and Export a Set of 2D Views to a DWG File.

1. In the practice files folder, open the **Office Phases** project that matches your discipline.

   - The views shown in this practice use the original version of **Office Phases-MEP.rvt**. Your practice file will vary according to the project you select and the work that has been done in the file.

---

2. In the *File* tab, expand 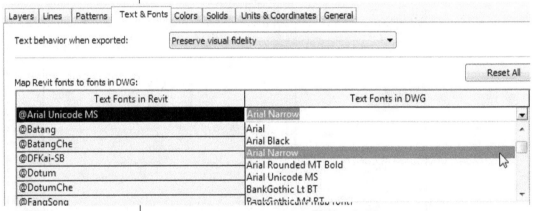 (Export), expand (CAD Formats), and click (DWG).

3. In the DWG Export dialog box, in the *Select Export Setup* area, click (Modify Export Setup).

4. In the Modify DWG/DXF Export Setup dialog box, *Layers* tab, *Load layers from standards* list, select the standard you are most likely to use.

5. In the *Text & Fonts* tab for *Text behavior when exported*, select **Preserve visual fidelity**.

6. Scroll down in the list of fonts and map *Arial* to **Arial Narrow**, as shown in Figure 3–55.

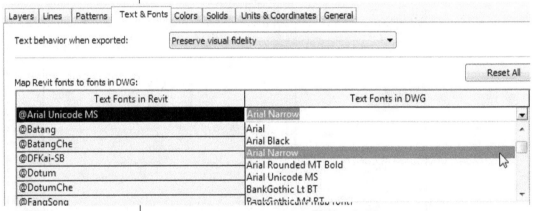

Figure 3–55

7. In the *General* tab, select **Export rooms, spaces and areas as polylines**. Click **OK**.

8. In the DWG Export dialog box, click (New Set).

9. In the New Set dialog box, type the name **Plans** and click **OK**.

10. Select at least two floor/structural plan views, as shown in Figure 3–56.

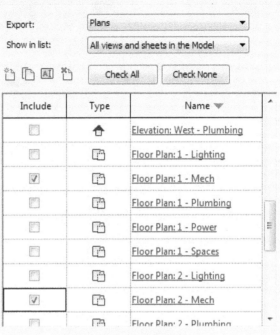

Figure 3–56

11. Click **Next...**.

The most recent AutoCAD file format is 2018 but using the older option is required for many users.

12. In the Export CAD Formats - Save to Target Folder dialog box, set the *Save In:* folder to the practice files folder. Set the *Files of Type:* to **AutoCAD 2013 DWG** files.

13. Set the *Naming* to **Automatic-Long (Specify prefix)** and type **Plans** in the *File name/Prefix* field.

14. Click **OK**. The software generates DWG files for the each selected view using the setup you defined.

Task 2 - Export a 3D View to AutoCAD.

1. Switch to a 3D view if you are not already in one.

2. In the *File* tab, expand (Export), expand (CAD Formats), and click (DWG Files).

3. In the DWG Export dialog box, set *Export* to **<Current View/Sheet only>**, as shown in Figure 3–57.

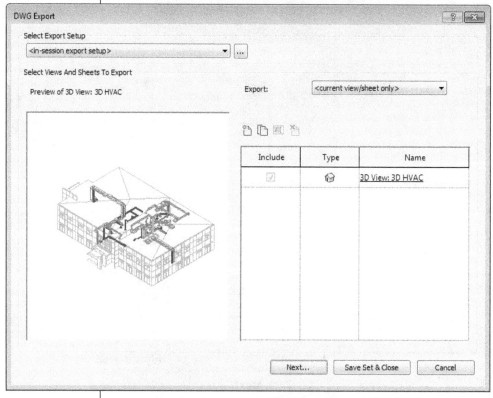

Figure 3–57

4. Click **Next...**. In the Export CAD Formats - Save to Target Folder dialog box, type a filename as required, and click **OK**.

5. If you have access to AutoCAD, you can open the files to see the exported geometry or view them in Windows Explorer, as shown in Figure 3–58 in the Extra Large Icons view.

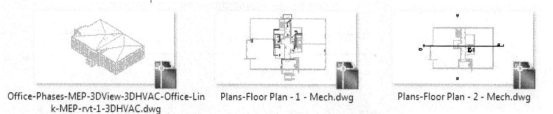

Office-Phases-MEP-3DView-3DHVAC-Office-Lin
k-MEP-rvt-1-3DHVAC.dwg

Plans-Floor Plan - 1 - Mech.dwg

Plans-Floor Plan - 2 - Mech.dwg

Figure 3–58

Task 3 - Export to DWF.

1. In the *File* tab, expand  (Export) and click

   (DWF/DWFx).

2. In the DWF Export Settings dialog box, click ⬚ (New Set).

3. In the New Set dialog box, type the name **Sheets** and click **OK**.

4. Change the *Show in list:* to **Sheets in the Model** and select the sheets, as shown in Figure 3–59.

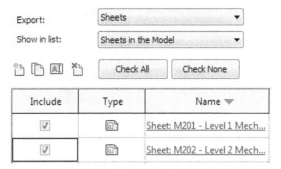

Figure 3–59

5. Switch to the *DWF Properties* tab and verify that **Element Properties** is selected.

6. Click **Next...**.

7. In the Export DWF - Save to Target Folder dialog box, note that **Combine selected views and sheets into a single dwf file** is selected by default.

8. Click **OK**.

9. If you have Autodesk Design Review, view the file.

10. If you have time, create a 3D DWF of the model and view the file.

3.5 Exporting for Energy Analysis

Green buildings and energy analysis are now a major component of design. Creating an energy-efficient building requires understanding of how lighting, heating, cooling, and other structures interact with the site, spaces, and materials used. For example, heating and cooling a 3-story space in a cold climate is very different from heating and cooling a room with an low ceiling in a desert area. The seasons and time of day also impact energy consumption, as shown in the shadow study in Figure 3–60.

Figure 3–60

Numerous programs do this type of analysis. Autodesk Revit projects are Building Information Models (BIM). Therefore, instead of time-consuming hand-takeoff, you can export Autodesk Revit projects to a gbXML file that can then be imported into the analysis program.

- gbXML stands for Green Building Extensible Markup Language. It is a standard used to transfer building information from a CAD BIM model to an engineering analysis tool.

- Engineering analysis tools include Green Building Studio, HVAC manufacturer programs (such as Trane or Carrier), and the United States Department of Energy's simulation tool.

- **Subscription-Only Feature**. You can enable the energy model directly in the Autodesk Revit software and run energy simulations in the cloud using Autodesk 360 and Autodesk Green Building Studio. This can be done early in a project using either the conceptual mass elements or the building elements without the spaces in place. This does not require exporting to gbXML The results are hosted in the cloud and you can compare results from different runs of the program.

Preparing a Project for Energy Analysis

Using the Export to gbXML tool enables you to send information from the energy analytical model based on the energy settings (subscription-only) or the volumes in the model identified by room (architecture) or spaces (MEP).

This topic covers exporting using the volumes of rooms and spaces.

- To prepare a project to export for gbXML you need to verify room height properties and ensure that the volume, as well as the area, is being calculated.

- All interior spaces, including plenums and chases, larger than the Sliver Space Tolerance need to have a room/space element placed in them for accurate analysis.

- For more information on preparing an MEP project for energy analysis, see the Autodesk Revit MEP Fundamentals learning guide from Ascent.

How To: Set Up Room Properties for Volumes

1. In the *Architecture* tab>Room & Area panel, click on the title to expand the options, and click ⌐ (Area and Volume Computations).
2. In the Area and Volume Computations dialog box, in the *Computations* tab, select **Areas and Volumes**, as shown in Figure 3–61, so that room volumes are calculated.

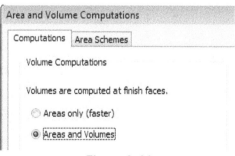

Figure 3–61

3. Click **OK** to close the dialog box
4. Add rooms to the project that define the spaces and areas for the energy analysis.
5. Modify the room properties so that **Upper Limit** and **Limit Offset** describe the height of the room, as shown in Figure 3–62.

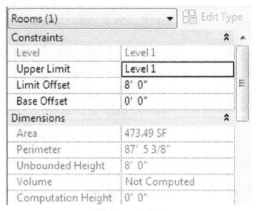

Figure 3–62

Exporting to gbXML

When you start the export process, you can modify the Project Information and ensure that the rooms and analytical surfaces display as expected. The program calculates the inner room volumes, analytical room models, shading surfaces, openings, and more.

How To: Export a File to gbXML

1. Open a 3D view of the model.

2. In the *File* tab, expand (Export) and click (gbXML).
3. In the Export gbXML dialog box, select **Use Room/Space Volumes** and click **OK**.

4. The Export gbXML dialog box, as shown in Figure 3–63, displays with a 3D view of the room volumes and information on the *General* and *Details* tabs.

In this example only one floor of rooms has been created for clarity.

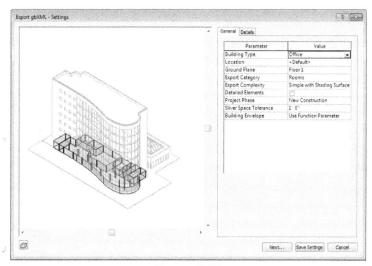

Figure 3–63

5. In the *General* tab, verify or apply the Project Information parameters, including how much complexity you want to export, as shown in Figure 3–64.

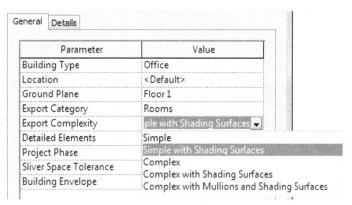

Figure 3–64

6. Select the *Details* tab and expand the levels to see the rooms for each level. Icons beside the room name show if the room has been able to be calculated, as shown in Figure 3–65.

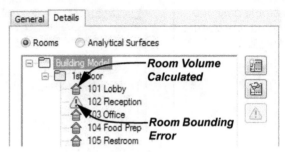

Figure 3–65

7. To view an error, click on the room name and then click ⚠ (Show Related Warnings). The warning dialog box, as shown in Figure 3–66, outlines the cause for the warning.

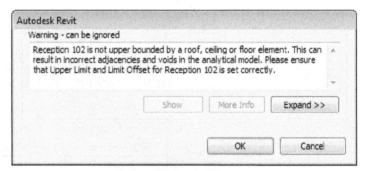

Figure 3–66

8. To see visual information about the room, select the room name and click 📋 (Highlight) to highlight the room in the 3D view, or click 📋 (Isolate) to toggle off all the display of the other rooms in the 3D view.

• Click the icons again to toggle them off.

9. Select **Analytical Surfaces** to see the surface calculation planes, as shown in Figure 3–67.

*The **Lobby** is isolated in Figure 3–67.*

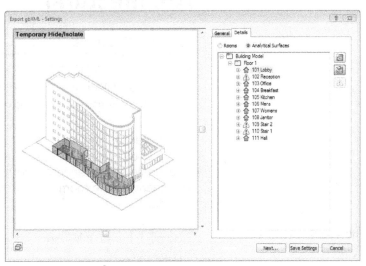

Figure 3–67

10. If you need to make changes to the model, click **Save Settings** to return to the model.
11. Run **Export gbXML** again and test the model. When you are ready to continue with the export, click **Next...**.
12. In the Export gbXML - Save to Target Folder dialog box, select the folder location and name for the file, and then click **Save**.
13. The resulting .XML file can then be imported into an energy analysis program.

The beginning of the .XML file contains project information about the building, including its location and type, as shown in Figure 3–68. Each room is then listed with its name, description, area, volume, and coordinate points.

```
<?xml version="1.0" encoding="UTF-8" ?>
- <gbXML temperatureUnit="F" lengthUnit="Feet" areaUnit="SquareFeet" volumeUnit="CubicFeet" useSIUnitsForResults="false"
  xmlns="http://www.gbxml.org/schema" version="0.37">
  - <Campus id="cmps-1">
    - <Location>
      <Name>Boston, MA, USA</Name>
      <Latitude>42.358300</Latitude>
      <Longitude>-71.060300</Longitude>
    </Location>
    - <Building id="bldg-1" buildingType="Office">
```

Figure 3–68

Practice 3e

Export for Energy Analysis - Architectural

Practice Objectives

- Prepare a project with room heights and locations.
- Test the gbXML export and identify issues that need to be corrected.
- Resolve the issues and export the project to gbXML.

In this practice you will modify room heights, as shown in Figure 3–69. You will also run the **Export to gbXML** command, investigate errors, and then correct the errors by adding ceilings and changing the room limits. You will then export the file to gbXML.

Estimated time for completion: 10 minutes

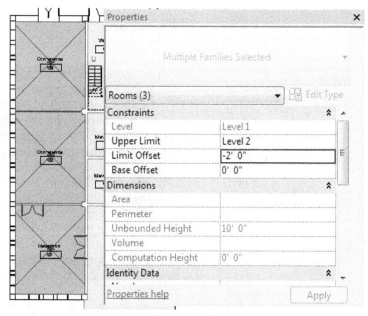

Figure 3–69

Task 1 - Prepare the Project for Export to gbXML.

1. In the practice files folder, open the project **Midrise-Energy-A.rvt**.

2. Open the Floor Plans: **Level 1 - Rooms** view.

3. Select the room **Entry 107**, as shown in Figure 3–70.

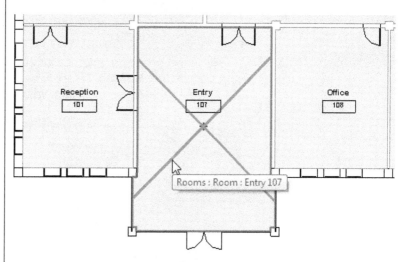

Figure 3–70

4. In Properties, change the *Upper Limit* to **Roof** and the *Limit Offset* to **0'-0"**, as shown in Figure 3–71.

5. Select the reception and two conference rooms to the left. In Properties, set the *Upper Limit* to **Level 2** and the *Limit Offset* to (negative) **-2'-0"**, as shown in Figure 3–72.

Figure 3–71

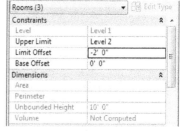

Figure 3–72

- The level-to-level distance is 12'-0"; therefore, this creates 10'-0" ceilings in these rooms.

- In Properties, note that the *Volume* is listed as **Not Computed**.

6. In the *Architecture* tab>Room & Area panel, click on the title to expand the options and click 🖳 (Area and Volume Computations).

7. In the Area and Volume Computations dialog box, in the *Computations* tab, select **Areas and Volumes**, as shown in Figure 3–73, so that room volumes are calculated.

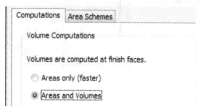

Figure 3–73

8. Click **OK** to close the dialog box.

9. Select one of the same rooms and view the *Volume* that displays in Properties.

10. Press <Esc> to clear the selection.

11. Save the project.

Task 2 - Test the Export to gbXML.

1. Open the default 3D view.

2. In the *File* tab, expand 🖺 (Export) and click 🖳 (gbXML).

3. In the Export gbXML dialog box, select **Use Room/space Volumes** and click **OK**.

4. In the Export gbXML dialog box, in the *General* tab, set the *Building Type* to **Office** from the list.

5. Click in the *Value* of the **Location** option and click

   ⬚ (Browse). In the Location Weather and Site dialog box, select a location for the building (as shown in Figure 3–74), and click **OK**.

6. In the Export to gbXML dialog box, switch to the *Details* tab and expand Level 1, as shown in Figure 3–75.

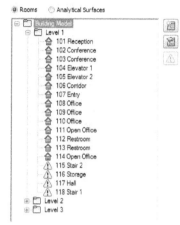

Figure 3–74   **Figure 3–75**

7. Select the room **115 Stair 2** and click ⚠ (Show Related Warnings). The warning displays as shown in Figure 3–76.

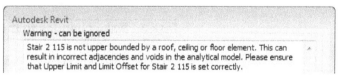

Figure 3–76

8. Select the other rooms with warnings on the first floor and display their warnings. In this case, all of the rooms that are not computed correctly are missing a boundary (such as a roof, ceiling, or floor).

9. Use 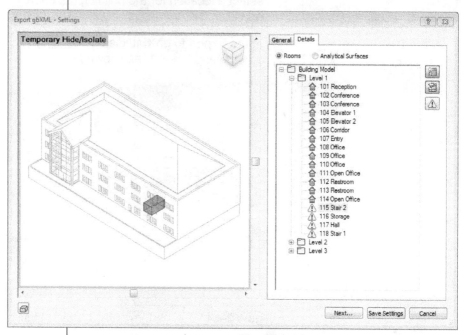 (Isolate) to identify the room locations, as shown in Figure 3–77.

Figure 3–77

10. Click **Save Settings** to close the Export gbXML dialog box and return to the model to modify it.

Task 3 - Make changes to the model.

1. Open the Ceiling Plans: **Level 1** view.

2. Add ceilings to rooms **Hall 117** and **Storage 116** using the **Compound Ceiling: GBW on Mtl. Stud** type and a *Height Offset From Level* of **8'-0"**, as shown in Figure 3–78.

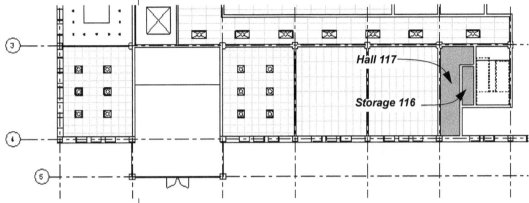

Figure 3–78

3. Open the Floor Plans: **Level 1 - Rooms** view. Select both of the stair room elements, as shown in Figure 3–79.

4. In Properties change the *Upper Limit* to **Roof** and the *Limit Offset* to **0'-0"**.

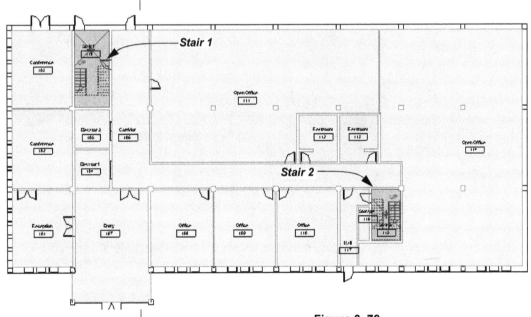

Figure 3–79

5. Save the project.

Task 4 - Rerun the Export to gbXML.

1. Return to a 3D view.

2. Start the **Export to gbXML** command again using the room/space volumes method.

3. Switch to the *Details* tab and expand **Level 1**. All the rooms on Level 1 should now be ready to export (as shown in Figure 3–80), with the two stair rooms isolated.

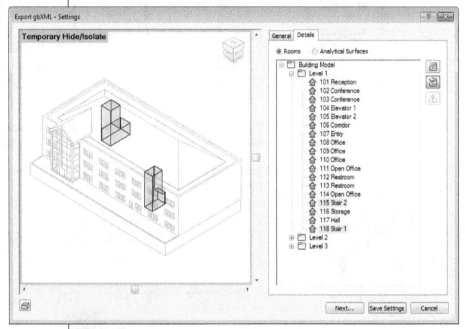

Figure 3–80

4. Click **Next...**.

5. In the Export gbXML - Save to Target folder dialog box, specify the practice files folder as the location for the file and click **Save**.

6. You can now import the resulting .XML file into an energy analysis program, or view it with Windows Explorer.

7. If you have time, you can fix the problems on Levels 2 and 3 and run the export to gbXML again.

Chapter Review Questions

1. Which of the following types of vector files can you import into the Autodesk Revit software? (Select all that apply.)

   a. DGN

   b. DWG

   c. DOC

   d. DXF

2. Which of the following settings can be specified before you import AutoCAD files (as shown in Figure 3–81) or Microstation files into a project?

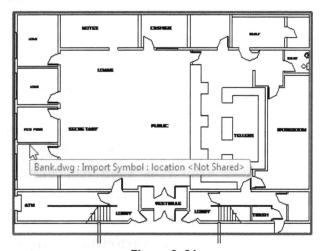

Figure 3–81

   a. Color to Line Weight

   b. Text and Dimension Styles

   c. Units

   d. Patterns

3. Once a vector file is imported into an Autodesk Revit project, can you change the visibility of elements in the imported instance?

   a. Yes

   b. No

4. When you explode an imported instance of a vector file, what type of elements do notes change to?

   a. Note Blocks

   b. Lines and Arcs

   c. Text

   d. Groups

5. Which of the following can you use to modify a raster image, such as the one shown in Figure 3–82? (Select all that apply.)

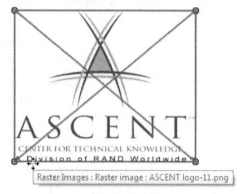

Raster Images : Raster image : ASCENT logo-11.png

Figure 3–82

   a. Delete portions of the graphic.

   b. Resize it by dragging the corners.

   c. Query the information inside the graphic.

   d. Change the foreground/background status.

6. Which of the following settings can be specified when you export a project to DWG/DXF or DGN? (Select all that apply.)

   a. Line Weight to Color

   b. Text

   c. Units

   d. Patterns

7. (Optional) What elements MUST be in an architectural project before exporting to gbXML for energy analysis?

   a. Ceilings

   b. Floors

   c. Rooms

   d. Roofs

Command Summary

Button	Command	Location
Vector Files		
	Coordination Model	• **Ribbon:** *Insert* tab>Link panel
	Delete Layers	• **Ribbon**: *Modify	[imported file name]* tab>Import Instance panel
	Explode	• **Ribbon**: *Modify	[imported file name]* tab>Import Instance panel
	Full Explode	• **Ribbon**: *Modify	[imported file name]* tab>Import Instance panel>Explode
	Import CAD	• **Ribbon**: *Insert* tab>Import panel
	Link CAD	• **Ribbon:** *Insert* tab>Link panel
	Partial Explode	• **Ribbon**: *Modify	[imported file name]* tab>Import Instance panel>Explode
	Query	• **Ribbon**: *Modify	[imported file name]* tab>Import Instance panel
	Scale	• **Ribbon**: *Modify* tab>Modify panel
Raster Files		
	Bring Forward	• **Ribbon**: *Modify	Raster Images* tab> Arrange panel
	Bring to Front	• **Ribbon**: *Modify	Raster Images* tab> Arrange panel
	Image	• **Ribbon**: *Insert* tab>Import panel
	Manage Images	• **Ribbon**: *Insert* tab>Import panel
	Send Backward	• **Ribbon**: *Modify	Raster Images* tab> Arrange panel>
	Send to Back	• **Ribbon**: *Modify	Raster Images* tab> Arrange panel

Exporting

	ACIS (SAT)	• *File* tab: Expand Export>CAD Formats
	Building Site	• *File* tab: Expand Export
	CAD Formats	• *File* tab: Expand Export
	DGN	• *File* tab: Expand Export>CAD Formats
	DWF/DWFx	• *File* tab: Expand Export
	DWG	• *File* tab: Expand Export>CAD Formats
	DXF	• *File* tab: Expand Export>CAD Formats
	Export	• *File* tab
	Export Setups DGN	• *File* tab: Expand Export>Options
	Export Setups DWG/DWF	• *File* tab: Expand Export>Options
	Family Types	• *File* tab: Expand Export
	FBX	• *File* tab: Expand Export
	gbXML	• *File* tab: Expand Export
	IFC	• *File* tab: Expand Export
	IFC Options	• *File* tab: Expand Export>Options
	Images and Animations	• *File* tab: Expand Export
	Mass Model gbXML	• *File* tab: Expand Export
	ODBC Database	• *File* tab: Expand Export
	Options	• *File* tab: Expand Export
	Reports	• *File* tab: Expand Export

Project Team Collaboration

Project team collaboration happens on many levels in a firm and between disciplines. When you have a very large project with more than one person working on that project at one time, you need to create and use worksets. Worksets enable you to work in one part of a project while someone else is working in another part of the same project. Not everyone needs to know how to set up worksets, but everyone can benefit from learning how to work with them.

Learning Objectives in this Chapter

- Understand worksharing workflow and definitions.
- Create and open a local file based on the central file.
- Synchronize a local file with the central file.
- Set the active workset and work in the local file.
- Request and approve permission to edit elements.
- Close the workshared project correctly.
- Control workset visibility by view.
- Temporarily enable the display of worksets.
- Set up worksets in a project.
- Place elements in worksets.
- Create a central file.
- Investigate tips for using worksets,

4.1 Introduction to Worksets

When a project becomes too big for one person, it needs to be subdivided so that a team of people can work on it. Since Autodesk® Revit® projects include the entire building model in one file, the file needs to be separated into logical components (as shown in Figure 4–1), without losing the connection to the whole. This process is called "worksharing" and its main component is worksets.

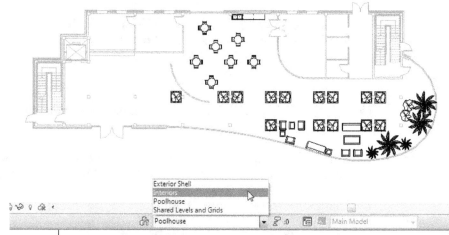

Figure 4–1

When worksets are established in a project, there is one **central file** and as many **local files** as required for each person on the team to have a file, as shown in Figure 4–2. All local files are saved back to the central file, and updates to the central file are sent out to the local files. This way, all changes remain in one file and all parts of the project, model views, and sheets are automatically updated.

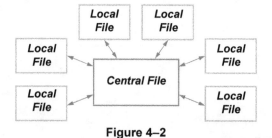

Figure 4–2

- The central file is created by the BIM Manager, Project Manager, or Project Lead, and stored on a server, enabling multiple user access.

Workset Definitions

Workset: A collection of related elements in a project. Each user-created workset matches a part of the project that an individual team member would work on (such as specific sections of the building or the exterior shell, site, or interior partitions). There are also worksets created automatically for Families, Project Standards (such as materials and line styles), and Views. Worksets can be checked out so that others cannot modify them without permission.

Central File: The main file that holds all of the worksets. This is the file to which everyone saves their changes. Typically, the file is not edited directly.

Local File: A copy of the central file that is saved to your local computer. This is the file that you modify. You then save the file locally and synchronize it with the central file.

Element borrowing: Refers to the process of modifying items in the project that are not part of the workset you have checked out. This either happens automatically (if no one else has checked out a workset), or specifically, when you request to have control of the elements (if someone else has a workset checked out).

General Process of Using Worksets

Close any worksets to which you do not need access. This saves system memory and frees up elements for other project team members to edit.

1. Create a local file from the central file that is set up by the project manager.
2. Open the local file and select the worksets on which you need to work.
3. Set a workset active. This is the workset on which any new elements are placed.
4. Add and modify elements, as required.
   - You may need to request access to elements in worksets that are currently checked out by other project team members.
5. Save the local file frequently as you would save any other project.
6. Synchronize the local file with the central file several times a day or as required by company policy or project status.
   - This reloads any changes from the central file to your local file and vice versa.
7. Save the local file every time you save to the central file.

4.2 Opening and Saving Workset-Related Projects

Some people recommend that you create a new local file every morning to ensure that you have the most up-to-date information.

The first step in using a workset-related project is to create a local file. This is the file you use to add and modify any of the elements in a project. Once you have a local file created, you can open it with only specific worksets opened. Local files are saved directly to your computer. You can also synchronize the local file with the central file.

How To: Create a Local File

1. Open the central file. Do not work in this file.
2. In the Open dialog box, when a central file is selected, use the option **Create New Local**, as shown in Figure 4–3.
3. Verify that it is selected and click **Open**.

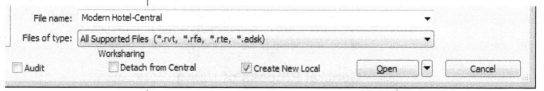

Figure 4–3

4. A copy of the project is created. It has the same name as the central file with Autodesk Revit *User Name* added to the end.

5. In the Quick Access Toolbar, click ![Save icon] (Save) if you want to use the default filename (*Central File Name-Local*.rvt). Alternatively, in the *File* tab, expand **Save As>Project** and name the file according to your office standard. It can include "Local" in the name to indicate that it is saved on your local computer or that you are the only one working with that copy of the file.
6. Click **Save**.

Hint: Setting the Username and Default File Location

The Autodesk Revit software checks the current *Username* to assign the local file name and determine which worksets are available for you to open after you create a local file. By default, it uses the login name you provided when you entered the operating system. To change the *Username*, in the *File* tab, click **Options**. Then, in the Options dialog box, in the *General* pane, type in the required *Username*, as shown in Figure 4–4.

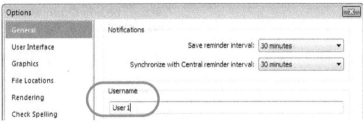

Figure 4–4

- This pane is also where you can set reminders to save and synchronize the local file with the central file.

In the *File Locations* pane, set the *Default path for user files*, as shown in Figure 4–5.

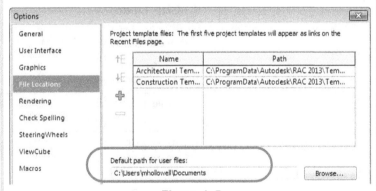

Figure 4–5

- This pane is also where you set location for project template files, family template files, and point cloud files.

How To: Open a Local File with Specific Worksets Editable

Once you have created a local file, you can open it with specific worksets editable.

1. Start the  (Open) command.
2. In the Open dialog box, select the local file set up on your computer.
3. Click ⬛ beside **Open** and select which worksets you want to open, as shown in Figure 4–6.

Figure 4–6

4. Click **Open**.

Open Worksets Options

All	Opens all worksets.
Editable	Opens all worksets that are editable (not checked out by someone else).
Last Viewed	Opens the worksets that were viewed last time you saved the local file. This is the default after the local file has been saved once.
Specify	Opens the Opening Worksets dialog box (once you click **Open**) where you select the worksets you want opened or closed.

- A rarely used option, **Detach from Central**, opens the file and detaches it from the central file. The new file name automatically has "detached" appended to the end of the name. You can either detach and preserve worksets, which you can then save as a different central file, or detach and discard worksets and all the related elements which removes all worksharing options from the file.

How To: Specify Opened or Closed Worksets

If you select **Specify...** when you open a workset-related file, it opens the Opening Worksets dialog box.

1. In the Opening Worksets dialog box (shown in Figure 4–7), select the name of the workset you want to open or close.

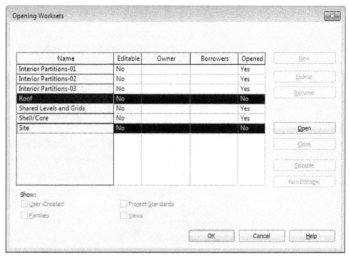

Figure 4–7

2. Click **Close** if a workset is opened and you want to close it. Click **Open** if a workset is closed and you want to open it.
3. Click **OK** to finish.

- You can select more than one workset by holding <Ctrl> or <Shift>. To select all of the worksets, press <Ctrl>+A.

Notes on Local Files

- When you open a local file, select only those worksets you need to open. Limiting the number of worksets speeds up the process of opening and saving the file.

- Only the user who created a local file should work on it, although others can open it. If you do open someone else's file, an alert box displays recommending that you change the user name or stop working on the file.

- If you try to save a file listed in someone else's name, you are alerted that it cannot be saved.

Saving Workset Related Files

To save workset-related files, you save them to your local machine as you would any other file. You also synchronize the file with the central file periodically and at the end of the day.

- Save the local file frequently (every 15-30 minutes). In the Quick Access Toolbar, click ▣ (Save) to save the local file as you would any other project.

- Synchronize to the central file periodically (every hour or two) or after you have made major changes to the project.

Synchronizing to the Central File

There are two methods for synchronizing to the central file.

Synchronize Now: Updates the central file and then the local file with any changes to the central file since the last synchronization without prompting you for any settings. It automatically relinquishes elements borrowed from any workset but retains worksets used by the current user.

The last used command is active if you click the top level icon.

- In the Quick Access Toolbar or *Collaborate* tab>Synchronize panel, expand ⚙ (Synchronize and Modify Settings or Synchronize with Central), and click ⚙ (Synchronize Now).

Synchronize and Modify Settings: Opens the Synchronize with Central dialog box, as shown in Figure 4–8, where you can set the location of the central file, add comments, save the file locally before and after synchronization, and set the options for relinquishing worksets and elements.

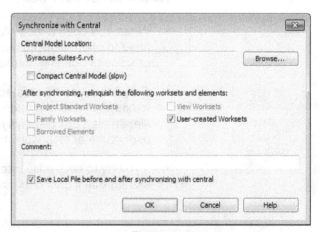

Figure 4–8

- In the Quick Access Toolbar or *Collaborate* tab>Synchronize panel, expand 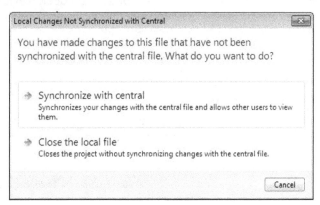 (Synchronize and Modify Settings or Synchronize with Central), and click (Synchronize and Modify Settings).

- Always save the local file after you have synchronized the file with central. Changes from the central file might have been copied into your file.

- When you close a local file without saving to the central file you are prompted to do so as shown in Figure 4–9.

Figure 4–9

Hint: Save As Options

If you want to save the central file as a new central file, use **Save As**. In the Save As dialog box, click **Options...**. In the File Save Options dialog box, select the **Make this a Central File after save** option, as shown in Figure 4–10. This option is toggled off by default because you typically create local files from the central file.

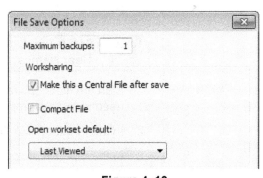

Figure 4–10

Practice 4a

Open Workset-Related Projects - Architectural

Practice Objectives

- Set up two copies of the Autodesk Revit software with different user names.
- Update an existing central file for use in the practice.
- Create a local file of the central file from each copy of the software.

Estimated time for completion: 10 minutes

In this practice you create two local files using two different copies of the Autodesk Revit software. You open the local files and select specific worksets to open in each project, as shown in Figure 4–11.

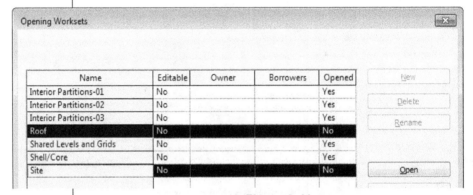

Figure 4–11

This practice uses a project that has been subdivided into worksets. To simulate a worksharing environment, you will open two sessions of the Autodesk Revit software and change the *Username* to **User1** and **User2**.

- **User1** focuses on the interiors of the condo units.

- **User2** focuses on the Exterior and Core.

Task 1 - Setup Two Copies of Autodesk Revit Using Different User Names.

1. Start the first copy of the Autodesk Revit software. You do not need to be in a project.

2. In the *File* tab, click **Options**.

3. In the Options dialog box, in the *General* tab, sign out of Autodesk® A360 if required, and change the *Username* to **User1**, as shown in Figure 4–12.

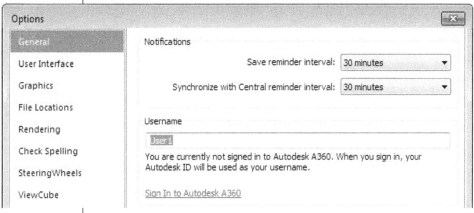

Figure 4–12

- Write down the existing name before you change it, so that you can return it to the original name at the end of these practices.

4. In the *File Locations* tab, change the *Default path for user files* to the practice files folder.

5. Click **OK** to close the dialog box.

6. Open a second copy of Autodesk Revit and repeat the steps above changing the *User Name* to **User 2**.

Task 2 - Update the Central File.

---

1. Working in the **User1** copy of Autodesk Revit, in the Quick Access Toolbar, click 📂 (Open). In the practice files folder, open **Condo-Project-A.rvt**.

2. Alert boxes about a Copied Central Model display. Read and then close the alert boxes.

3. In the *File* tab, expand 💾 (Save As) and click 🗒 (Project).

4. In the Save As dialog box, click **Options**....

5. In the File Save Options dialog box, select **Make this a Central File after save** and then click **OK**.

6. Verify that the name is still set to **Condo-Project-A.rvt**, and then click **Save**.

7. When the Workset File Already Exists dialog box displays, click **Yes** to replace the existing file.

A central file needs to be repathed if it has been relocated. This typically does not happen in an office environment, but does in the training environment, depending on where the central file is saved.

8. Close the project.

Task 3 - Create the Local File for User1.

1. Continue working in the **User1** copy of Autodesk Revit. In the Quick Access Toolbar, click 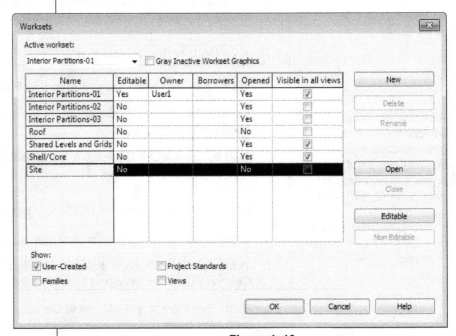 (Open). In the practice files folder, open **Condo-Project-A.rvt**.

   - Do not select central files from the startup screen, as that opens the central file itself. Instead, use the **Open** command to create a new local file.

2. Verify that **Create New Local** is selected and click **Open**. A file with the name **Condo-Project-A_User1.rvt** is opened.

3. In the *Collaborate* tab>Manage Collaboration panel, click (Worksets) or in the Status Bar, click (Worksets).

4. In the Worksets dialog box, make **Interior Partitions-01** the Active Workset. Set *Editable* to **Yes** and select **Visible in all views** for this workset. Select the worksets **Roof** and **Site**. Click **Close** so that the worksets are not open in this session, as shown in Figure 4–13.

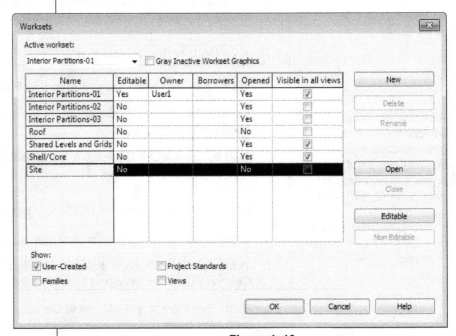

Figure 4–13

5. Click **OK** to finish.

6. In the Quick Access Toolbar, click 💾 (Save) to save the local file.

Task 4 - Create the Local File for User2.

1. Work in the **User2** copy of Autodesk Revit.

2. In the Quick Access Toolbar, click 📂 (Open) and select the file **Condo-Project-A.rvt**. Verify that **Create New Local** is selected, click the arrow next to **Open**, and select **Specify...** in the drop-down list, as shown in Figure 4–14.

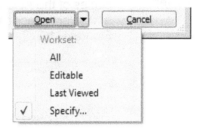

Figure 4–14

3. Click **Open** to open the project.

4. In the Opening Worksets dialog box, select the three **Interior Partition** worksets and click **Close** so that these worksets are not opened in this session, as shown in Figure 4–15.

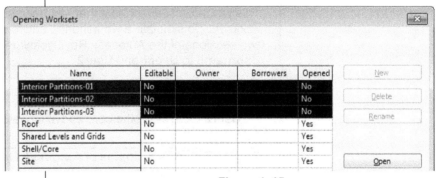

Figure 4–15

5. Click **OK** to finish. The file is opened and automatically named **Condo-Project-A_User2.rvt**.

6. Save the local file.

7. Leave both copies of the Autodesk Revit software open for the next practices.

Practice 4b

Open Workset-Related Projects - Structural

Practice Objectives

- Set up two copies of the Autodesk Revit software with different user names.
- Update an existing central file for use in the practice.
- Create a local file of the central file from each copy of the software.

Estimated time for completion: 10 minutes

In this practice you create two local files using two different copies of the Autodesk Revit software. You open the local files and select specific worksets to open in each project, as shown in Figure 4–16.

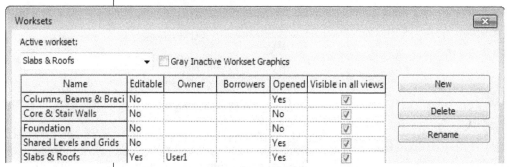

Figure 4–16

This practice uses a project that has been subdivided into worksets. To simulate a worksharing environment, you will open two sessions of the Autodesk Revit software and change the **Username** to **User1** and **User2**.

- **User1** focuses on the floor slabs.

- **User2** focuses on the core and stair walls.

Task 1 - Setup Two Copies of Autodesk Revit Using Different User Names.

1. Start the first copy of the Autodesk Revit software. You do not need to be in a project.

2. In the *File* tab, click **Options**.

3. In the Options dialog box, in the *General* tab, sign out of Autodesk A360 if required, and change the *Username* to **User1**, as shown in Figure 4–17.

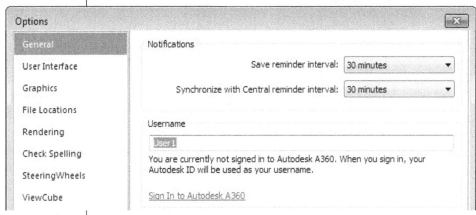

Figure 4–17

- Write down the existing name before you change it, so that you can return to the original name at the end of these practices.

4. In the *File Locations* tab, change the *Default path for user files* to the practice files folder.

5. Click **OK** to close the dialog box.

6. Open a second copy of Autodesk Revit and repeat the steps above changing the *User Name* to **User 2**.

Task 2 - Update the Central File.

---

1. Working in the **User1** copy of Autodesk Revit, in the Quick Access Toolbar, click 🗁 (Open). In the practice files folder, open **Syracuse-Suites-S.rvt**.

2. Alert boxes about a Copied Central Model display. Read and then close the alert boxes.

3. In the *File* tab, expand 💾 (Save As) and click 🗂 (Project).

4. In the Save As dialog box, click **Options...**.

5. In the File save Options dialog box, select **Make this a Central File after save**, and then click **OK**.

6. Verify that the name is still set to **Syracuse-Suites-S.rvt** and then click **Save**.

7. When the Workset File Already Exists dialog box displays, click **Yes** to replace the existing file.

A central file needs to be repathed if it has been relocated. This typically does not happen in an office environment, but does in the training environment, depending on where the central file is saved.

8. Close the project.

Task 3 - Create the Local File for User1.

1. Continue working in the **User1** copy of Autodesk Revit. In the Quick Access Toolbar, click 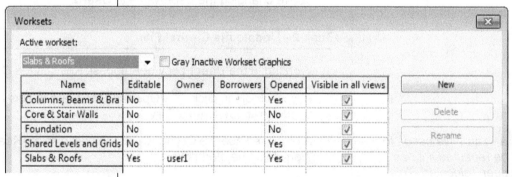 (Open). In the practice files folder, open **Syracuse-Suites-S.rvt**.

    *   Do not select central files from the startup screen as it opens the central file directly. Instead, use the **Open** command and create a new local file.

2. Verify that **Create New Local** is selected and click **Open**. A file with the name **Syracuse-Suites-S_User1.rvt** is opened.

3. In the *Collaborate* tab>Manage Collaboration panel, click (Worksets) or in the Status Bar, click (Worksets).

4. In the Worksets dialog box, make **Slabs & Roofs** the Active Workset. Set *Editable* to **Yes** and select **Visible in all views** for this workset. Select the **Core & Stair Walls** and **Foundation** worksets. Click Close so the worksets are not open in this session, as shown in Figure 4–18.

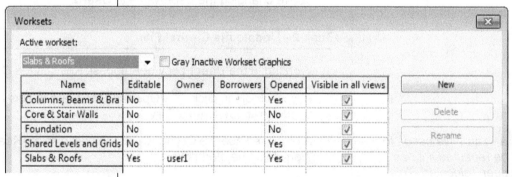

Worksets						
Active workset:						
Slabs & Roofs ▼	☐ Gray Inactive Workset Graphics					
Name	Editable	Owner	Borrowers	Opened	Visible in all views	New
Columns, Beams & Bra	No			Yes	☑	Delete
Core & Stair Walls	No			No	☑	
Foundation	No			No	☑	Rename
Shared Levels and Grids	No			Yes	☑	
Slabs & Roofs	Yes	user1		Yes	☑	

Figure 4–18

5. Click **OK** to finish.

6. In the Quick Access Toolbar, click (Save) to save the local file.

Task 4 - Create the Local File for User2.

1. Work in the **User2** copy of Autodesk Revit.

2. In the Quick Access Toolbar, click 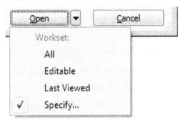 (Open) and select the file **Syracuse-Suites-S.rvt**. Verify that **Create New Local** is selected, click the arrow next to **Open**, and select **Specify...** in the drop-down list, as shown in Figure 4–19.

Figure 4–19

3. Click **Open** to open the project.

4. In the Opening Worksets dialog box, select the **Columns, Beams & Bracing**, and **Slabs & Roofs** worksets and click **Close** so these worksets are not opened in this session, as shown in Figure 4–20.

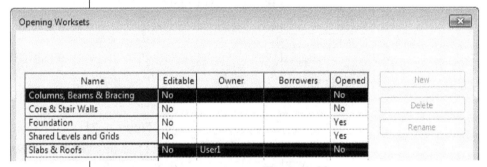

Name	Editable	Owner	Borrowers	Opened
Columns, Beams & Bracing	No			No
Core & Stair Walls	No			No
Foundation	No			Yes
Shared Levels and Grids	No			Yes
Slabs & Roofs	No	User1		No

Figure 4–20

5. Click **OK** to finish. The file is opened and automatically named **Syracuse-Suites-S_User2.rvt**.

6. Save the local file.

7. Leave both copies of the Autodesk Revit software open for the next practices.

Practice 4c

Open Workset-Related Projects - MEP

Practice Objectives

- Set up two copies of the Autodesk Revit software with different user names.
- Update an existing central file for use in the practice.
- Create a local file of the central file from each copy of the software.

Estimated time for completion: 10 minutes

In this practice you create two local files using two different copies of the Autodesk Revit software. You open the local files and select specific worksets to open in each project, as shown in Figure 4–21.

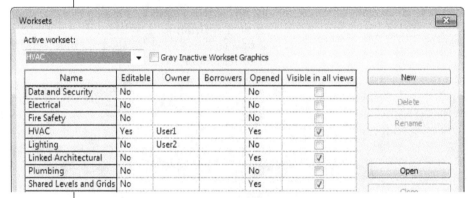

Figure 4–21

This practice uses a project that has been subdivided into worksets. To simulate a worksharing environment, you will open two sessions of the Autodesk Revit software and change the **Username** to **User1** and **User2**.

- **User1** focuses on the HVAC portion of the project.

- **User2** focuses on the Lighting portion of the project.

Task 1 - Setup Two Copies of Autodesk Revit Using Different User Names.

1. Start the first copy of the Autodesk Revit software. You do not need to be in a project.

2. In the *File* tab, click **Options**.

3. In the Options dialog box, in the *General* tab, sign out of Autodesk A360 if required, and change the *Username* to **User1**, as shown in Figure 4–22.

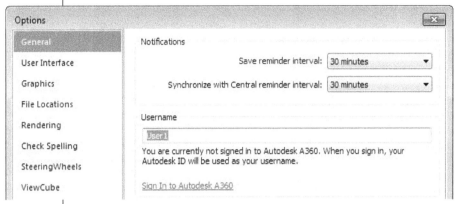

Figure 4–22

- Write down the existing name before changing it, so that you can return to the original name at the end of these practices.

4. In the *File Locations* tab, change the *Default path for user files* to the practice files folder.

5. Click **OK** to close the dialog box.

6. Open a second copy of Autodesk Revit and repeat the steps above, changing the *User Name* to **User 2**.

Task 2 - Update the Central File

---

1. Working in the **User1** copy of Autodesk Revit, in the Quick Access Toolbar, click 📂 (Open). In the practice files folder, open **Elementary-School-MEP.rvt**.

2. Alert boxes about a Copied Central Model display. Read and then close the alert boxes.

3. In the *File* tab, expand 💾 (Save As) and click 🗔 (Project).

4. In the Save As dialog box, click **Options...**.

5. In the File save Options dialog box, select **Make this a Central File after save** and then click **OK**.

6. Verify that the name is still set to **Elementary-School-MEP.rvt** and then click **Save**.

A central file needs to be repathed if it has been relocated. This typically does not happen in an office environment, but does in the training environment, depending on where the central file is saved.

7. When the Workset File Already Exists dialog box displays, click **Yes** to replace the existing file.

8. Close the project.

Task 3 - Create the Local File for User1.

1. Continue working in the **User1** copy of Autodesk Revit. In the Quick Access Toolbar, click 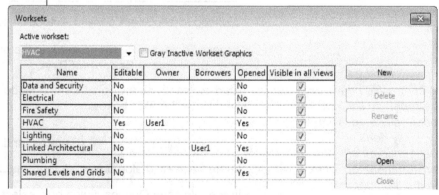 (Open). In the practice files folder, open **Elementary-School-MEP.rvt**.

   - Do not select central files from the startup screen as it opens the central file directly. Instead, use the **Open** command and create a new local file.

2. Verify that **Create New Local** is selected and click **Open**. A file with the name **Elementary-School-MEP_User1.rvt** is opened.

3. In the *Collaborate* tab>Manage Collaboration panel, click (Worksets) or in the Status Bar, click (Worksets).

4. In the Worksets dialog box, make **HVAC** the Active Workset. Set *Editable* to **Yes** and select **Visible in all views** for this workset.

5. Select all the other worksets except **Linked Architectural** and **Shared Levels and Grids**. Click **Close** so that the worksets are not open in this session, as shown in Figure 4–23.

Name	Editable	Owner	Borrowers	Opened	Visible in all views
Data and Security	No			No	✓
Electrical	No			No	✓
Fire Safety	No			No	✓
HVAC	Yes	User1		Yes	✓
Lighting	No			No	✓
Linked Architectural	No		User1	Yes	✓
Plumbing	No			No	✓
Shared Levels and Grids	No			Yes	✓

Active workset: HVAC — Gray Inactive Workset Graphics

New / Delete / Rename / Open / Close

Figure 4–23

6. Click **OK** to finish.

7. In the Quick Access Toolbar, click (Save) to save the local file.

Task 4 - Create the Local File for User2.

1. Work in the **User2** copy of Autodesk Revit.

2. In the Quick Access Toolbar, click 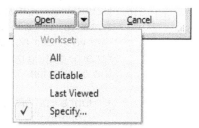 (Open) and select the file **Elementary-School-MEP.rvt**. Verify that **Create New Local** is selected, click the arrow next to **Open**, and select **Specify...** in the drop-down list, as shown in Figure 4–24.

Figure 4–24

3. Click **Open** to open the project.

4. In the Opening Worksets dialog box, select **Data and Security**, **Fire Safety**, **HVAC**, and **Plumbing** worksets and click **Close** so that these worksets are not opened in this session, as shown in Figure 4–25.

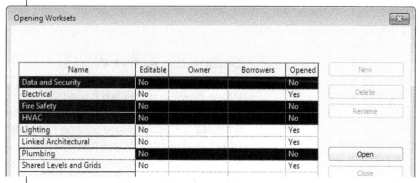

Figure 4–25

5. Click **OK** to finish. The file is opened and automatically named **Elementary-School-MEP_User2.rvt**.

6. Save the local file.

7. Leave both copies of the Autodesk Revit software open for the next practices.

4.3 Working in Workset-Related Projects

Most of the work you do in a workset is no different to working in any other project. You draw and modify elements. You create views, sheets, and schedules. You even create families and modify family types, if you have permissions to do so.

Several workset-specific methods and tools can increase your effectiveness as you work. You can edit elements in worksets that you have not checked out, check out worksets, request and receive editing permissions, and save the worksets locally and to the central file.

- Once you are in a workset-related project, select the *Collaborate* tab, as shown in Figure 4–26. The workset-related tools are in the Worksets and Synchronize panels.

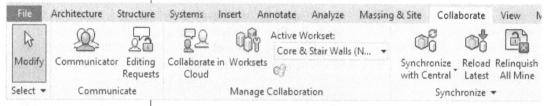

Figure 4–26

Setting the Active Workset

When new elements are added to the project, they are placed on the active workset. It is therefore important to set the active workset correctly before adding new elements. Not doing so can result in visibility and permissions-related issues.

How To: Set the Active Workset

1. Open your local file.
2. In the Status Bar, expand the *Active Workset* list and select a workset, as shown in Figure 4–27.

You can also set the active workset in the Collaborate tab>Manage Collaboration panel.

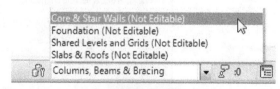

Figure 4–27

- It does not matter if the workset says (**Not Editable**); you can still add elements to it. **Not Editable** means that you have not checked out the workset but are working on the basis of borrowing elements.

- You can gray out inactive worksets in a view to easily distinguish between active and inactive worksets, as shown in Figure 4–28. In the *Collaborate* tab>Manage Collaboration panel, toggle 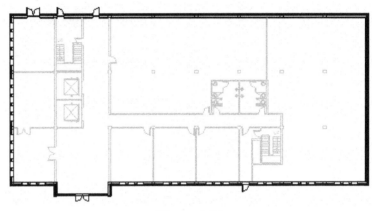 (Gray Inactive Workset Graphics) on. You can also select **Gray Inactive Workset Graphics** in the Worksets dialog box.

Figure 4–28

Editing Elements in Worksets

There are two different ways to edit elements in worksets:

1. Borrow elements: If you *borrow* the elements as you make changes, no one has to wait for permission to make modifications even if someone else is working on the same workset. This can speed up the work if you have a fairly small group of people working on the project, especially when there is some overlap between the purposes of the users or when the project has only been divided into a few worksets.

2. Check out a workset: When you *check out* a specific workset and make it editable, no one else can modify elements in that workset without expressed permission.

Check with your project coordinator to see which method your office uses.

Borrowing Elements

When you select an element and see the **Make element editable** icon, as shown in Figure 4–29, it means you have not checked out that particular workset or that you are not currently borrowing the element.

It is not necessary to click the icon; simply proceed to edit the element as required.

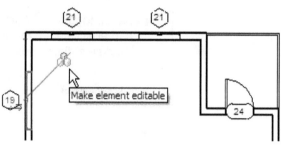

Figure 4–29

- If you modify the element and it enables you to do so, then no one else has that workset checked out and you were given automatic permission to modify this element.

- If someone else has borrowed the element or checked out the workset to which it belongs, you are prompted to request permission to edit the element.

How To: Check Out Worksets

1. In the *Collaborate* tab>Manage Collaboration panel, click (Worksets).

You can also open the Worksets dialog box from the Status Bar.

2. In the Worksets dialog box, select **Yes** in the *Editable* column next to the workset name that you want to checkout and edit, as shown in Figure 4–30. More than one workset can be checked out and made editable at a time, but ensure that you only check out those that you really need.

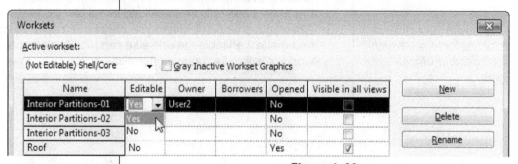

Figure 4–30

3. Select **Active workset** in the menu. You can also set the active workset from the list in the Manage Collaboration panel and Status Bar.

4. Click **OK**.

- When editing elements, you can control which ones can be picked by selecting the **Editable Only** option in the Options Bar, as shown in Figure 4–31. If **Editable Only** is selected, you can only select items that are available in the editable worksets or those which you borrowed. If it is cleared, you can select anything.

Figure 4–31

Permissions to Edit

If you try to edit an element that is being used by someone else, an alert box opens stating that you cannot edit the element without their permission, as shown in Figure 4–32. First, you must request an edit. Second, the owner of the workset either grants or denies the request. If the request is granted, you can update your local file and have control of the element until you relinquish it.

Figure 4–32

How To: Request an Edit

1. When the alert box opens stating that you need to have permission to modify an element, click **Place Request** to ask to borrow the element.
2. An alert box opens, stating the request has been made, as shown in Figure 4–33. If you expect a quick reply, leave the message in place. If you want to continue working, click **Close** and cancel out of the alert box. The request is still active.

Figure 4–33

How To: Grant or Deny an Editing Request

1. When a user sends an editing request for an element you are currently borrowing or which belongs to a workset which you have checked out (editable), an alert displays as shown in Figure 4–34.

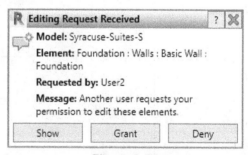

Figure 4–34

2. In the Editing Request Received dialog box, click **Show** to zoom into the element requested, **Grant** to allow the other user to modify the element, or **Deny** to stop the other user from modifying the element.

3. If you do not respond right away to the editing request, you can always access it again. In the *Collaborate* tab>Synchronize panel, click  (Editing Requests) or in the Status Bar, click (Editing Request). The information on the Status Bar includes the number of requests outstanding, as shown in Figure 4–35.

Figure 4–35

4. In the Editing Requests dialog box, as shown in Figure 4–36, select the pending request. Click on the date.

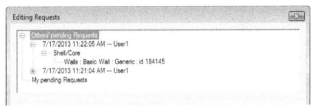

Figure 4–36

- When you select the editing request date, the elements included in the request are highlighted in the project. Click **Show** to zoom in on the elements if required.

5. Click **Grant** to enable the other user to make the changes or **Deny/Retract** to deny the request. (The original user can also retract the request with this button.) You can also grant the request by saving the entire workset back to the central file and relinquishing the items.

Applying an Editing Request

When an editing request is granted, a confirmation alert box opens in the program of the user who requested it, as shown in Figure 4–37. Close the alert box.

Once a request is granted, you can make modifications to the element again without having to request to edit the feature, although the icon still displays.

Figure 4–37

- If the requesting user canceled out of the Error dialog box, when they are notified that they have permission, click

   (Reload Latest) or type **RL** to make the ownership modification.

- If the Error dialog box is still open, the Editing Request Placed dialog box displays that the request has been granted, as shown in Figure 4–38. Click **Close** and the element is modified.

An additional note "Reload Latest is required to edit the elements" might display in the dialog box depending on what the other user did with the borrowed elements.

Figure 4–38

Editing Request Frequency

To control the frequency of updates to editing requests (and worksharing display modes), in the Options dialog box, in the *General* tab, move the slider bar between *Less Frequent* and *More Frequent*, as shown in Figure 4–39.

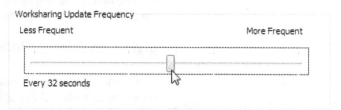

Figure 4–39

- If the bar is moved to the far side of *Less Frequent*, it changes to manual and updates only when you borrow elements or synchronize with the central file. This can improve the performance of the program but also causes the other user to wait until you receive the request.

Relinquishing Worksets

After you have been working with borrowed elements or have checked out worksets, you should return them to the central file when you are finished. In the Quick Access Toolbar or

Collaborate tab>Synchronize panel, click 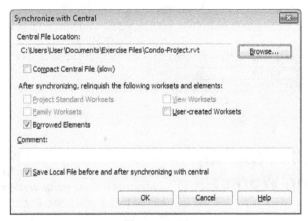 (Synchronize and Modify Settings). The Synchronize with Central dialog box displays, as shown in Figure 4–40. In this dialog box, select the worksets and/or elements you want to relinquish. Only those of which you have ownership are available.

Figure 4–40

Synchronize with Central Options

- The **Borrowed Elements** option is selected by default. This relinquishes any elements you borrowed from another workset.

- Select the **Save the Local File before and after synchronizing with central** option to save extra steps.

- If the central file location changes, select the new central file using **Browse...**.

- Periodically, use the **Compact Central File (slow)** option when you save to the central file. This reduces the file size, but also increases the time required to save.

Adding comments at key points and for significant changes in the project is useful in case the project backup needs to be restored in the future.

- You can add comments to the central file for others to see. To view the comments, in the *Collaborate* tab>Synchronize panel, click 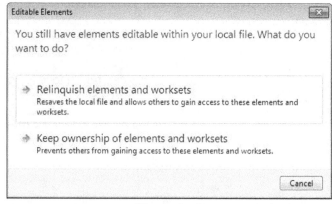 (Show History), and select the central file whose history you want to view. The History dialog box displays with the *Date/Time Stamp*, *Modified by*, and *Comments* columns populated with information, as shown in Figure 4–41.

History

Click on a column heading to sort by that column.

Date/Time Stamp	Modified by	Comments	
7/17/2013 11:29:21 AM	User1		Close
7/17/2013 11:19:44 AM	User1		Export...
7/17/2013 11:19:36 AM	User2		Help
7/17/2013 11:18:52 AM	User1		
7/17/2013 11:18:35 AM	User2		

Figure 4–41

Ending the Day Using Worksets

IMPORTANT: When you have finished working on the project for the day, you need to save to the central file and relinquish all user-created editable worksets. Then, you must save your local file before exiting the Autodesk Revit software. This way, the two files are in sync and you are able to save to the central file next time you work on the local file.

- If you close a project, but have not relinquished all worksets when you saved to the central file, the alert shown in Figure 4–42 displays.

If you are working on a project with other people, you need to relinquish all your worksets when closing a project so they can edit them. This is correct worksharing etiquette.

Editable Elements

You still have elements editable within your local file. What do you want to do?

→ Relinquish elements and worksets
Resaves the local file and allows others to gain access to these elements and worksets.

→ Keep ownership of elements and worksets
Prevents others from gaining access to these elements and worksets.

Cancel

Figure 4–42

- To relinquish worksets without saving to the central file, in the *Collaborate* tab>Synchronize panel, click ⬜ (Relinquish All Mine)

Do not delete any files in these directories.

- The backup directory for central and local files, as shown in Figure 4–43, holds information about the editability of worksets, borrowed elements, and workset/element ownership. If required, you can restore the backup directory. In the *Collaboration* tab>Synchronize panel, click ⬜ (Restore Backup).

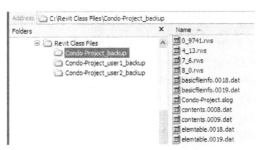

Figure 4–43

4.4 Visibility and Display Options with Worksharing

While using worksets, there are certain display tools to help you as you work. Worksets can be toggled off and on in the Visibility/Graphics dialog box. You can use the Worksharing Display settings to graphically show by color information, such as the Owners of different elements and the elements that need to be updated.

Controlling Workset Visibility

Not all worksets need to be visible in every view. For example, the exterior shell of a building should display in most views, but interior walls or the site features only need to be displayed in related views. The default workset visibility is controlled when the workset is first created, but can be managed in the Visibility/Graphics dialog box, as shown in Figure 4–44.

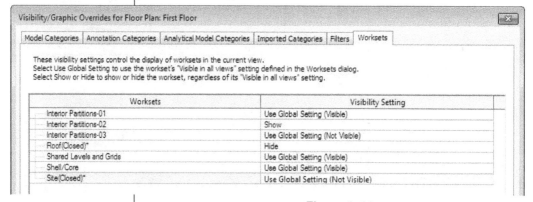

Figure 4–44

How To: Change the Visibility of Worksets

1. Type **VV** or **VG** to open the Visibility/Graphics dialog box.
2. Select the *Worksets* tab. Modify the *Visibility Setting* for each workset, as required. Changing the setting to **Show** or **Hide** only impacts the current view.
3. Click **OK** to close the dialog box.

- Worksets marked with an asterisk (*) have not been opened in this session of the Autodesk Revit software and are therefore not visible in any view.

- Closing worksets toggles off element visibility in all views. It also saves more computer memory than just toggling off the display of worksets.

- The *Worksets* tab in the Visibility/Graphics dialog box is only available if worksets have been enabled.

- These overrides can also be setup in a view template.

Worksharing Display Options

A handy way to view the status of elements in worksharing is to set the Worksharing Display. For example, when you set the Worksharing Display to Worksets, as shown in Figure 4–45, the elements in each workset are highlighted in a different color.

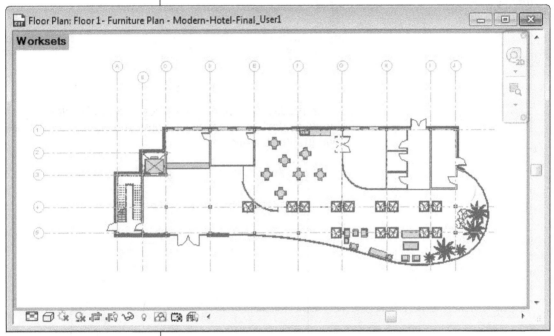

Figure 4–45

There are several type of Worksharing displays: Checkout Status, Owners, Model Updates, and Worksets. You can access those in the Status Bar, as shown in Figure 4–46.

Figure 4–46

- As you hover the cursor over elements in a view, with Worksharing Display selected, information about the element displays, depending on the type you selected, as shown in Figure 4–47.

Toggling on Gray Inactive Worksets while using Worksharing Display might change the display status of elements in two tones of the same color.

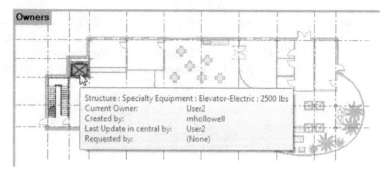

Figure 4–47

- You can modify the colors in the Worksharing Display Settings, as well as select which items you want to display, as shown in Figure 4–48.

Figure 4–48

4.5 Worksharing and Linked Models

When you are working in a workshared project, each linked model should be in a separate workset. For example, before linking in a structural model, specify and set a related workset, as shown in Figure 4–49. When you open a local file, you can specify which worksets you want to display, as shown in Figure 4–50.

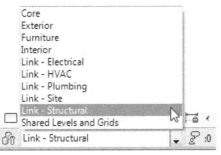

Figure 4–49   Figure 4–50

The same is true if you are linking in a model that has been workshared. You can control which worksets are open and which worksets display. In this case, the worksets from the linked model are not available for modification or use in the host project (which might have its own worksets).

- Remember that limiting the number of worksets speeds up the process of opening and saving the file. It is recommended that you close a workset that is not required rather than change its visibility. When working with linked files, you can also unload them, as shown in Figure 4–51.

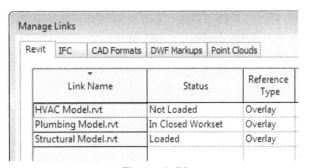

Figure 4–51

Managing Links in Local Files

When you open a local file that includes linked models setup in separate worksets, you can choose to unload each link for just yourself or for all users. In the Manage Links dialog box, as shown in Figure 4–52, select the link and in the *Unload* area, select either **For all users** or **For me**.

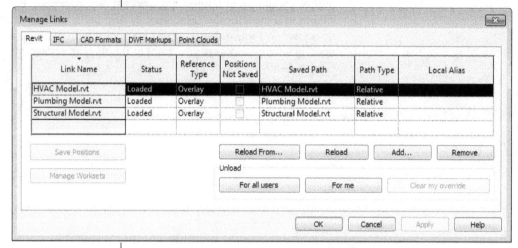

Figure 4–52

- If you unload for all users, the link will still be available but will be unloaded by default anytime someone else opens a local file. You will need to place a request to reload it if the original person that unloaded the link has not relinquished it.

- If you unload a link just for yourself, this action is remembered when you synchronize with the central file. If you want to reload the link, select it and click **Clear my override**.

Managing Worksets in Linked Models

Linked models that include worksets can be managed at two levels. You can load and unload the entire link or you can open and close the individual worksets in the linked model. For example, you might want the Site workset on in some views but not in others, as shown in Figure 4–53.

- Worksets can also be set as visible in some views and not in other views.

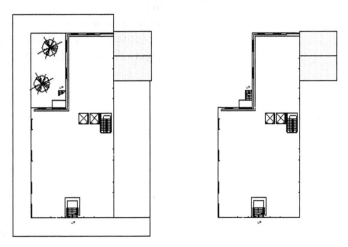

Figure 4–53

How To: Open and Close Worksets in a Linked Model

1. Open the Manage Links dialog box.
2. In the Manage Links dialog box, select the Link that includes worksets, as shown in Figure 4–54, and click **Manage Worksets**.

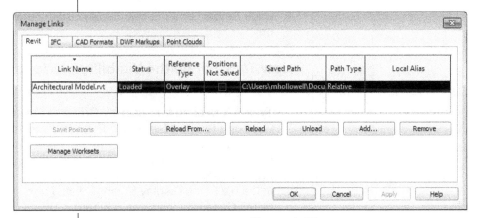

Figure 4–54

- The **Manage Worksets** button will be grayed out if there are no worksets associated with a link.

3. In the Manage Worksets for Link dialog box, select the workset(s) you want to close and click **Close** or the workset(s) you want to open and click **Open**. For example, in Figure 4–55, the Linked - Site workset has been closed.

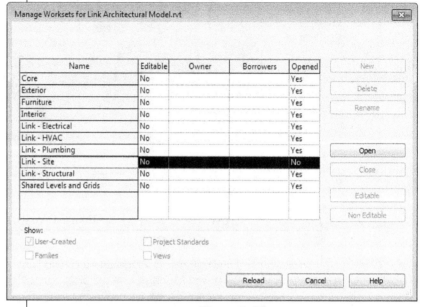

Figure 4–55

4. Click **Reload** and the link displays only the worksets that are on.

How To: Change the Visibility of Worksets in a Linked model

1. Type **VG** to open the Visibility/Graphics Overrides dialog box.
2. Click on the *Revit Links* tab. This tab displays if there are links in the project.
3. In the *Display Settings* column, beside the link, click **<By host view>**.
4. In the RVT Link Display Settings dialog box, in the *Basics* tab, select **Custom** as shown in Figure 4–56.

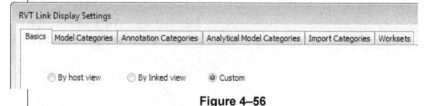

Figure 4–56

5. Select the *Worksets* tab and set the *Worksets* to **<Custom>.** This enables you to modify the visibility of individual worksets as required. For example, in Figure 4–57, the **Roof** workset is cleared indicating that it is set as not to be visible in the current view.

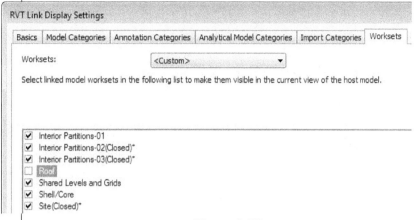

Figure 4–57

6. Click **OK** to close the dialog boxes.

•   Worksets that are closed do not display in any view.

Practice 4d

Work in Workset-Related Projects - Architectural

Practice Objectives

- Add and Modify Elements in Worksets.
- Request and grant permissions to edit.
- Save, synchronize, and reload files to display the changes made by each user.

Estimated time for completion: 20 minutes

In this practice you will work with two different sessions of the Autodesk Revit software. In the first session, you will make worksets visible and add, modify elements in worksets without having to get permission. You will then switch to a different user and make a workset editable. The first user requests an edit to the workset owned by the second user. Permission will be granted and the first user will make the change. You save the local file, save to central file, and reload the latest file. An example of Worksets dialog box used in this practice is shown in Figure 4–58.

Name	Editable	Owner	Borrowers	Opened	Visible in all views
Interior Partitions-01	Yes	User1		Yes	☑
Interior Partitions-02	No			Yes	☐
Interior Partitions-03	No			Yes	☐
Roof	No			No	☐
Shared Levels and Grids	No			Yes	☑
Shell/Core	No	User2	user1	Yes	☑
Site	No			No	☐

Figure 4–58

- You must complete **Practice 4a: Open Workset-Related Projects - Architectural** before beginning this practice.

Task 1 - Add and Modify Elements in Worksets.

1. Working as **User1** in the file **Condo-Project-A_User1.rvt**, verify that you are in the **Floor Plans: First Floor** view.

2. Zoom in on Unit 1C, and add several walls using an interior wall type with the *Height* set to **Second Floor**. Include one that butts up against an existing window, as shown in Figure 4–59. A warning displays, noting that the Insert conflicts with the joined wall.

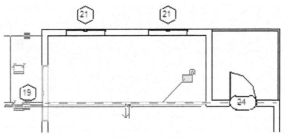

Figure 4–59

3. Close the warning.

4. Click ➋ (Modify) and select the window. It has an icon connected to it (as shown in Figure 4–60), indicating that it belongs to another workset. Click the **Make element editable** icon.

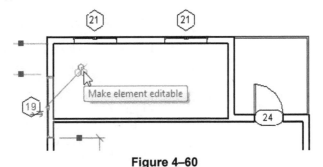

Figure 4–60

5. Move the window so it does not conflict with the wall.

6. Open the Worksets dialog box. **User1** is noted as the *Owner* of the **Interior Partitions-01** workset and a *Borrower* of **Shell/Core** workset, as shown in Figure 4–61.

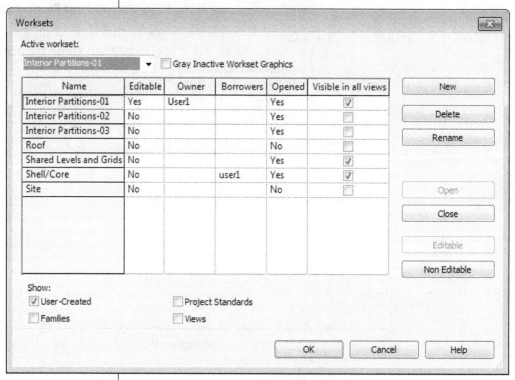

Figure 4–61

7. Click **OK** to close the dialog box.

8. In the *Collaborate* tab>Synchronize panel or in the Quick Access Toolbar, click (Synchronize and Modify Settings) to open the Synchronize with Central dialog box, as shown in Figure 4–62. The **Borrowed Elements** option should be selected. Add a comment about moving the window and select the **Save Local File before and after synchronizing with central** option.

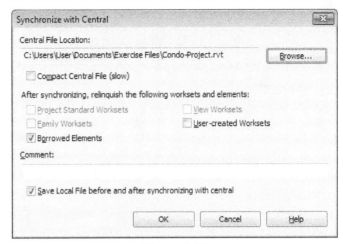

Figure 4–62

9. Click **OK**.

Task 2 - Check out a Workset.

1. Open the session of the Autodesk Revit software used by **User2** and open the **Floor Plans: First Floor** view if it is not already open. None of the changes show in the local file.

2. In the *Collaborate* tab>Synchronize panel, click (Reload Latest or type **RL**. The window location changes but you do not see the new walls because that workset is not open.

3. Click (Worksets) to open the dialog box.

4. Select **Shell/Core** in the *Active workset* drop-down list and make it editable (select **Yes** in the *Editable* column). The *Owner* should display **User 2**, as shown in Figure 4–63.

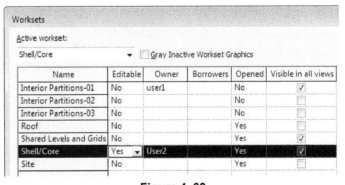

Figure 4–63

5. Click **OK** to close the dialog box.

6. Move door number 5 in Unit 1A down in the wall so that it is no longer opposite to door number 6.

7. In the Quick Access Toolbar, click 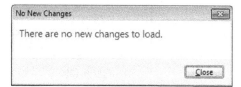 (Save) to save the local file.

8. Switch to the **User1** session and type **RL** (Reload Latest). There are no new changes to load, as shown in Figure 4–64, because User 2 has not saved back to the central file. Close the dialog box.

No New Changes	
There are no new changes to load.	
	Close

Figure 4–64

9. Switch to the **User2** session and click 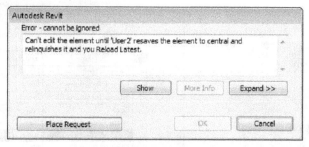 (Synchronize Now). This saves the changes to the central file without relinquishing the Shell/Core workset.

Task 3 - Request Permission to Edit.

1. Switch to the **User1** session and type **RL** (Reload Latest) again. This time, the door moves in response to the change made in the central file.

2. Try to move the door back where it was. This time, an error message displays that cannot be ignored, as shown in Figure 4–65. **User2** has made the Shell/Core workset editable. Therefore, anyone else cannot edit elements in it without permission.

Autodesk Revit		
Error - cannot be Ignored		
Can't edit the element until 'User2' resaves the element to central and relinquishes it and you Reload Latest.		
	Show	More Info	Expand >>
Place Request	OK	Cancel

Figure 4–65

3. Click **Place Request**. The Editing Request Placed dialog box opens. Close the dialog boxes.

4. Switch to the **User2** session. An alert box displays, as shown in Figure 4–66.

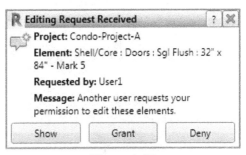

Figure 4–66

5. Hover the cursor over the **Show** button to highlight the door. Move the dialog box out of the way if required, to see the door.

6. The other user can have permission to modify the placement of this door. Click **Grant**. By doing this, you enable the other user full control over this one element in the workset.

7. Switch to the **User1** session. The Editing Request is granted, as shown in Figure 4–67.

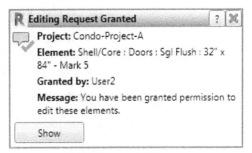

Figure 4–67

8. Close the Editing Request Granted dialog box. Your request was granted and the door moves.

9. Move the door again to exactly where you want it. This time, you are not prompted to ask to move the door because you are still borrowing it.

10. Try to move another door. You do not have permission to move this door. Click **Cancel** rather than place the request. The door returns to its original location.

11. In the View Control Bar, expand the Worksharing display and click 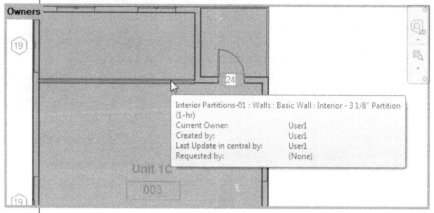 (Owners). Different colors highlight the elements and their respective owners. Hover the cursor over one of the walls to display information about the owner, as shown in Figure 4–68.

Figure 4–68

- The color on your display might be different.

12. Zoom out so you can see the full floor plan.

13. Click (Synchronize and Modify Settings) and relinquish **User created Worksets** and **Borrowed Elements.**

14. The new interior walls once displayed as owned by **User1** are now not in color and the door that was borrowed returns to the original owner User 2.

15. Toggle the Worksharing Display off.

16. Save the local file.

17. Switch to the **User2** session.

18. Click (Synchronize Now). The door moves to the location where **User1** moved it. When you save to the central file, it also reloads the latest changes.

19. Close the project. When the Editable Elements dialog box opens, as shown in Figure 4–69, click **Relinquish elements and worksets**.

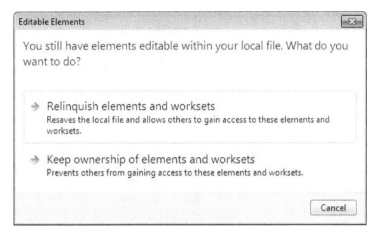

Figure 4–69

20. Close the **User2** session of the Autodesk Revit software.

21. In the **User1** session of the Autodesk Revit software, return the *Username* to the original name at the start of this set of practices.

22. Close the project and synchronize with central if required.

Practice 4e

Work in Workset-Related Projects - Structural

Practice Objectives

- Add and Modify Elements in Worksets.
- Request and grant permissions to edit.
- Save, synchronize, and reload files to display the changes made by each user.

Estimated time for completion: 20 minutes

In this practice you will work with two different sessions of the Autodesk Revit software. In the first session, you will make worksets visible and add, modify elements in worksets without having to get permission. You will then switch to a different user and make a workset editable. The first user requests an edit to the workset owned by the second user. Permission will be granted and the first user will make the change. You save the local file, save to central file, and reload the latest file. An example of Worksets dialog box used in this practice is shown in Figure 4–70.

Name	Editable	Owner	Borrowers	Opened	Visible in all v
Columns, Beams & Bracing	No			Yes	☑
Core & Stair Walls	No	User2	User1	Yes	☑
Foundation	No			No	☐
Shared Levels and Grids	No			Yes	☑
Slabs & Roofs	Yes	User1		Yes	☑

Figure 4–70

- You must complete **Practice 4b: Open Workset-Related Projects - Structural** before beginning this practice.

Task 1 - Add and Modify Elements in Worksets.

1. Working as **User1** in the file **Syracuse-Suites-S_User1.rvt**, open the **Structural Plans: 1ST FLOOR** view.

2. Zoom in on the beam system between grids 6 and 7 and C and D. Stay far enough out so that you can see the edge of the building as shown in Figure 4–71. Do not select the beam system.

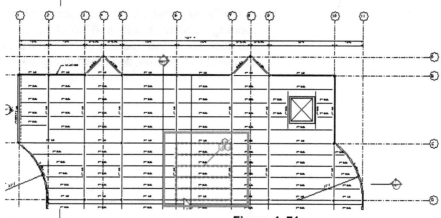

Figure 4–71

3. Select the second beam from the top and type **UP** to unpin it from the beam system. Move it **2'-0"** up so that the distance between the beams is **7'-0"** as shown in Figure 4–72.

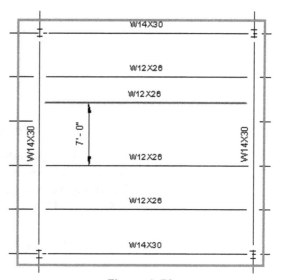

Figure 4–72

4. Hover the cursor over the edge of the building and press <Tab> until the floor is highlighted. Select the floor.

5. In the *Modify | Floors* tab>Mode panel, click 🔲 (Edit Boundary).

6. In the Draw panel, click ⌐ (Boundary Line) and draw a rectangle approximately **4'-0"x6'-0"** to add a new opening in the floor. Move the opening inside the framing system between two beams, as shown in Figure 4–73. An exact location is not required for this practice.

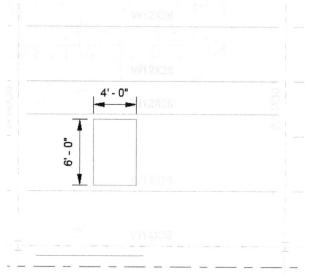

Figure 4–73

7. Click ✓ (Finish Edit Mode).

8. In the *Collaborate* tab>Manage Collaboration panel, in the Active Workset drop-down list, select the **Columns, Beams & Bracing** workset to make it the active workset. It should be listed as (Not Editable).

9. In the *Structure* tab>Structure panel, click ✏ (Beam).

10. In the *Modify | Place Beam* tab>Tag panel, click 👆① (Tag on Placement) to toggle it, on as required.

11. In the Type Selector, verify that the selected beam is **W-Wide Flange: W12x26**. In the Options Bar, set the *Structural Usage* to **Joist**, and verify that the **Chain** option is cleared, as shown in Figure 4–74.

Figure 4–74

12. Add two beams to frame the new opening on the unsupported sides, as shown in Figure 4–75.

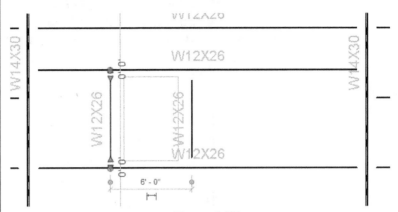

Figure 4–75

13. In the *Collaborate* tab>Manage Collaboration panel or in the Status Bar, click (Worksets).

14. In the Worksets dialog box, **User1** is noted as the Owner of the Slabs & Roofs workset and as a Borrower of Columns, Beams & Bracing, as shown in Figure 4–76.

Name	Editable	Owner	Borrowers	Opened	Visible in all v
Columns, Beams & Bracing	No		User1	Yes	✓
Core & Stair Walls	No			No	✓
Foundation	No			No	✓
Shared Levels and Grids	No			Yes	✓
Slabs & Roofs	Yes	User1		Yes	✓

Figure 4–76

15. Close the dialog box.

16. In the Quick Access Toolbar, click (Synchronize and Modify Settings).

17. In the Synchronize with Central dialog box, the **Borrowed Elements** option should be selected. Add a comment about adding an opening to the First Floor Slab, and select the **Save the Local File before and after synchronizing with central** option, as shown in Figure 4–77.

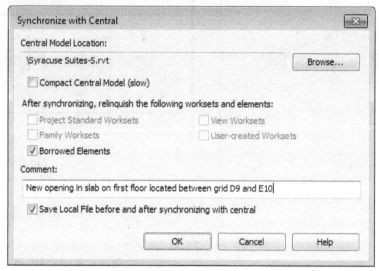

Figure 4–77

18. Click **OK** to finish synchronizing.

Task 2 - Check Out a Workset.

1. Open the session of the Autodesk Revit software that is designated to **User2**.

2. Open the **Structural Plans: 1ST FLOOR** view if it is not already open. None of the changes display in the local file yet.

3. In the Status Bar, click (Worksets).

4. In the Worksets dialog box, open the **Columns, Beams & Bracing** and **Slabs & Roofs** worksets by setting the *Opened* column to **Yes**, as shown in Figure 4–78. Click **OK**.

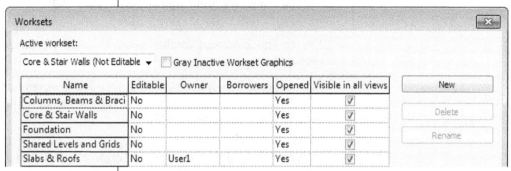

Figure 4–78

5. In the **Structural Plans: 1ST FLOOR** view, the changes are still not displayed.

6. In the *Collaborate* tab>Synchronize panel, click 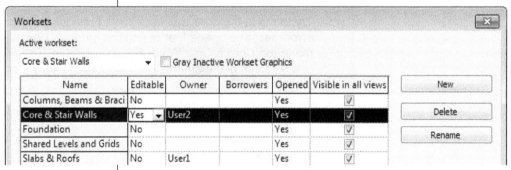 (Reload Latest) or type **RL**. The new opening and joist display.

7. Open the Worksets dialog box.

8. In the Worksets dialog box, select **Core & Stair Walls** in the list of worksets and make it **Editable**. The Owner should change to **User2**, as shown in Figure 4–79.

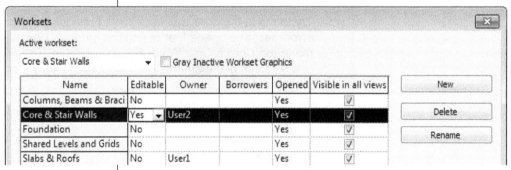

Figure 4–79

9. Click **OK**.

10. Zoom in on the elevator in the upper right of the building.

11. Move the core's north wall approximately **1'-0"** up.

12. In the Quick Access Toolbar, click 🖫 (Save) to save the local file.

13. Switch to the **User1** session and type **RL** (**Reload Latest**). There are no new changes to load because User2 has not saved back to the central file.

14. Switch to the **User2** session and click 🗗 (Synchronize Now). This saves the changes to the central file without relinquishing the Core & Stair Walls workset.

Task 3 - Request Permission to Edit.

1. Switch to the **User1** session.

2. Open the Worksets dialog box.

3. Select **Core & Stair Walls** in the list of worksets and click **Open**. Click **OK** to exit the dialog box.

4. Type **RL** (**Reload Latest**) again. This time, the core wall moves in response to the change made by **User2**.

5. Try to move the core wall back to its previous position. An error message opens that cannot be ignored. **User2** has made the Core & Stair Walls workset editable. Therefore, no one else can edit elements in it without permission, as shown in Figure 4–80.

Figure 4–80

6. Click **Place Request**. The Editing Request Placed dialog box opens. Leave it open.

7. Switch to the **User2** session.

8. The Editing Request Received dialog box opens as shown in Figure 4–81.

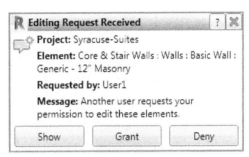

Figure 4–81

9. Hover the cursor over the **Show** button to highlight the door. (Move the box out of the way as required to display the modified wall.)

10. The other user can have permission to modify the placement of this core wall. Click **Grant**. By doing so, you enable the other user to have full control over this element in the workset.

11. Switch to the **User1** session.

12. The Editing Request Granted dialog box opens.

13. After a moment or two, the Editing Request Placed dialog box updates to prompt you that your request has been granted. Because your request was granted, the core wall moves.

14. Close the dialog boxes.

15. Move the core wall again. This time, you are not prompted to ask permission to move the core wall because you are still borrowing it.

16. Try to move another core wall. You do not have permission to move this wall. Cancel rather than place the request. The core wall returns to its original location.

Task 4 - View Information About the Worksets.

1. Continue working as **User1**.

2. In the Status Bar, expand the Worksharing display, and select **Owners** as shown in Figure 4–82.

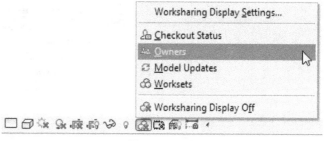

Figure 4–82

3. The view displays in color showing the two owners. Different colors highlight the elements and their respective owners. as shown in Figure 4–83. Hover the cursor over one of the walls to display information about the owner.

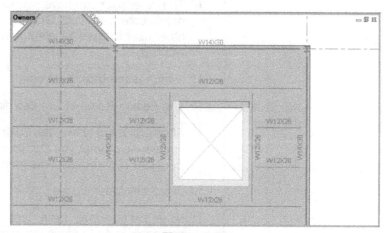

Figure 4–83

4. Open the Worksets dialog box. The owner of Core & Stair Walls is listed as **User2**, but **User1** is also listed as a borrower. Click **Cancel**.

5. Toggle the **Worksharing Display** off and zoom out to see the full building.

6. In the *Collaborate* tab>Manage Collaboration panel, click

   (Gray Inactive Worksets) to gray-out the elements that you cannot modify without requesting permission. This also grays out the core walls, although you have a right to edit the wall that you borrowed.

7. Click (Synchronize and Modify Settings) and verify that all of the worksets will be relinquished before clicking **OK**.

8. Close the project.

9. Switch to the **User2** session.

10. Click (Synchronize Now). The core wall moves to the location selected by **User1**. When you sync with the central file, it also reloads the latest changes.

11. Close the project. When the Editable Elements dialog box opens, select **Relinquish elements and worksets**.

12. If you will not be continuing into the next section, close the **User2** session of the Autodesk Revit software. In addition, in the **User1** session of the Autodesk Revit software, return the Username to the original name used at the beginning of this practice.

Practice 4f

Work in Workset-Related Projects - MEP

Practice Objectives

- Add and Modify Elements in Worksets.
- Request and grant permissions to edit.
- Save, synchronize, and reload files to display the changes made by each user.

Estimated time for completion: 20 minutes

In this practice you will work with two different sessions of the Autodesk Revit software. In the first session, you will make worksets visible and add, modify elements in worksets without having to get permission. You will then switch to a different user and make a workset editable. The first user requests an edit to the workset owned by the second user. Permission will be granted and the first user will make the change. You save the local file, save to central file, and reload the latest file. An example of Worksets dialog box used in this practice is shown in Figure 4–84.

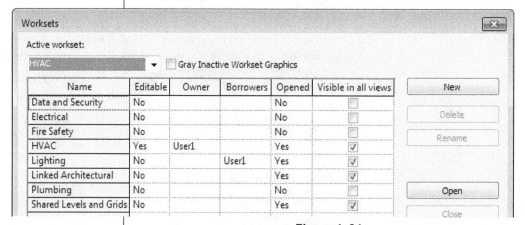

Figure 4–84

- You must complete **Practice 4c: Open Workset-Related Projects - MEP** before beginning this practice.

Task 1 - Add and Modify Elements in Worksets.

1. Working as **User1** in the file **Elementary-School-MEP_User1.rvt**, open the **Coordination>MEP>Ceiling Plans:01 RCP** view.

2. Zoom in on the lower left classroom. You should see elements related to HVAC.

3. Move a couple of air terminals similar to that shown in Figure 4–85. Reattach the flex duct, if required.

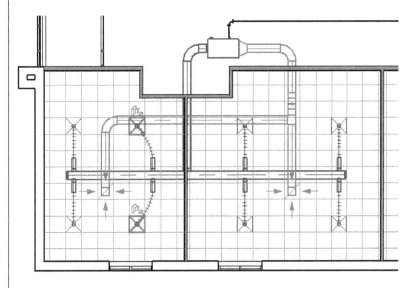

Figure 4–85

4. Open the Worksets dialog box and select the Lighting workset. Open it and make it visible in all views. Click **OK**. Now the air terminals are on top of lights.

5. Select one of the lighting fixtures. It has an icon connected to it, as shown in Figure 4–86, indicating that it belongs to another workset. Click the icon to make the element editable.

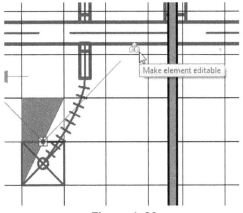

Make element editable

Figure 4–86

6. Move the lighting fixture so it does not conflict with the air terminal.

7. Open the Worksets dialog box. **User1** is noted as the *Owner* of the **HVAC** workset and a *Borrower* of **Lighting** and **Linked Architectural** worksets, as shown in Figure 4–87.

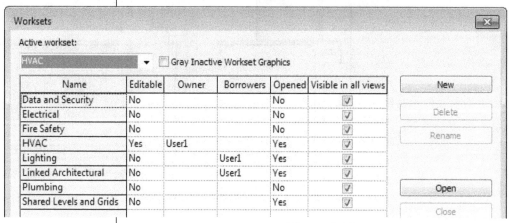

Figure 4–87

8. Click **OK** to close the dialog box.

9. In the *Collaborate* tab>Synchronize panel, or the Quick Access Toolbar, click 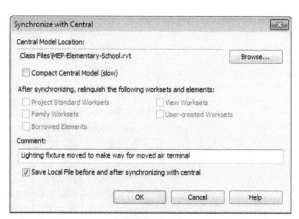 (Synchronize and Modify Settings) to open the Synchronize with Central dialog box, as shown in Figure 4–88. The **Borrowed Elements** option should be selected. Add a comment about moving the light and select the **Save Local File before and after synchronizing with central** option.

Figure 4–88

10. Click **OK**.

Task 2 - Check out a Workset.

---

1. Work in **User2** and open the **Coordination>MEP>Ceiling Plans: 01 RCP**. Neither the HVAC elements nor the changes show in the local file.

2. In the *Collaborate* tab>Synchronize panel, click 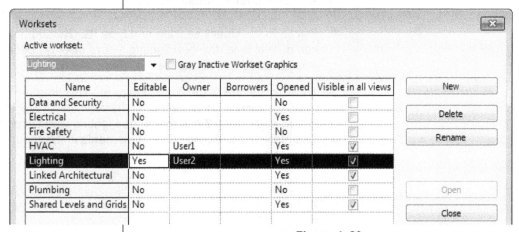 (Reload Latest or type **RL**. The light fixture location changes but you do not see the air terminals because that workset is not open.

3. Click (Worksets) to open the dialog box and open the HVAC workset. Verify that it is Visible in all views.

4. Select **Lighting** in the *Active workset* drop-down list and make it editable (select **Yes** in the *Editable* column). The *Owner* should display **User 2**, as shown in Figure 4–89.

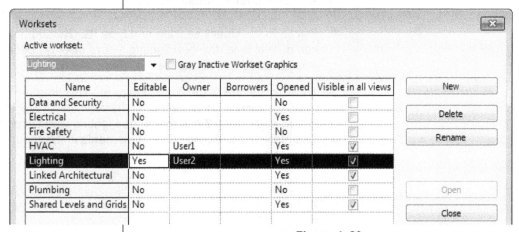

Name	Editable	Owner	Borrowers	Opened	Visible in all views
Data and Security	No			No	
Electrical	No			Yes	
Fire Safety	No			No	
HVAC	No	User1		Yes	☑
Lighting	Yes	User2		Yes	☑
Linked Architectural	No			Yes	☑
Plumbing	No			No	
Shared Levels and Grids	No			Yes	☑

Figure 4–89

5. Click **OK** to close the dialog box.

6. Add another lighting fixture in the room.

7. In the Quick Access Toolbar, click (Save) to save the local file.

---

8. Switch to the **User1** session and type **RL** (Reload Latest). There are no new changes to load, as shown in Figure 4–90, because User 2 has not saved back to the central file. Close the dialog box.

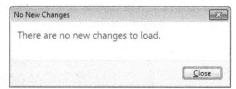

Figure 4–90

9. Switch to the **User2** session and click  (Synchronize Now). This saves the changes to the central file without relinquishing the Lighting workset.

Task 3 - Request Permission to Edit.

1. Switch to the **User1** session and type **RL** (Reload Latest) again. This time, the new lighting fixture displays because it was saved to the central file.

2. Try to move one of the lighting fixtures. This time, an error message displays that cannot be ignored, as shown in Figure 4–91. **User2** has made the Lighting workset editable. Therefore, no one else can edit elements in it without permission.

Figure 4–91

3. Click **Place Request**. The Editing Request Placed dialog box opens.

4. Switch to the **User2** session. An alert box displays, as shown in Figure 4–92.

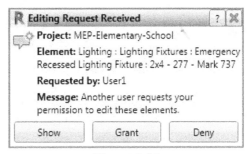

Figure 4–92

5. Hover the cursor over the **Show** button to highlight the door. Move the dialog box out of the way if required to see the modified lighting fixture.

6. The other user can have permission to modify the placement of this lighting fixture. Click **Grant**. By doing this, you enable the other user full control over this one element in the workset.

7. Switch to the **User1** session. The Editing Request is granted, as shown in Figure 4–93.

Figure 4–93

8. Close the Editing Request Granted dialog box. Your request was granted and the lighting fixture moves.

9. Move the lighting fixture again to exactly where you want it. This time, you are not prompted to ask to move the element because you are still borrowing it.

10. Try to move another lighting fixture. You do not have permission to move this or any others. Click **Cancel** rather than place the request. The lighting fixture returns to its original location.

11. In the View Control Bar, expand the Worksharing display and click 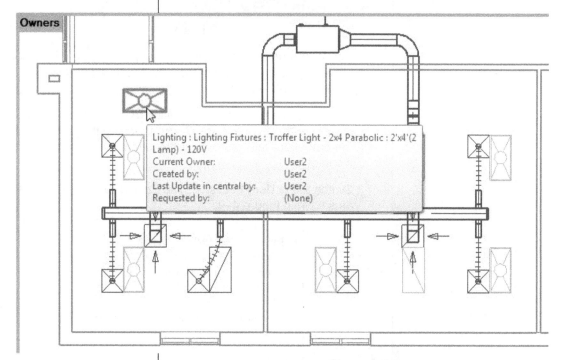 (Owners). Different colors highlight the elements and their respective owners. Hover the cursor over one of the elements to display the information about the owner, as shown in Figure 4–94.

Owners

Lighting : Lighting Fixtures : Troffer Light - 2x4 Parabolic : 2'x4'(2 Lamp) - 120V

Current Owner:	User2
Created by:	User2
Last Update in central by:	User2
Requested by:	(None)

Figure 4–94

• The color on your display might be different.

12. Click (Synchronize and Modify Settings) and relinquish **User created Worksets** and **Borrowed Elements.**

13. Toggle the Worksharing Display off and zoom out to see the full building.

14. Save the local file.

15. Switch to the **User2** session.

16. Click 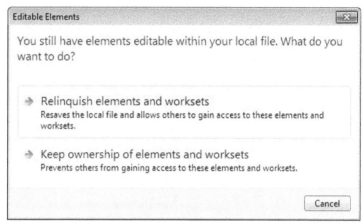 (Synchronize Now). The lighting fixture moves to the location where **User1** moved it. When you save to the central file, it also reloads the latest changes.

17. Close the project. When the Editable Elements dialog box opens, as shown in Figure 4–95, click **Relinquish elements and worksets**.

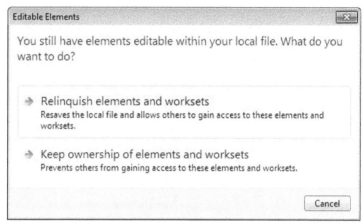

Figure 4–95

18. Close the **User2** session of the Autodesk Revit software.

19. In the **User1** session of the Autodesk Revit software, return the *Username* to the original name at the start of this set of practices.

20. Close the project.

4.6 Setting Up Worksets

Building projects are complex, requiring multiple team members. Therefore, the Autodesk Revit software designed *worksets* to help project teams work together. Individual worksets are subsets of a project with only specific elements available to view or edit. Worksets are created in the Worksets dialog box, as shown in Figure 4–96.

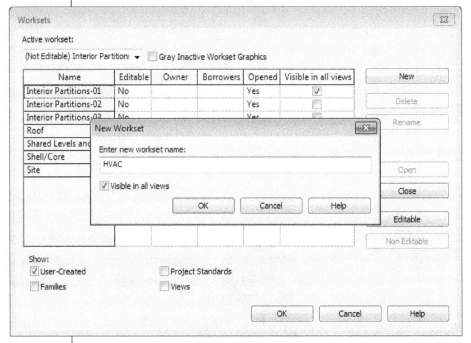

Figure 4–96

- It is important to have one user start a project and develop most of the views, families, and other settings before sharing.

- Worksets are designed for multiple team members working on one building. If you have multiple buildings in a project, you use linking to show the relationships between the buildings. Each building can have its own worksets.

- To divide a project into worksets depends on the complexity of the project, the need to be able to load only parts of the model, and the need to control visibility by workset.

- If your company is primarily checking out worksets rather than borrowing on the fly, dividing the project depends on the different tasks to be done and the number of people working on the project.

- You can also have worksets for electrical, site and structural work that are not visible to other users, and separate worksets for linked Autodesk Revit files.

Setting Up Worksets Process Overview

1. Add user-created worksets.
2. If the design of the building has already been started in the project, move the building elements to the appropriate workset.
3. Create a central file.

- You can add additional worksets to the project as you involve more specialties.

How To: Create Worksets

1. Open the project that becomes your central file.
2. In the *Collaborate* tab>Manage Collaboration panel, click

   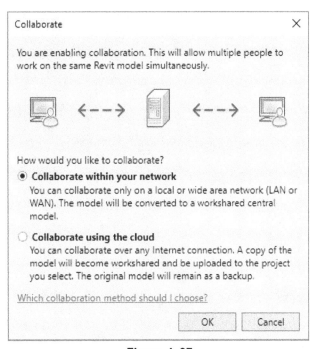 (Collaborate).
3. In the Collaborate dialog box, select **Collaborate within your network**, as shown in Figure 4–97. Then, click **OK**.

This learning guide focuses on network collaboration.

Collaborate   ×

You are enabling collaboration. This will allow multiple people to work on the same Revit model simultaneously.

How would you like to collaborate?

◉ **Collaborate within your network**
You can collaborate only on a local or wide area network (LAN or WAN). The model will be converted to a workshared central model.

○ **Collaborate using the cloud**
You can collaborate over any Internet connection. A copy of the model will become workshared and be uploaded to the project you select. The original model will remain as a backup.

Which collaboration method should I choose?

OK   Cancel

Figure 4–97

4. In the *Collaborate* tab>Manage Collaboration panel or in the Status Bar, click ⚇ (Worksets).

- Four types of worksets are created by default, as described below:

Project Standards	Worksets are set up for standards such as materials, fill patterns, line styles, and other settings.
Families	A workset is created for each family that is loaded in the project (such as doors, windows, and furniture components).
Views	A workset is assigned to each view. This is where view-specific elements (such as text and dimensions) are placed automatically when you work on user-created worksets.
User-created	These worksets hold the building elements. The Autodesk Revit software creates two of these by default: *Shared Levels and Grids* and *Workset1*.

5. In the Worksets dialog box, click **New** and type a name for the workset in the New Workset dialog box, as shown in Figure 4–98.

As they are created, the worksets are open and editable by the person who set them up.

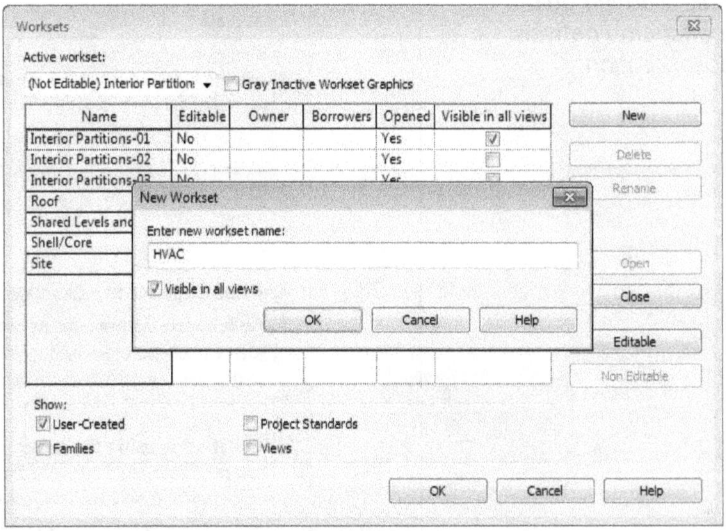

Figure 4–98

6. Select or clear the **Visible in all views** option, as required. For example, a workset showing the exterior of the building is required in all views, while a furniture layout is only required in the current workset.
7. Click **OK**.
8. Continue to create new worksets, as required.
9. Set the *Active workset*. You might also want to select the **Gray Inactive Workset Graphics** option to give a visual understanding of which elements in a drawing are active and inactive.
10. Click **OK** to close the dialog box.

• The new worksets are automatically made **Editable**.

• You can change existing workset names in the Worksets dialog box. Select the workset and click **Rename**.

• If you delete a workset and there are elements in the workset, the dialog box shown in Figure 4–99 displays, prompting you what to do with any elements in the workset. They can either be deleted or moved to another workset.

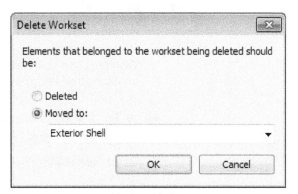

Figure 4–99

• To rename or delete a workset, it must first be made editable.

Placing Elements in Worksets

Before sharing the worksets with everyone, place existing building elements in the appropriate worksets. For example, move any furniture already in a project to a furniture workset, as shown in Figure 4–100.

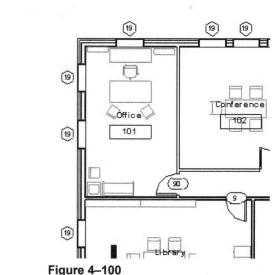

Figure 4–100

- Worksets can span levels; therefore, you can select elements on each level and move them into the appropriate workset.

How To: Move Elements to the Appropriate Worksets

1. Open the view that holds the elements that you need to move to a workset.
2. Select the element(s).
3. In Properties, change the *Workset* parameter to the workset in which you want the elements to be, as shown in Figure 4–100.

- You can select multiple types of building elements and move them to a workset. However, you will need to filter out any annotation elements such as views and tags that are automatically assigned to the related View workset.

- Curtain wall subcomponents (grids, mullions, and panels) must be filtered out of a selection set. Select just the base curtain wall element when you want to move it to a workset.

- If you have added elements to a workset that is not visible in the current workset, the elements do not display in the view. This is what you want in some cases. If you need elements to be visible, open the Visibility/Graphic Overrides dialog box. Select the *Worksets* tab and select the worksets you want to be visible in the current workset, as shown in Figure 4–101.

Worksets	Visibility Setting
Exterior Shell	Use Global Setting (Visible)
Furniture	Use Global Setting (Visible)
Plumbing	Use Global Setting (Not Visible)
Shared Levels and Grids	Use Global Setting (Visible)

Figure 4–101

Hint: Setting a Starting View

To save time when opening a complex model with worksharing activated, you can specify a *Starting View*. This could be a cover sheet or a drafting view with information about the project. The idea is that the contents of the starting view are simple elements rather than model elements.

- To set the starting view, in the *Manage* tab>Manage Project

  panel, click 🗗 (Starting View). In the Starting view dialog box, select the view name, as shown in Figure 4–102.

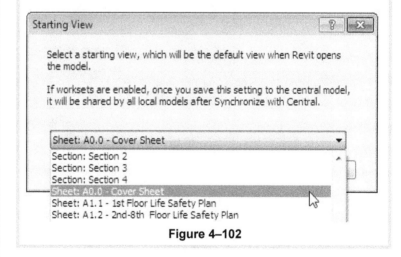

Figure 4–102

Creating the Central File

The central file keeps track of available worksets, and coordinates the changes made in each one with the rest of the worksets. It needs to be accessible to all team members, though typically no one should work in it directly.

Once you have created the worksets for a project and moved elements to them, it is time to create the *central file* to which the worksets are saved.

How To: Create a Central File

1. In the project file in which you have defined the worksets, in the Quick Access Toolbar, click 💾 (Save).

2. As the worksets were enabled, the file automatically becomes a central file. If required, in the Save dialog box, click **Options...** to open the File Save Options dialog box, as shown in Figure 4–103 and specify the number of backups. **Make this a Central Model after save** is selected and grayed out. Click **Save** to complete the process.

Figure 4–103

3. In the *Collaborate* tab>Synchronize panel, or in the Quick Access Toolbar, click 🔄 (Synchronize and Modify Settings.)

4. In the Synchronize with Central dialog box, select **User-created Worksets** so that they are released and available to everyone, as shown in Figure 4–104. You can also add a comment. Click **OK**.

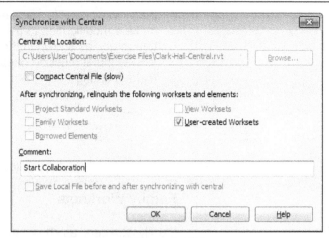

Figure 4–104

5. Close the central file.

Other Workset Types

User-created worksets are the main ones you work in as you add and modify elements in a project. There are also three other types of worksets you can use: View, Family, and Project Standards.

View Worksets

View worksets (shown in Figure 4–105) are automatically created for each view that is in place when the workset is first created. When you make a change to a view (such as turning elements on or off), or create a new view, you do not need to have permission unless someone else has checked out the view by making it editable.

In the Show area, you can select the type of Worksets that you want to view.

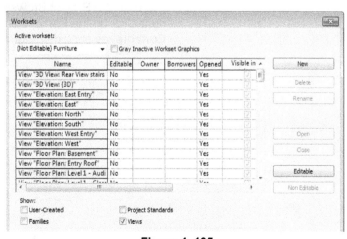

Figure 4–105

- If a View workset is made editable and a different user tries to make a modification to the view, the change is only temporary, as shown in the warning in Figure 4–106. The view workset must be released by the owner for anyone to make a change.

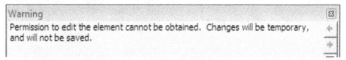

Figure 4–106

Family Worksets

Family worksets, as shown in Figure 4–107, control the status of each family in the project. To make a change to a family (such as a door style, lighting fixture or mechanical equipment), similar to view worksets, you can make this change on-the-fly as long as someone else has not checked out the family.

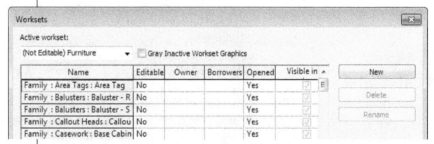

Figure 4–107

- If you need to check out a family so no one else can modify it, you can change the editable status in the Worksets dialog box or in the Project Browser. Expand the Families branch, right-click on the Family name, and select **Make Workset Editable**, as shown in Figure 4–108.

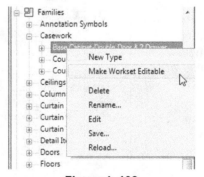

Figure 4–108

- A family workset made editable cannot be changed by any other user. The owner must release it and synchronize it with the central file before anyone else can modify it.

Project Standards Worksets

Project Standards worksets (shown in Figure 4–109) hold information such as the materials, line styles, wall types, text types, and any other settings. These should only be modified by a project leader or a delegated person to help maintain these standards.

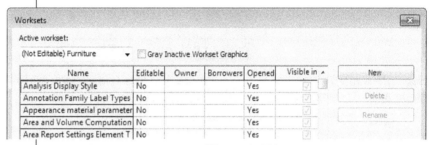

Figure 4–109

- You can create new family types for floors, roofs, and walls using Type Properties without making them editable. Once they have been saved to the central file, they need to be made editable to modify them again.

- Relinquishing ownership of any Project Standard workset you are not working on is especially important so that others can have access to it.

Practice 4g

Set Up Worksets - Architectural

Practice Objectives

- Set up worksets and move existing elements to the worksets.
- Create a central file and local files.
- Modify project standards and views worksets, and save them to the central file.

In this practice you will set up a default workset, add user-created worksets, move building elements to different worksets, and create a central file.

Task 1 - Set up Worksets.

Estimated time for completion: 20 minutes

1. In the practice files folder, open **Midrise-A.rvt**

2. In the *Collaborate* tab>Manage Collaboration panel, click (Collaborate).

3. In the Collaborate dialog box, select **Collaborate within your network** and click **OK**.

4. In the *Collaborate* tab>Manage Collaboration panel or in the Status Bar, click (Worksets).

5. In the Worksets dialog box, rename *Workset 1* to **Exterior**. Then create the new worksets shown in Figure 4–110. The **Visible in all views** option should be off in all new worksets, except for *Vertical Circulation* and *Support Equipment*.

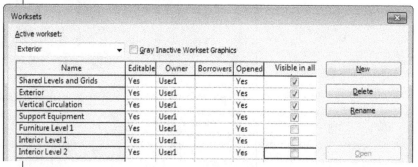

Name	Editable	Owner	Borrowers	Opened	Visible in all	
Shared Levels and Grids	Yes	User1		Yes	☑	New
Exterior	Yes	User1		Yes	☑	
Vertical Circulation	Yes	User1		Yes	☑	Delete
Support Equipment	Yes	User1		Yes	☑	Rename
Furniture Level 1	Yes	User1		Yes	☐	
Interior Level 1	Yes	User1		Yes	☐	
Interior Level 2	Yes	User1		Yes	☐	Open

Active workset: Exterior

Figure 4–110

6. Verify that the *Active workset* is **Exterior**. Select **Gray Inactive Workset Graphics** and click **OK** to close the Worksets dialog box.

7. If prompted to change the active workset, click **No**. Elements on the *Shared Levels and Grids* worksets as well as the view-specific room tags are grayed out. Everything in the *Exterior* workset displays in black.

Task 2 - Move Building Elements to Worksets.

1. In the **Floor Plans: Level 1** view, select all of the interior walls, columns, and doors. Use ▽ (Filter) to remove other items from the selection set. Ensure that you do not select any exterior doors, especially the curtain wall door.

2. In Properties, change the *Workset* for the selected elements to **Interior-Level 1**. The items should be removed from the view if you toggled off the **Visible by default** option when you created the workset.

3. Repeat the same procedure to move the furniture to the **Furniture – Level 1** workset.

4. Repeat the same procedure and move the elevators and stairs to the **Vertical Circulation** workset, and the bathroom items to the **Support Equipment** workset. These elements are still visible but grayed out, as shown in Figure 4–111.

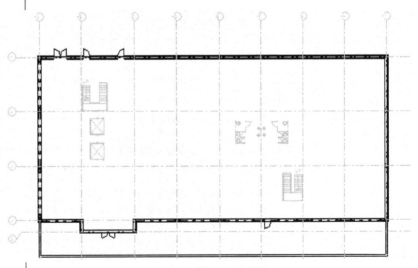

Figure 4–111

5. To verify that the elements are in the correct workset, in the Status bar, expand Worksharing Display and click

   ⚘ (Worksets). The elements in the Exterior, Vertical Circulation, and Support Equipment worksets should be in different colors.

6. Make any required modifications and toggle off the Worksharing Display.

Task 3 - Create a Central File.

1. In the *File* tab, expand 🖫 (Save As) and click

   📄 (Project).

2. Name the file **Midrise-1234.rvt** and locate it in your practice files directory. Click **Save**.

3. In the Status Bar, click 🗗 (Worksets). All of the files are now *Editable* with your user name listed as the owner, as shown in Figure 4–112.

Name	Editable	Owner	Borrowers	Opened	Visible in all
Exterior	Yes	User1		Yes	☑
Furniture Level 1	Yes	User1		Yes	☐
Interior Level 1	Yes	User1		Yes	☐
Interior Level 2	Yes	User1		Yes	☐
Shared Levels and Grids	Yes	User1		Yes	☑
Support Equipment	Yes	User1		Yes	☑
Vertical Circulation	Yes	User1		Yes	☑

Figure 4–112

4. Click **OK** to close the dialog box.

5. In the Quick Access Toolbar, click 🗗 (Synchronize and Modify Settings). In the Synchronize with Central dialog box, select the option to relinquish **User-created Worksets** so that they are available to everyone.

6. Click **OK** to Synchronize with Central and close the file. Remember that you do not want to work directly in the central file.

Task 4 - Modify a Project Standards Workset.

1. In the *File* tab, click **Options**. Change the *Username* to **User1** if it is not already set. (Sign out of Autodesk A360, if required.)

Do not use the link on the introductory screen or from Recent Documents as these options open the central file directly.

2. In the Quick Access Toolbar, click ⌂ (Open). Select **Midrise-1234.rvt**. Verify that **Create New Local** is selected and click **Open**. This creates a new file named **Midrise-1234 _User1.rvt**.

3. Open the Worksets dialog box.

4. Select the **Project Standards** option in the *Show* area.

5. Scroll through the list until you find *Text Types*. Make *Text Types* editable and click **OK** to close the dialog box.

*You do not have to make the **Text Types** editable to complete the following steps; however, it does indicate how the Synchronize and Modify Settings process works.*

6. Create a new text type. Start the **Text** command.

7. In Properties, click ⊞ (Edit Type).

8. In the Type Properties dialog box, click **Duplicate**. Name the text type and select a size and font. The exact ones are not important at this time.

9. Add some text in the project.

10. Zoom All.

11. Click ⌬ (Synchronize and Modify Settings). In the dialog box, note that you are automatically asked to relinquish the **Project Standard Worksets**. Click **OK**.

12. Click ⊟ (Save) to save the file locally.

Task 5 - Create New Views.

1. Open a second session of the Autodesk Revit software. In **Options**, change the *Username* to **User2**.

2. Create a local copy of **Midrise-1234.rvt.** It is automatically named **Midrise-1234_User2.rvt**.

3. Start the **A** (Text) command and, in Properties, view the list of Text Types. The new text type is available for **User2**. Cancel the text command.

4. In the Project Browser, duplicate the **Level 1** floor plan view and rename it **First Floor Plan**.

5. Type **VG** to open the Visibility Graphic Overrides dialog box. Select the *Worksets* tab and change the *Visibility Setting* for **Interior – Level 1** to **Show**, as shown in Figure 4–113.

Worksets	Visibility Setting
Exterior	Use Global Setting (Visible)
Furniture Level 1	Use Global Setting (Not Visible)
Interior Level 1	Show
Interior Level 2	Use Global Setting (Not Visible)
Shared Levels and Grids	Use Global Setting (Visible)
Support Equipment	Use Global Setting (Visible)
Vertical Circulation	Use Global Setting (Visible)

Figure 4–113

6. Click **OK**. The Interior walls now display in the view as shown in Figure 4–114.

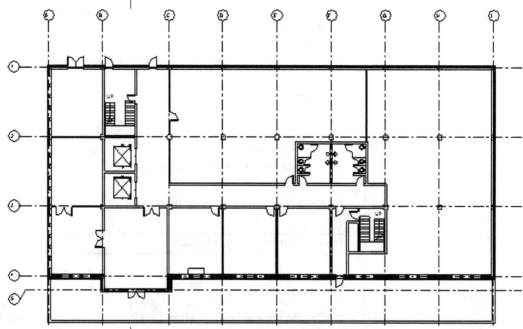

Figure 4–114

7. Create a new sheet using the default title block. Name it **A201-First Floor Plan**.

8. Drag and drop the view **Floor Plans – First Floor Plan** to the sheet.

9. Open the Worksets dialog box. Select the **Views** option in the *Show* section and scroll down to see the new view worksets. These were automatically created when you added the views. **User2** is the owner of these views, as shown in Figure 4–115. Close the dialog box.

Name	Editable	Owner	Borrowers	Opened	Visibl
View "3D View: Interior Perspective	No			Yes	
View "3D View: {3D}"	No			Yes	
View "Elevation: East"	No			Yes	
View "Elevation: North"	No			Yes	
View "Elevation: South"	No			Yes	
View "Elevation: West"	No			Yes	
View "Floor Plan: Basement"	No			Yes	
View "Floor Plan: First Floor Plan"	Yes	User2		Yes	
View "Floor Plan: Level 1"	No			Yes	

Figure 4–115

10. Save the project to the central file and locally. The view worksets are automatically relinquished.

11. Switch to the **User1** session of the Autodesk Revit software. The new views are not yet visible, as shown in Figure 4–116.

12. Type **RL** (Reload Latest). The new view, as shown in Figure 4–117, and sheet are now visible.

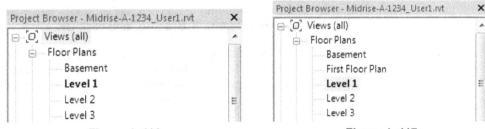

Figure 4–116   Figure 4–117

13. Save the file locally and close it. You do not need to save back to the central file because you did not make any changes to the file.

14. Close the **User2** session of the Autodesk Revit software.

15. In the **User1** session of the Autodesk Revit software, change the username back to the original name at the start of this set of practices.

Practice 4h

Set Up Worksets - Structural

Practice Objectives

- Set up worksets and move existing elements to the worksets.
- Create a central file and local files.
- Modify project standards and views worksets, and save them to the central file.

Estimated time for completion: 20 minutes

In this practice you will set up a default workset, add user-created worksets, move building elements to different worksets, and create a central file.

Task 1 - Set up Worksets.

1. In the practice files folder, open **Bon-Air-Office-S.rvt**.

2. In the *Collaborate* tab>Manage Collaboration panel, click (Collaborate).

3. In the Collaborate dialog box select **Collaborate within your network** and click **OK**.

4. In the *Collaborate* tab>Manage Collaboration panel or in the Status Bar, click (Worksets).

5. In the Worksharing dialog box, rename *Workset 1* as **Columns, Beams & Bracing**, and click **OK**.

6. In the Worksets dialog box, create the new worksets shown in Figure 4–118. The **Visible in all views** option should be off in all new worksets.(The Shared Levels and Grids workset has already been created.)

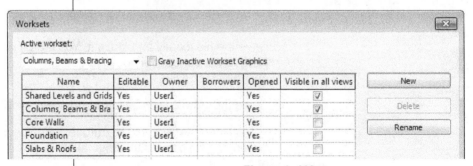

Figure 4–118

7. Verify that the *Active workset* is **Columns, Beams & Bracing**. Select **Gray Inactive Workset Graphics** and click **OK** to close the Worksets dialog box.

8. If prompted to change the active workset, click **No**.

9. Open the **Structural Plans: Level 1** view. Elements on the *Shared Levels and Grids* workset and the view-specific view and section markers are grayed out. Everything else is black because they are in the Columns, Beams & Bracing workset that was formerly named Workset1.

Task 2 - Move Building Elements to Worksets.

---

1. Open the **Elevations (Building Elevation): East** view.

2. Select all of the elements from Level 1 down to the lowest footing as shown in Figure 4–119.

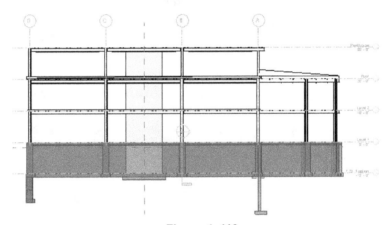

Figure 4–119

Although you are changing the workset for the wall foundations, analytical wall foundations do not automatically follow and it is not possible to manually change their workset. When starting a project from scratch, as would typically be the case, it is important to set the right workset before creating the wall foundations.

3. In Properties, change the workset for the selected elements to **Foundation**. (The elements should be removed from the view if you toggled off the **Visible in all views** option when you created the workset.)

4. Repeat the procedure by opening the appropriate views and moving the slabs and roofs to the **Slabs & Roofs** workset. Ensure that you include the slab edges. (Hint: Use

   ▽ (Filter).)

5. Repeat the procedure by opening the appropriate views and moving the elevator walls to the **Core Walls** workset.

Task 3 - Create a Central File.

1. In the *File* tab, expand 🖫 (Save As), and click
   🗋 (Project).

2. In the Save As dialog box, click **Options...**. The **Make this a Central File Model after save** option is selected but grayed out. This project must become the central file because you have initiated worksets. Click **OK** to close the dialog box.

3. Name the file **Bon-Air-Office-1234.rvt** and locate it in your practice files folder. Click **Save**.

4. Click 🗐 (Worksets). All of the files are listed as *Editable* with your user name listed as the owner, as shown in Figure 4–120.

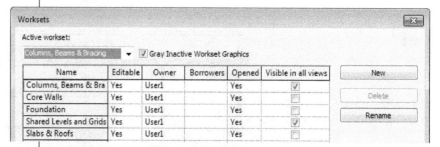

Figure 4–120

5. Click **OK** to close the dialog box.

6. Click 🗐 (Synchronize and Modify Settings). In the Synchronize with Central dialog box, select the option to relinquish **User-created Worksets** so that they are available to everyone.

7. Click **OK** to Synchronize with Central and close the file. Remember that you do not want to work directly in the central file.

Task 4 - Modify a Project Standards Workset.

1. In the *File* tab, click **Options**. Change the *Username* to **User1** if it is not already set. (Sign out of Autodesk A360 if required.)

Do not use the link on the introductory screen or from Recent Documents as these options open the central file directly.

2. In the Quick Access Toolbar, click ⌂ (Open). Select **Bon-Air-Office-1234.rvt**. Verify that **Create New Local** is selected and click **Open**. This creates a new file named **Bon-Air-Office-1234_User1.rvt**.

3. Open the **Structural Plans: Level 1** view.

4. Open the Worksets dialog box.

5. Select the **Project Standards** option in the *Show* area.

*You do not have to make the **Text Types** editable to do the following steps but it does indicate how the Synchronize and Modify Settings process works.*

6. Scroll through the list to locate **Text Types**. Make **Text Types** editable and click **OK** to close the dialog box.

7. Create a new text type. Start the **Text** command.

8. In Properties, click ⊞ (Edit Type).

9. In the Type Properties dialog box, click **Duplicate**. Name the text type and select a size and font. The exact ones are not important at this time.

10. Add some text in the project.

11. **Zoom All**.

12. Click ⊚ (Synchronize and Modify Settings). In the dialog box, note that you are automatically prompted to relinquish the **Project Standard Worksets**. Click **OK**.

13. Click 💾 (Save) to save the file locally.

Task 5 - Create New Views.

1. Open a second session of the Autodesk Revit Structure software. In **Options**, change the *Username* to **User2**.

2. Create a local copy of **Bon-Air-Office-1234.rvt.** It is automatically named **Bon-Air-Office-1234_User2.rvt**.

3. Click A (Text). In Properties, display the list of Text Types. The new text type is available for **User2**.

4. In the Project Browser, duplicate the **Structural Plans: Level 1** view and rename it **Foundation**.

5. Open the Visibility/Graphic Overrides dialog box. Select the *Worksets* tab and change the *Visibility Setting* for **Foundation** to **Show**, as shown in Figure 4–121.

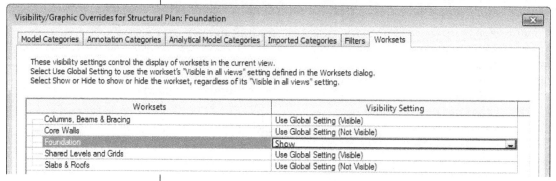

Figure 4–121

6. Click **OK**. The foundation elements now display in the view as shown in Figure 4–122.

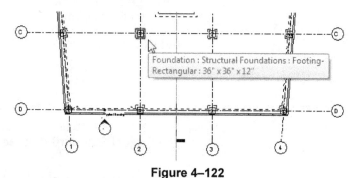

Figure 4–122

7. Create a new sheet using the default title block. Name it **S201-Foundation Plan**.

8. Drag-and-drop the **Structural Plans: Foundation** view to the sheet.

9. Open the Worksets dialog box. Select the **Views** option in the *Show* area and scroll down to display the new view worksets. These were automatically created when you added the views. **User2** is the owner of these views, as shown in Figure 4–123. Close the dialog box.

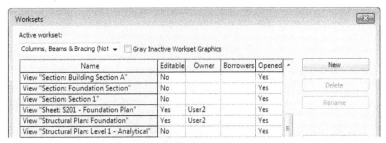

Figure 4–123

10. Save the project in the central file and locally. The view worksets are automatically relinquished.

11. Switch to the **User1** session of the Autodesk Revit software. The new views are not yet visible, as shown in Figure 4–124.

12. Type **RL** (**Reload Latest**). The new view, as shown in Figure 4–125, and the sheets are now visible.

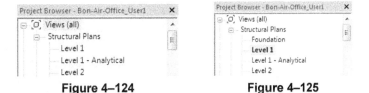

Figure 4–124   **Figure 4–125**

13. Save the file locally and close it. You do not need to save back to the central file because you did not make any changes to the file.

14. Close the **User2** session of the Autodesk Revit software.

15. In the **User1** session of the Autodesk Revit software, change the username back to the original name at the start of this set of practices.

Practice 4i

Set Up Worksets - MEP

Practice Objectives

- Set up worksets and move existing elements to the worksets.
- Create a central file and local files.
- Modify project standards and views worksets, and save them to the central file.

Estimated time for completion: 20 minutes

In this practice you will set up a default workset, add user-created worksets, move building elements to different worksets, and create a central file.

Task 1 - Set up Worksets.

1. In the practice files folder, open **Olethe-Building-MEP.rvt**.

2. In the *Collaborate* tab>Manage Collaboration panel, click

   (Collaborate).

3. In the Collaborate dialog box select **Collaborate within your network** and click **OK**.

4. In the *Collaborate* tab>Manage Collaboration panel or in the

   Status Bar, click (Worksets).

5. In the Worksets dialog box, rename *Workset1* to **HVAC** (the majority of the existing elements need to be in this workset) and create the new worksets shown in Figure 4–126. The **Visible in all views** option should be off in all new worksets, except for *Architectural* Link

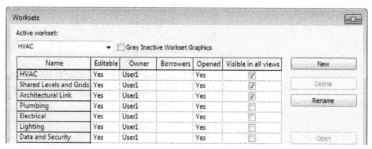

Figure 4–126

6. Verify that the Active workset is HVAC and select the **Gray Inactive Workset Graphics** option and click **OK** to close the Worksets dialog box.

7. If prompted to change the active workset, click **No**.

Task 2 - Move Building Elements to Worksets.

1. Select some of the ducts and equipment. In Properties, you can see that the *Workset* is **HVAC**.

2. If the link is not selected, in the Status Bar click 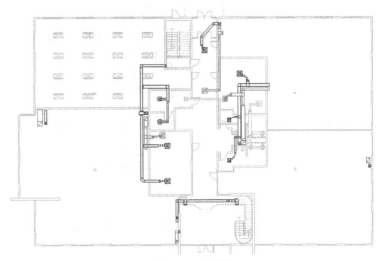 (Select Links) to toggle it on.

3. Select the linked architectural model. It is also set to HVAC. Change the *Workset* to **Architectural Link**.

4. Open the Electrical>Lighting>Floor Plans>**1-Lighting** view.

5. Select all of the lighting fixtures and move them to the *Workset* Lighting. The elements are removed from the view because the Lighting workset is set to not visible.

6. Open the Mechanical>Plumbing>Floor Plans>**1-Plumbing** view and move the plumbing fixtures to the Plumbing workset. These elements are also removed from the view because the Plumbing workset is set to not visible.

7. Open the Coordination>MEP>Floor Plans>**1 - MEP** view.

8. Open the Worksets dialog box and make the Lighting and Plumbing worksets visible. Click **OK**. The view displays with the HVAC workset in color but the other worksets are grayed out, as shown in Figure 4–127.

Figure 4–127

9. To verify that the elements are in the correct workset, in the Status bar, expand Worksharing Display and click

   ⬡ (Worksets). The elements in the worksets should be in different colors as shown in Figure 4–128.

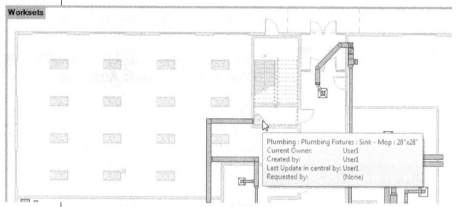

Figure 4–128

10. Make any required modifications and toggle off the Worksharing Display.

Task 3 - Create a Central File.

1. In the *File* tab, expand 🖫 (Save As) and click

   📄 (Project).

2. Name the file **Olethe-Building-1234.rvt** and locate it in your practice files directory. Click **Save**.

3. Click 👥 (Worksets). All of the files are now *Editable* with your user name listed as the owner. Clear **Visible in all views** for Lighting and Plumbing, as shown in Figure 4–129.

Name	Editable	Owner	Borrowers	Opened	Visible in all views
Architectural Link	Yes	User1		Yes	☑
Data and Security	Yes	User1		Yes	☐
Electrical	Yes	User1		Yes	☐
HVAC	Yes	User1		Yes	☑
Lighting	Yes	User1		Yes	☐
Plumbing	Yes	User1		Yes	☐
Shared Levels and Grids	Yes	User1		Yes	☑

Figure 4–129

4. Click **OK** to close the dialog box.

5. Click ⬚ (Synchronize and Modify Settings). In the Synchronize with Central dialog box, select the option to relinquish **User-created Worksets** so that they are available to everyone.

6. Click **OK** to Synchronize with Central and close the file. Remember that you do not want to work directly in the central file.

Task 4 - Modify a Project Standards Workset.

---

1. In the *File* tab, click **Options**. Change the *Username* to **User1** if it is not already set. (Sign out of Autodesk A360, if required.)

Do not use the link on the introductory screen or from Recent Documents as these options open the central file directly.

2. In the Quick Access Toolbar, click 🗁 (Open). Select **Olethe-Building-1234.rvt**. Verify that **Create New Local** is selected and click **Open**. This creates a new file named **Olethe-Building-1234_User1.rvt**.

3. Open the Worksets dialog box.

4. Select the **Project Standards** option in the *Show* area.

*You do not have to make the **Text Types** editable to complete the following steps, but it does indicate how the Synchronize and Modify Settings process works.*

5. Scroll through the list until you find *Text Types*. Make *Text Types* editable and click **OK** to close the dialog box.

6. Create a new text type. Start the **Text** command.

7. In Properties, click ⬚ (Edit Type).

8. In the Type Properties dialog box, click **Duplicate...**. Name the text type and select a size and font. The exact ones are not important at this time.

9. Add some text in the project.

10. Zoom All.

11. Click ⬚ (Synchronize and Modify Settings). In the dialog box, note that you are automatically asked to relinquish the **Project Standard Worksets**. Click **OK**.

12. Click ⬚ (Save) to save the file locally.

Task 5 - Create New Views.

1. Open a second session of the Autodesk Revit software. In **Options**, change the *Username* to **User2**.

2. Create a local copy of **Olethe-Building-1234.rvt.** It is automatically named **Olethe-Building-1234_User2.rvt**.

3. Start the **A** (Text) command and, in Properties, view the list of Text Types. The new text type is available for **User2**. Cancel the text command.

4. In the Coordination>MEP>Floor Plans>1 - MEP view, open the Visibility Graphic Overrides dialog box.

5. In the *Worksets* tab, change the *Visibility Setting* for the Worksets **Lighting** and **Plumbing** to **Show**, as shown in Figure 4–130.

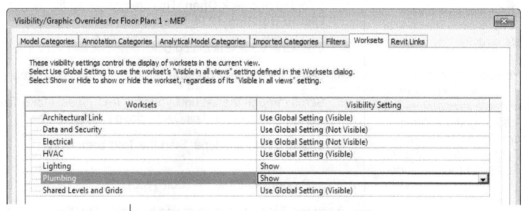

Figure 4–130

6. Click **OK**. The lighting and plumbing elements now display in the view as shown in Figure 4–131.

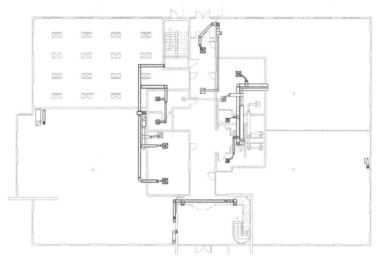

Figure 4–131

7. Create a new sheet using the default title block. Name it **C201-First Floor Coordination**.

8. Drag and drop the **1 - MEP** view to the sheet.

9. Open the Worksets dialog box. Select the **Views** option in the *Show* section and scroll down to see the new view worksets. These were automatically created when you added the views. **User2** is the owner of these views, as shown in Figure 4–132. Close the dialog box.

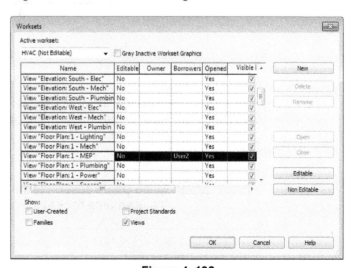

Figure 4–132

10. Save the project to the central file and locally. The view worksets are automatically relinquished.

11. Switch to the **User1** session of the Autodesk Revit software. The 1 - MEP view has not changed and the new sheet is not visible, as shown in Figure 4–133.

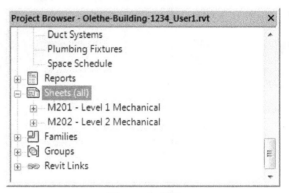

Figure 4–133

12. Type **RL** (Reload Latest). The new sheet is now visible, as shown in Figure 4–134.

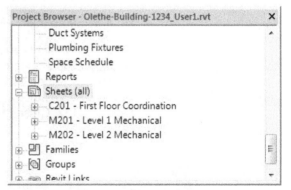

Figure 4–134

13. Save the file locally and close it. You do not need to save back to the central file because you did not make any changes to the file.

14. Close the **User2** session of the Autodesk Revit software.

15. In the **User1** session of the Autodesk Revit software, change the username back to the original name at the start of this set of practices.

4.7 Best Practices for Worksets

Working with Company Policies

There are different practices regarding the frequency of synchronizing with central. Some companies ask users to synchronize before lunch and at the end of the day. Other companies require users to synchronize every 30 - 60 minutes. As the file size gets larger, synchronizing more often prevents the loss of data and also makes the synchronization finish quicker than if there are several hours worth of work to synchronize. However, there can be many reasons to change this frequency or to do additional synchronizations at specific points in time. They are:

- Major or critical changes to the project, such as moving an elevator core, reorienting the building on the site, etc.

- Users working in close proximity inside the model, to reduce permission issues.

When users need to leave their work for an hour or more (for lunch or a meeting, or at the end of the day), it is best to synchronize and relinquish all. Then, upon returning, they should create a new local file (with a new name if you want the previous file saved as a backup). This ensures their file is up to date and eliminates the update time.

Tips for Using Worksets

Working with the Local File

- Be selective about which worksets you open. Avoid opening worksets that are not required for the work you are doing in the project. Limiting the number of worksets speeds up the process of opening and saving the file.

- Close unused views on a regular basis as you are working on a project.

- Use a Starting View that is a drafting view, 2D plan, or elevation view. The Autodesk Revit software only loads into memory what it displays, so this saves memory the next time the file is opened. This can also be used before plotting to increase the amount of available RAM.

- If you have been away from an active project for some time, it is better to create a new local file rather than depend on the **Reload Latest** command to update your current local file for you.

- If you are not sure what workset to put certain elements in, you can use *Workset1* or a specific temporary workset to put them in until the decision can be finalized.

- Restart the software before performing memory-intensive operations, such as printing an entire document set.

Saving to the Central File

- Stagger your saves to the central file.

- Type **RL** (Reload Latest) to update your copy of the project without changing the central file. This saves time by eliminating the need to reload as part of the **Synchronize and Modify Settings** command.

- Periodically synchronize with the central file using the **Compact File** option. This takes longer to save, but frees up more memory.

- If you get an error, such as *Unable to Save* or *File not found*, you might have run out of memory. Close the major worksets so that the Autodesk Revit software releases some of the virtual memory that can be used to then save the file.

Requesting Edits

- Enable elements, not worksets, whenever possible. The Autodesk Revit software automatically borrows the unowned elements without user intervention. This saves time by not having to request an edit in the first place.

- Communicate with the team members working on a project to avoid working on the same elements at the same time.

Tips for Creating Worksets

Worksets and the Team

- Assign one person to create worksets.

- Create your project team structure to correspond with the new way of working with the building model. For example, architects and engineers do much of the work directly without needing an intern or drafter to create working drawings until the later parts of a project.

- Divide worksets according to components of a building rather than drawing types (such as plans, elevations, and sections), as these are created automatically.

- Key considerations when determining how to divide a project into worksets, include the ability to load only those worksets that are required at the time and the ability to control visibility by worksets.

- As the project progresses, more worksets can be added.

- Using worksets does not negate the need for good team communication. You still need to have scheduling and planning meetings.

- Be sure that everyone knows exactly which part of the model for which they are responsible.

- File sharing should be a tool that is used in the workflow of the project; it should not be something that is disruptive.

Creating Worksets

- A multi-floor building does not need to have a workset for each floor until you are working on the floor-specific layouts.

- If you have a project with a large floor plate that needs to be divided by match lines to fit on sheets, you should divide the various parts of the building into separate worksets.

- If you have imported files into a project, each import should be in a separate workset that is not visible by default. They should also be closed when not in use.

- Every linked file should also be in a separate workset not visible by default. They should also be closed when not in use.

- Worksets cannot be included in templates.

Default Workset Visibility

- As you create worksets, you should set the visibility. For example, the exterior and core of a building should be visible in all views, but furniture layouts or tenant partitions only need to be visible in specific views.

- Set up a standard for typical workset visibility designations. There are always exceptions, but working with the standard first is simpler.

Chapter Review Questions

1. When setting up a project to be workshared, which of the following is performed first?

   a. Use Save As and, in Options, select **Make this a Central Model** after save.

   b. Start the project using a Central File template.

   c. Start the **Worksets** command and add worksets.

   d. All of the grids and levels need to be in place.

2. Where should a central file be located?

   a. On your computer.

   b. On the company server.

   c. On each of the computers used by the team.

3. When you want to update the work that you have done and receive any changes others have made, but you do not want to change anything else, which command do you use?

   a. (Synchronize and Modify Settings)

   b. (Synchronize Now)

   c. (Relinquish All Mine)

   d. (Reload Latest)

4. Where should a local file be located?

   a. On the project manager's computer.

   b. On the company server.

   c. On each team member's computer.

5. What do you need to do so that any new elements you add are placed in a particular workset, as shown in Figure 4–135?

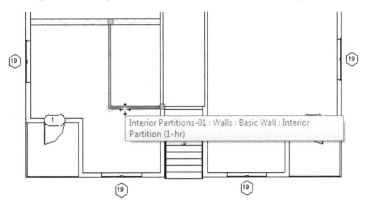

Figure 4–135

a. Gray out inactive worksets so you know not to work in them.

b. Make the workset editable.

c. Set the workset active.

d. Create a new workset.

6. When selecting an element to edit, the icon shown in Figure 4–136 displays. What do you need to do?

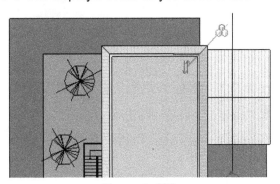

Figure 4–136

a. Nothing, you can edit the element without checking it out.

b. Click the icon and an error dialog box displays indicating that you cannot edit the element.

c. Click the icon and an error dialog box displays indicating that you cannot edit the element but you can request permission to edit it.

d. Click the icon and a dialog box displays granting you permission to edit the element.

7. You have the most recent updates from the central file but some elements in a workset are not displaying, as shown in Figure 4–137. Which of the following should you check? (Select all that apply.)

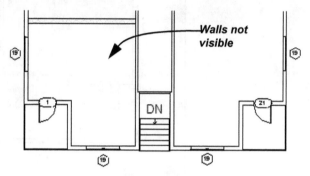

Figure 4–137

a. In the Visibility/Graphics Overrides dialog box, change the Visibility Setting of the workset to **Visible**.

b. In the Worksets dialog box, request permission to edit.

c. Set the workset as active.

d. On the Status Bar, change the Worksharing Display.

e. In the Worksets dialog box, verify if the workset is open.

Command Summary

Button	Command	Location
	Collaborate	• **Ribbon**: *Collaborate* tab>Manage Collaboration panel
	Editing Requests	• **Ribbon**: *Collaborate* tab> Synchronize panel • **Status Bar**
	Gray Inactive Worksets	• **Ribbon**: *Collaborate* tab>Manage Collaboration panel
Options	Options	• **Ribbon**: *File* tab
	Owners (Display)	• **Status Bar**: expand Worksharing Display Off
	Relinquish All Mine	• **Ribbon**: *Collaborate* tab> Synchronize panel
	Reload Latest	• **Ribbon**: *Collaborate* tab> Synchronize panel • **Shortcut**: RL
	Restore Backup	• **Ribbon**: *Collaborate* tab> Synchronize panel
	Show History	• **Ribbon**: *Collaborate* tab> Synchronize panel
	Synchronize and Modify Settings	• **Quick Access Toolbar** • **Ribbon**: *Collaborate* tab> Synchronize panel>expand Synchronize with Central
	Synchronize Now	• **Quick Access Toolbar** • **Ribbon**: *Collaborate* tab> Synchronize panel>expand Synchronize with Central
	Worksets	• **Ribbon**: *Collaborate* tab>Manage Collaboration panel>Worksets • **Status Bar**
	Worksets (Display)	• **Status Bar**: expand Worksharing Display Off
	Worksharing Display Off	• **Status Bar**

Additional Information

When you are working with links in Autodesk® Revit®, several additional features can help you with some specific situations, such as copying elements from a link into the host project, converting links into groups (or groups into links), and acquiring or publishing coordinates between linked files.

Learning Objectives in this Appendix

- Copy individual items from a linked file into the host file.
- Convert links into groups and groups into links.
- Publish coordinates of the host project to linked models.
- Acquire coordinates from a linked model for a host project.
- Select named locations for multiple instances of linked models in a host project.

A.1 Linked Model Conversion

There are times when you require information stored in a linked file that is brought into your host file. The information required might be about one or more individual elements or an entire link. A link can be converted to a group by binding it to the project. The group becomes a part of the project and does not update if the original file is modified. You can also convert a group to a link, which creates a new project file containing the elements of the group. Links and groups display differently when selected, as shown in Figure A–1.

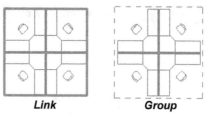

Link   **Group**

Figure A–1

How To: Copy Individual Elements in a Linked File to the Host File

1. Select an individual element in a linked model by moving the cursor over the element and pressing <Tab>.
2. When the element you want to use highlights, click on it.
3. In the *Modify | RVT Links* tab>Clipboard panel, click

   (Copy to the Clipboard).

4. Click (Paste from Clipboard) to insert the individual element into the project, as shown in Figure A–2.

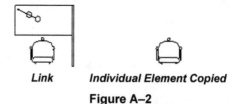

Link   **Individual Element Copied**

Figure A–2

- This is not the same as copying and monitoring elements.

Individual items in a linked model can be copied into the host project or into another project file.

How To: Convert a Link to a Group

1. Select the link. In the *Modify | RVT Links* tab>Link panel, click (Bind Link).

2. The Bind Link Options dialog box opens, as shown in Figure A–3. Select the items that you want to include and click **OK**.

Figure A–3

- An alert box might open, warning you about duplicate types. The types in the current project override the types in the linked project.

- If there is an existing group with the same name as the link in the project, an alert box opens, as shown in Figure A–4.

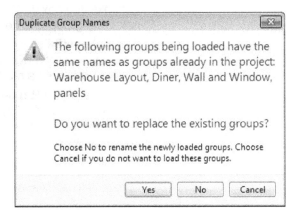

Figure A–4

How To: Convert Groups to Links

1. Select the group(s) you want to convert. You can select multiple copies, but they must be the same group.
2. In the *Modify | Model Groups* tab>Group panel, click 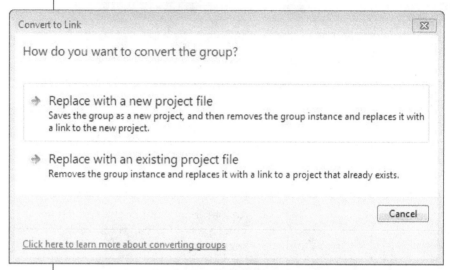 (Link).
3. In the Convert to Link dialog box, select the method for converting the group, as shown in Figure A–5.

Convert to Link   ⊠

How do you want to convert the group?

→ **Replace with a new project file**
Saves the group as a new project, and then removes the group instance and replaces it with a link to the new project.

→ **Replace with an existing project file**
Removes the group instance and replaces it with a link to a project that already exists.

     Cancel

Click here to learn more about converting groups

Figure A–5

4. When you select **Replace with a new project file,** the Save Group dialog box displays. Navigate to the appropriate folder, name the group (the default is the same as the group name), and click **Save**.
    *   Select **Include attached detail groups as views** when you have both a model group and detail group together.
5. When you select **Replace with an existing project file,** the Open dialog box displays. Navigate to the appropriate folder, select the file you want to use to replace the selected group and click **Open**.

A.2 Shared Positioning

Each project created in the Autodesk Revit software has a set of internal coordinates that are only used by that project. As long as you are working in a stand-alone project, you do not need to reference these coordinates. However, if you are linking projects together, you might want to have one coordinate system that is referenced throughout the connected projects. This is when you need to share coordinates.

The Project Base Point, typically visible in a site plan, establishes the coordinate system.

- Shared Sites can be specified in the Properties of the linked model, as shown in Figure A–6.

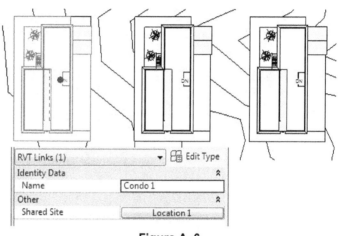

Figure A–6

- Linked models that share coordinates can be created in the Autodesk Revit software or a combination of files created in the Autodesk Revit software and DWG and DXF files created in the AutoCAD software.

- Shared coordinates should only be derived from one file. You can acquire coordinates from a linked project or drawing or publish them from the host project to the other files.

Publishing and Acquiring Coordinates

Shared coordinates are often used with site plans to which multiple buildings are linked. The buildings can all be different or can be copies of the same project, such as in an apartment complex. The site project typically controls the coordinates.

- If you are working in the site project, you can select the links and publish the coordinates to them.

- If you are working in a building project, you can acquire the coordinates from the site project.

- Typically, the architectural project acquires the coordinates from a site project and then the other disciplines link the architectural model into their projects using Origin to Origin or **Project Base Point to Project Base Point**.

How To: Publish Coordinates to Linked Models

1. Open the host project that has the coordinates you want to use and contains the linked models.
2. In the *Manage* tab>Project Location panel, expand

    (Coordinates) and click (Publish Coordinates).
3. Select the linked model to which you want to publish the shared coordinate system. The Location Weather and Site dialog box opens with the *Site* tab active, as shown in Figure A–7.

Click (Location) in the Manage tab>Project Location panel to open the dialog box at any time.

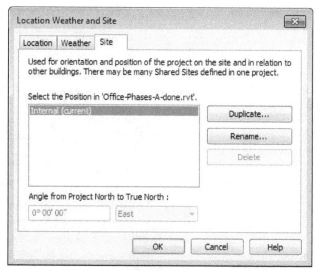

Figure A–7

4. The Internal named location of the linked model is the default. Click **Rename...** to give the default location a different name. Click **Duplicate...** to create a new name for the instance location. Each instance of the linked model should have a differently named location.
5. Select the location that you want to use and click **OK**.
6. You are still in the command and can select another linked project to which to publish the coordinates or press <Esc> to end the command.

- You only need to publish coordinates to a linked model once. However, you can use this method on multiple instances to create the named locations.

How To: Save the Modifications to the Linked Model

When the coordinates have been published, they still need to be saved to the linked model.

1. In the *Manage* tab>Manage Project panel, click 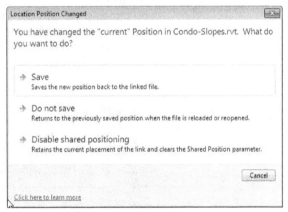 (Manage Links).
2. In the Manage Links dialog box, select the *Revit* tab.
3. A checkmark displays in the *Positions Not Saved* column, as shown in Figure A–8, indicating that the published coordinates have not yet been saved to the linked model.

Linked File	Status	Reference Type	Positions Not Saved
Townhouse.r	Loaded	Overlay	✓

Figure A–8

4. Select the name in the *Linked File* column and click **Save Positions**.
5. In the Location Position Changed dialog box shown in Figure A–9, select the method that you want to use.

Figure A–9

6. If you selected **Save**, the **Positions Not Saved** option is cleared in the Manage Links dialog box
7. Click **OK** to close the dialog box.

- If you make a change to the location or save the project before managing the links, you are prompted to make a selection in the same dialog box.

Acquiring Coordinates

If you are working in a project with linked models and want to use the coordinates from one of the linked models rather than from the host project, you can acquire the coordinates, as shown in Figure A–10. For example, you might have a drawing site plan that was created in the AutoCAD software linked to a project created in the Autodesk Revit Architecture software and want to use the coordinates from the DWG file.

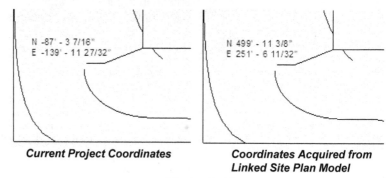

Current Project Coordinates   *Coordinates Acquired from Linked Site Plan Model*

Figure A–10

New in 2018

To maintain a consistent geographic location between models, you can use the GIS coordinates stored in a linked DWG file that includes a Geographic Marker, as shown in AutoCAD in Figure A–11. When you acquire the coordinates from the linked DWG, these are shared with the Revit project.

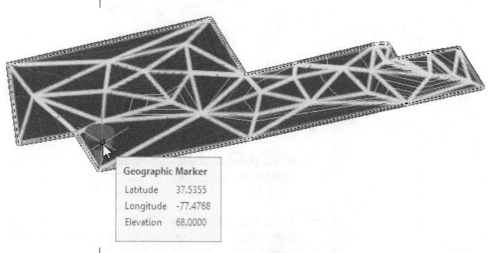

Figure A–11

When you acquire coordinates from a Geographic Marker, as shown in Figure A–12, the Autodesk Revit model updates to show the real-world position of the model, which improves energy analysis.

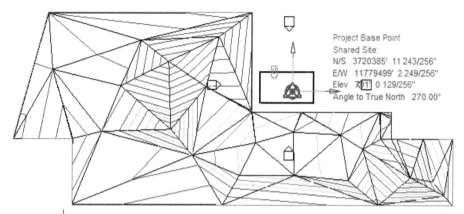

Figure A–12

How To: Acquire Coordinates from a Linked Project

1. In the *Manage* tab>Project Location panel, expand

    (Coordinates) and click (Acquire Coordinates).
2. Select a linked model from which to acquire the shared coordinate system. The current project now uses the new coordinates.

- If you move or rotate a linked instance after it has been shared and saved, a Warning box opens as shown in Figure A–13. You can click **Save Now** to save the position or click **OK** to continue working in the project. You can save the linked model later using the Manage Links dialog box.

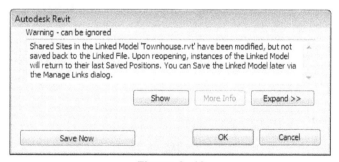

Figure A–13

Selecting Locations

It is possible to select locations for multiple instances of linked models using the **Publish Coordinates** command. Another way of specifying locations is to use the Properties of the linked model. If you have not already published coordinates to the linked project, you are prompted to reconcile the link before proceeding. Through Properties, you can move a linked instance to a new location, record the current position to a named location, or stop sharing the location of the linked instance.

How To: Select or Specify a Named Location for a linked model

1. Select the linked model.
2. In Properties, next to *Shared Site*, click **<Not Shared>**.
3. If the linked model is already reconciled, the Select Location dialog box opens, as shown in Figure A–14.

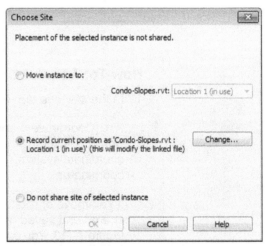

Figure A–14

*   You can move the instance to an existing named location. Select **Move instance to:** and select the location from the list.
*   If you do not want to select a named location, select **Do not share location of selected instance**.

- If you need to create a new named location, select **Record current position...** and click **Change...**. The Location Weather and Site dialog box opens, in which you can create a new named location as shown in Figure A–15. Make the new location current.

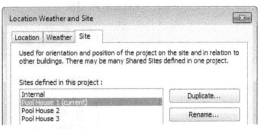

Figure A–15

4. Click **OK** to close the dialog box.
5. The value of the **Shared Site** option is now the new location name, as shown in Figure A–16.

Figure A–16

Hint: Identifying Coordinates

To identify a coordinate point: in the *Manage* tab>Project Location panel, expand ⬐ (Coordinates) and click
⬐ (Report Shared Coordinates). The cursor icon ⬐ displays. Move it over a point on the project and click on it. The Shared Coordinates display in the Options Bar, as shown in Figure A–17.

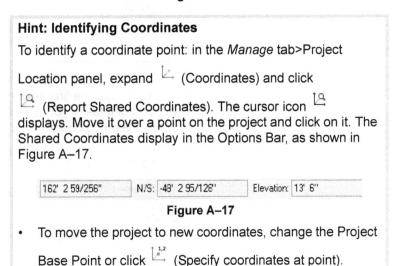

Figure A–17

- To move the project to new coordinates, change the Project Base Point or click ⬐ (Specify coordinates at point).

Reconciling Links

When you select a linked model and in Properties, select **Shared Site**, and the link has not been reconciled with the host project, the Share Coordinates dialog box opens, as shown in Figure A–18.

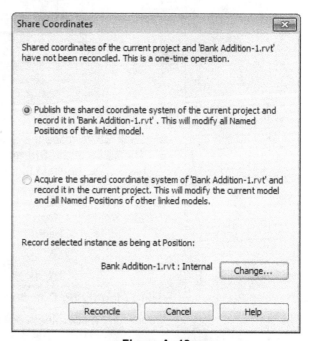

Figure A–18

- This only occurs the first time you select a file that does not share coordinates. If you select other instances of the same link, this dialog box does not open.

How To: Reconcile Links

1. In the Share Coordinates dialog box, select **Publish** or **Acquire**.
2. Click **Change...** to record the location of the instance.
3. In the Location Weather and Site dialog box, specify the named location and click **OK**.
4. In the Share Coordinates dialog box, click **Reconcile**.

Practice A1

Shared Positioning

Practice Objectives

- Link a model to a site host project multiple times.
- Publish Coordinates and Share Locations.
- Test different locations

Estimated time for completion: 15 minutes

In this practice you will link a project to a site multiple times, publish coordinates, and share locations. You will also test different locations using shared coordinates, as shown in Figure A–19.

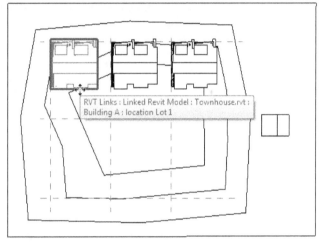

Figure A–19

Task 1 - Link a Model to a Site multiple times.

1. In the practice files folder, open **Townhouse-Site.rvt**.

2. In the *Insert* tab>Link panel, click (Link Revit).

3. In the Import/Link RVT dialog box, select **Townhouse.rvt** with the *Positioning:* set to **Auto - Origin to Origin**.

4. Move the link so that the upper left corner meets the intersection of the two reference planes, as shown in Figure A–20.

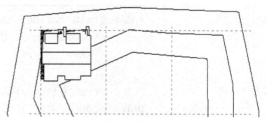

Figure A–20

5. Copy the link to the other two reference plane intersections, as shown in Figure A–21.

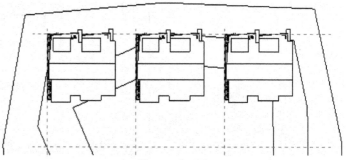

Figure A–21

6. Select the first link. In Properties, set the value of the *Name* to **Building A**, as shown in Figure A–22. Do not modify the **Shared Site** at this time.

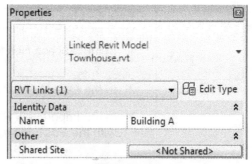

Figure A–22

7. Repeat the process with the other two instances of the linked model. Name them **Building B** and **Building C**.

Task 2 - Publish Coordinates and Share Locations.

1. In the *Manage* tab>Project Location panel, expand ∠ (Coordinates) and click ⤷ (Publish Coordinates).

2. Select **Building A**.

3. In the Location Weather and Site dialog box, in the *Site* tab, click **Rename...**. Rename the location as **Lot 1**, as shown in Figure A–23.

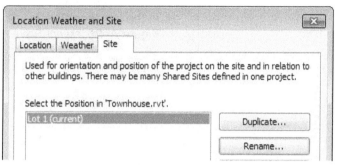

Figure A–23

4. Click **OK** and click ⌖ (Modify) to end the command. (You could continue using the **Publish Coordinates** command to assign named locations to the other instances of the link, but the next steps show you how to do it using Properties.)

5. Select **Building B**. In Properties, next to *Shared Site*, click **<Not Shared>**

6. Select **Record current position...** and click **Change...**.

7. Click **Duplicate...** to create a new named location named **Lot 2**.

8. Click **OK** twice to close the dialog boxes. The *Shared Site* is now set to **Lot 2**.

9. Repeat the process with the third link.

10. In the *Manage* tab>Manage Project panel, click ▥ (Manage Links).

11. In the Manage Links dialog box, select the *Revit* tab.

12. The **Positions Not Saved** option is selected in the list (as shown in Figure A–24) indicating that the published coordinates have not been saved to the linked model.

Linked File	Status	Reference Type	Positions Not Saved
Townhouse.r	Loaded	Overlay	☑

Figure A–24

13. Select the *Link Name* **Townhouse.rvt** and click **Save Positions**.

14. In the Location Position Changed dialog box shown in Figure A–25, select **Save**.

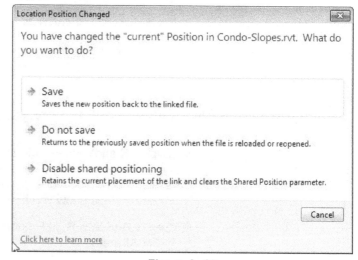

Figure A–25

15. The **Positions Not Saved** option is cleared. Click **OK** to close the Manage Links dialog box.

16. Zoom out to see the entire site.

17. Do not close the project.

Task 3 - Test different locations.

1. In the practice files folder, open **Poolhouse.rvt**.

2. In the *Manage* tab>Project Location panel, click

   🌐 (Location).

3. In the Location Weather and Site dialog box, in the *Site* tab, three named locations are listed in addition to the **Internal** location, as shown in Figure A–26. These were created when the model was previously linked to the host site project.

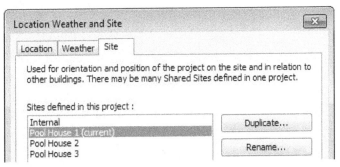

Figure A–26

4. Close the dialog box, close the project, and verify that you are in the **Townhouse-Site.rvt** project.

5. In the *Insert* tab>Link panel, click (Link Revit).

6. Select the **Poolhouse.rvt** project. Set the *Positioning:* to **Auto-By Shared Coordinates**, as shown in Figure A–27, and click **Open**.

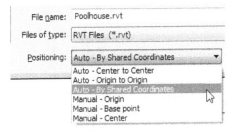

Figure A–27

7. In the Location Weather and Site dialog box, in the *Site* tab, select one of the named locations and click **OK**. The pool house is automatically inserted at that location.

8. Select the pool house.

9. In Properties, click the button next to *Shared Site*.

10. In the Choose Site dialog box, select **Move Instance to:** and select one of the other named locations in the list, as shown in Figure A–28.

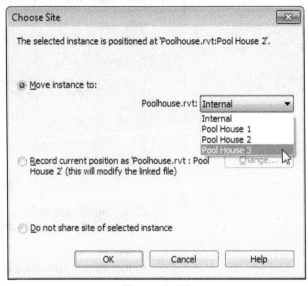

Figure A–28

11. Close the dialog boxes. The pool house moves to the named location. The three locations are shown in Figure A–29.

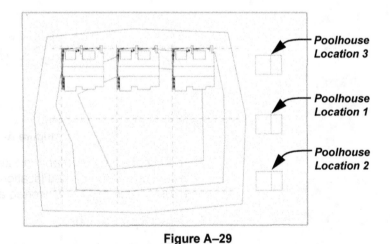

Figure A–29

12. Save and close the project.

Command Summary

Button	Command	Location
Groups and Links		
	Bind Link	• **Ribbon**: Modify | Revit Link tab>Link panel
	Link	• **Ribbon**: Modify | Revit Link tab>Link panel
Shared Coordinates		
	Acquire Coordinates	• **Ribbon**: Manage tab>Project Location panel>expand Coordinates
	Coordinates	• **Ribbon**: Manage tab>Project Location panel
	Location	• **Ribbon:** Manage tab>Project Location panel
	Publish Coordinates	• **Ribbon**: Manage tab>Project Location panel>expand Coordinates
	Report Shared Coordinates	• **Ribbon:** Manage tab>Project Location panel>expand Coordinates
	Specify Coordinates at Point	• **Ribbon**: Manage tab>Project Location panel>expand Coordinates

Autodesk Revit Architecture Certification Exam Objectives

The following table will help you to locate the exam objectives in the chapters of the Autodesk® Revit® learning guides to help you prepare for the Autodesk Revit Architecture Certified Professional exam.

Exam Topic	Exam Objective	Learning Guide	Chapter & Section(s)
Collaboration			
	Copy and monitor elements in a linked file	• Revit Collaboration Tools	• 2.3
	Use worksharing	• Revit Collaboration Tools	• 4.1, 4.2, 4.3
	Import DWG and image files	• Revit Architecture Fundamentals	• 3.4
		• Revit Collaboration Tools	• 3.1, 3.2, 3.3
	Use Worksharing Visualization	• Revit Collaboration Tools	• 4.4
	Assess review warnings in Revit	• Revit Architecture Fundamentals	• 12.1

Exam Topic	Exam Objective	Learning Guide	Chapter & Section(s)
Documentation			
	Create and modify filled regions	• Revit Architecture Fundamentals	• 16.3
	Place detail components and repeating details	• Revit Architecture Fundamentals	• 16.2
	Tag elements (doors, windows, etc.) by category	• Revit Architecture Fundamentals	• 15.1
	Use dimension strings	• Revit Architecture Fundamentals	• 14.1
	Set the colors used in a color scheme legend	• Revit Architecture: Conceptual Design and Visualization	• 2.3
	Work with phases	• Revit Collaboration Tools	• 1.1
Elements and Families			
	Change elements within a curtain wall (grids, panels, mullions	• Revit Architecture Fundamentals	• 6.2, 6.3, 6.4
	Create compound walls	• Revit BIM Management	• 3.1
	Create a stacked wall	• Revit BIM Management	• 3.3
	Differentiate system and component families	• Revit BIM Management	• 3.1 • 4.1
	Work with family parameters	• Revit BIM Management	• 4.2
	Create a new family type	• Revit Architecture Fundamentals	• 5.3
		• Revit BIM Management	• 4.4
	Use family creation procedures	• Revit BIM Management	• 4.1 to 4.4

Exam Topic	Exam Objective	Learning Guide	Chapter & Section(s)
Modeling			
	Create a building pad	• Revit Architecture: Site and Structure	• 1.2
	Define floor for a mass	• Revit Architecture: Conceptual Design and Visualization	• 1.7
	Create a stair with a landing	• Revit Architecture Fundamentals	• 12.1
	Create elements such as floors, ceilings, or roofs	• Revit Architecture Fundamentals	• 9.1 • 10.1 • 11.2, 11.4
	Generate a toposurface	• Revit Architecture: Site and Structure	• 1.1
	Model railings	• Revit Architecture Fundamentals	• 12.3
	Edit a model element's material (door, window, furniture)	• Revit Architecture Fundamentals	• 5.3 • B.4
	Change a generic floor / ceiling / roof to a specific type	• Revit Architecture Fundamentals	• 9.1 • 10.1 • 11.2
	Attach walls to a roof or ceiling	• Revit Architecture Fundamentals	• 11.2
	Edit room-aware families	• Revit BIM Management	• 5.1
Views			
	Define element properties in a schedule	• Revit Architecture Fundamentals	• 15.3
	Control visibility	• Revit Architecture Fundamentals	• 7.1
	Use levels	• Revit Architecture Fundamentals	• 3.1
	Create a duplicate view for a plan, section, elevation, drafting view, etc.	• Revit Architecture Fundamentals	• 7.2
	Create and manage legends	• Revit Architecture Fundamentals	• 14.4
	Manage view position on sheets	• Revit Architecture Fundamentals	• 13.2
	Organize and sort items in a schedule	• Revit Architecture Fundamentals	• B.10
		• Revit BIM Management	• 2.2

Appendix C

Autodesk Revit MEP Electrical Certification Exam Objectives

The following table will help you to locate the exam objectives in the chapters of the Autodesk® Revit® learning guides to help you prepare for the Autodesk Revit MEP Electrical Certified Professional exam.

Exam Topic	Exam Objective	Learning Guide	Chapter & Section(s)
Collaboration	Import AutoCAD files into Revit	• Revit Collaboration Tools	• 3.1
	Link Revit models	• Revit MEP Fundamentals	• 4.1
	Copy levels and setup monitoring	• Revit MEP Fundamentals	• 4.2 & 4.3
	Create floor plans	• Revit MEP Fundamentals	• 4.2
	Use Worksets	• Revit Collaboration Tools	• 4.1 to 4.3
	Resolve Coordination Review Errors	• Revit MEP Fundamentals	• 4.5
Documentation	Electrical: Tag components	• Revit MEP Fundamentals	• 14.1
	Create sheets	• Revit MEP Fundamentals	• 12.1
	Electrical: Create panel schedules	• Revit MEP Fundamentals	• 11.4
	Add and modify text	• Revit MEP Fundamentals	• 13.2
	Add and modify dimensions	• Revit MEP Fundamentals	• 13.1
Elements	Differentiate system and component families	• Revit BIM Management	• 3.1 • 4.1
	Edit Family Connectors	• Revit BIM Management	• 5.1
	Create a new family type	• Revit BIM Management	• 4.4

Exam Topic	Exam Objective	Learning Guide	Chapter & Section(s)
Modeling	Electrical: Add and modify receptacles	• Revit MEP Fundamentals	• 11.2
	Electrical: Add and modify panels	• Revit MEP Fundamentals	• 11.2
	Electrical: Create and modify circuits	• Revit MEP Fundamentals	• 11.3
	Electrical: Add and modify lighting fixtures	• Revit MEP Fundamentals	• 11.2
	Electrical: Add and modify switches	• Revit MEP Fundamentals	• 11.2
	Electrical: Create and modify lighting circuits	• Revit MEP Fundamentals	• 11.3
	Electrical: Create and modify switching circuits	• Revit MEP Fundamentals	• 11.3
	Electrical: Add and modify conduit	• Revit MEP Fundamentals	• 11.5
	Electrical: Use cable trays	• Revit MEP Fundamentals	• 11.5
	Electrical: Add and modify switch systems	• Revit MEP Fundamentals	• 11.3
	Electrical: Create Distribution System	• Revit MEP Fundamentals	• 11.1
	Electrical: Add and modify security devices	• Revit MEP Fundamentals	• 11.2
	Electrical: Add and modify wiring	• Revit MEP Fundamentals	• 11.3
	Electrical: Generate automatic wire layouts	• Revit MEP Fundamentals	• 11.3
	Electrical: Check circuits and disconnects	• Revit MEP Fundamentals	• 11.6
	Perform interference check	• Revit Collaboration Tools	• 2.4
	Electrical: Work with Spaces	• Revit MEP Fundamentals	• 6.1 to 6.3
	Electrical: Perform a Lighting Analysis	• Revit MEP Fundamentals	• 11.6
	Electrical: Work with Fire Alarm Devices	• Revit MEP Fundamentals	• 11.2
	Electrical: Work with Site Lighting	• Revit MEP Fundamentals	• 11.2
Views	View models	• Revit MEP Fundamentals	• 1.4
	Apply view templates	• Revit MEP Fundamentals	• 6.1
	Create detail views	• Revit MEP Fundamentals	• 15.1
	Electrical: Create and label wiring plans	• Revit MEP Fundamentals	• 5.2 • 11.3 • 13.1 to 13.3 • 14.1

Autodesk Revit MEP Mechanical Certification Exam Objectives

The following table will help you to locate the exam objectives in the chapters of the Autodesk® Revit® learning guides to help you prepare for the Autodesk Revit MEP Mechanical Certified Professional exam.

Exam Topic	Exam Objective	Learning Guide	Chapter & Section(s)
Collaboration	Import AutoCAD files into Revit	• Revit Collaboration Tools	• 3.1
	Link Revit models	• Revit MEP Fundamentals	• 4.1
	Copy levels and setup monitoring	• Revit MEP Fundamentals	• 4.2 & 4.3
	Create floor plans	• Revit MEP Fundamentals	• 4.2
	Use Worksets	• Revit Collaboration Tools	• 4.1 to 4.3
	Resolve Coordination Review Errors	• Revit MEP Fundamentals	• 4.5
Documentation	Mechanical: Tag ducts and piping	• Revit MEP Fundamentals	• 14.1
	Create sheets	• Revit MEP Fundamentals	• 12.1
	Add and modify text	• Revit MEP Fundamentals	• 13.2
	Add and modify dimensions	• Revit MEP Fundamentals	• 13.1
	Mechanical: Create duct/pipe legends	• Revit MEP Fundamentals	• B.3

Exam Topic	Exam Objective	Learning Guide	Chapter & Section(s)
Elements	Differentiate system and component families	• Revit BIM Management	• 3.1 • 4.1
	Edit Family Connectors	• Revit BIM Management	• 5.1
	Create a new family type	• Revit BIM Management	• 4.4
Modeling	Mechanical: Add and use mechanical equipment	• Revit MEP Fundamentals	• 8.1
	Mechanical: Add and modify air terminals	• Revit MEP Fundamentals	• 8.1
	Mechanical: Add and modify ducts	• Revit MEP Fundamentals	• 8.2 & 8.3
	Mechanical: Add and modify return ducts	• Revit MEP Fundamentals	• 8.2 & 8.3
	Mechanical: Add and modify duct accessories and fittings	• Revit MEP Fundamentals	• 8.3
	Mechanical: Work with heating and cooling zones	• Revit MEP Fundamentals	• 7.1
	Plumbing: Add and modify fixtures	• Revit MEP Fundamentals	• 9.1
	Plumbing: Add and modify piping	• Revit MEP Fundamentals	• 9.2
	Plumbing: Add and use plumbing equipment	• Revit MEP Fundamentals	• 9.1
	Plumbing: Create a plumbing system	• Revit MEP Fundamentals	• 10.1
	Plumbing: Add and modify pipe accessories	• Revit MEP Fundamentals	• 9.3
	Mechanical: Add and modify placeholder duct	• Revit MEP Fundamentals	• 8.2
	Mechanical: Define a duct system	• Revit MEP Fundamentals	• 10.1
	Mechanical: Add and modify placeholder duct	• Revit MEP Fundamentals	• 8.2 & 8.3
	Mechanical: Define a duct system	• Revit MEP Fundamentals	• 10.1
	Mechanical: Work with spaces	• Revit MEP Fundamentals	• 6.1 to 6.3
	Plumbing: Add and modify placeholder pipe	• Revit MEP Fundamentals	• 9.2
	Size duct and pipe systems	• Revit MEP Fundamentals	• 8.3
	Perform interference check	• Revit Collaboration Tools	• 2.4
	Check duct and pipe systems and disconnects	• Revit MEP Fundamentals	• 10.3

Exam Topic	Exam Objective	Learning Guide	Chapter & Section(s)
Views	View models	• Revit MEP Fundamentals	• 1.4
	Apply view templates	• Revit MEP Fundamentals	• 6.1
	Create detail views	• Revit MEP Fundamentals	• 15.1
	Mechanical: Create and label HVAC plans	• Revit MEP Fundamentals	• 5.2 • 13.1 to 13.3 • 14.1
	Plumbing: Create a plumbing view	• Revit MEP Fundamentals	• 5.1
	Plumbing: Create and label plumbing plans	• Revit MEP Fundamentals	• 5.2 • 13.1 to 13.3 • 14.1

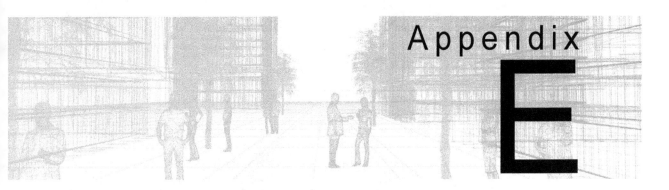

Autodesk Revit Structure Certification Exam Objectives

The following table will help you to locate the exam objectives within the chapters of the Autodesk® Revit® learning guides to help you prepare for the Autodesk Revit Structure Certified Professional exam.

Exam Topic	Exam Objective	Learning Guide	Chapter & Section(s)
Collaboration	Create and modify levels	• Revit Structure Fundamentals	• 3.3
	Create and modify structural grids	• Revit Structure Fundamentals	• 5.1
	Import AutoCAD files into Revit	• Revit Structure Fundamentals	• 3.1
		• Revit Collaboration Tools	• 3.1
	Link Revit models	• Revit Structure Fundamentals	• 3.2
		• Revit Collaboration Tools	• 2.1
	Control the visibility for linked objects	• Revit Collaboration Tools	• 2.2
Documentation	Using temporary dimensions	• Revit Structure Fundamentals	• 2.1
	Annotate beams	• Revit Structure Fundamentals	• 13.3
	Add and modify text annotations	• Revit Structure Fundamentals	• 13.2
	Add and use dimensions and dimension labels	• Revit Structure Fundamentals	• 13.1
	Use detail components	• Revit Structure Fundamentals	• 14.2
	Create and modify column schedules	• Revit Structure Fundamentals	• 15.2

Exam Topic	Exam Objective	Learning Guide	Chapter & Section(s)
Documentation (continued)	Create and modify footing schedules	• Revit Structure Fundamentals	• 15.3 • B.8
		• Revit BIM Management	• 2.2
	Create and modify standard sheets	• Revit Structure Fundamentals	• 12.1, 12.2
Modeling	Place and modify structural columns	• Revit Structure Fundamentals	• 5.2
	Place and modify walls	• Revit Structure Fundamentals	• 6.1
	Create custom wall types	• Revit BIM Management	• 3.1
	Place footings	• Revit Structure Fundamentals	• 6.2, 6.4
	Create concrete slabs and/or floors	• Revit Structure Fundamentals	• 8.1
	Create and modify stepped walls in foundations	• Revit Structure Fundamentals	• 6.2
	Place rebar	• Revit Structure Fundamentals	• 9.2
	Add beams	• Revit Structure Fundamentals	• 7.1
	Add beam systems	• Revit Structure Fundamentals	• 7.1
	Add joists	• Revit Structure Fundamentals	• 7.1
	Add cross bracing to joists	• Revit Structure Fundamentals	• 7.1
	Create and use trusses	• Revit Structure Fundamentals	• 7.3
	Create and modify floors	• Revit Structure Fundamentals	• 8.1
	Create and modify custom floors	• Revit BIM Management	• 3.1
	Create and modify sloped floors	• Revit Architecture Fundamentals	• 9.3
	Add floor openings for stairs	• Revit Structure Fundamentals	• 8.2
	Create and modify stairs	• Revit Architecture Fundamentals	• 12.1
	Create and modify ramps	• Revit Architecture Fundamentals	• 12.5
	Model and use roofs	• Revit Structure Fundamentals	• 8.1
		• Revit Architecture Fundamentals	• 11.2, 11.4
Views	Create section views	• Revit Structure Fundamentals	• 4.4
	Create framing elevations	• Revit Structure Fundamentals	• 4.4
	Use callout views	• Revit Structure Fundamentals	• 4.3

Index